VALENTINA HARRIS'
COMPLETE ITALIAN COOKERY COURSE

For Ben and Jamie.
This one is for you.
Vi voglio tanto di quel bene!

VALENTINA HARRIS'

Complete Italian Cookery Course

BBC BOOKS

ACKNOWLEDGEMENTS

Valentina would very much like to thank
Suzanne Webber, Anna Ottewill and Frank Phillips at BBC Books;
Wendy Hobson and her kitchen; Maxime Clarke (and helpers);
Helen Payne and Graham Kirk (and his assistant)
and anybody else who had any part in this book – however small!

Editing and testing of recipes: Wendy Hobson
Photographer: Graham Kirk
Home economist: Maxime Clarke
Stylist: Helen Payne
Illustrator: Kate Simunek

Published by BBC Books,
a division of BBC Enterprises Limited,
Woodlands, 80 Wood Lane, London W12 0TT

First published 1992
© Valentina Harris 1992
ISBN 0 563 36162 X
Set in Monotype Garamond
Printed and bound in Great Britain by Clays Ltd, St Ives plc
Colour separations by Technic, Berkhamsted
Jacket printed by Belmont Press, Northampton

Designed and produced by Toucan Books Limited

Contents

Foreword

The COMPLETE ITALIAN COOKERY COURSE *is a celebration of Italian cookery. As people become more and more interested in cookery, they need and want to cook dishes from countries other than their own as authentically as possible. As far as the cooking of Italy is concerned, that is where this book comes in useful, because every single technique and every recipe in this book is absolutely Italian. I very much hope that you will find it interesting and entertaining as well as being instructive, as I firmly believe that food should be enjoyable above all other considerations.*

The book begins with the absolute basics — what I like to think of as the supporting columns for all the recipes which follow. These include recipes for such things as stock and mayonnaise, to prepare you for the dishes which follow. The point is that you cannot make a good risotto or soup without having a proper stock, and there is no real substitute for home-made fresh mayonnaise.

As you move on through the book, you'll go through antipasti into soups, then on to wonderful risottos, through pastas and then on to the main courses. Here I begin with meat dishes, followed by poultry and game and finally into fish, which is divided into freshwater fish, saltwater fish and seafood. Then there is a section devoted to vegetables, and finally the dessert chapter. The last recipe chapter is devoted to dishes that cannot be considered to be classic Italian dishes, but are my own innovations: more unusual combinations of ingredients that result in dishes that are original and very different.

There is a new generation of Italian cooks who are moving into a lighter, more modern style of cooking, preparing dishes similar to these. This book could not really call itself complete without at least a nod in the direction of this currently very fashionable style of cuisine.

But although the rest of the book is devoted mostly to classic Italian cuisine, this does not for a moment mean that the recipes are lacking in sparkle and imagination. All aspects of Italian cuisine are based on flair and a passion for food that tastes good and looks good. It is these basic principles which I have tried to convey above all else in this book, and it is these principles which make Italian food so popular all over the world.

You will see from the recipes that most Italian cookery is based on simplicity. There are none of the complicated techniques which exist in the cooking of some other countries. Practically all Italian cookery is born out of family recipes handed down from one generation to another, using ingredients which were readily available.

The principles have not changed, even in this new supermarket era that means we can go out and buy all manner of ingredients, from all over the world, so easily. Fresh ingredients, cooked with love and care, remain at the very core of all good Italian food.

I hope you enjoy using this book as much as I have enjoyed writing it and that you will soon be cooking authentic Italian food like a native! For me, there is no other cuisine which comes anywhere near the style and simplicity of these dishes and I am so glad that more and more people are learning to appreciate it. I wish you buon appetito *and happy reading.*

NOTES ON THE RECIPES
Eggs are size 2.
Wash all fresh produce before preparation.
Spoon measurements are level.
Follow one set of measurements only; do not mix metric and Imperial.
Adjust seasoning or strongly flavoured ingredients to taste.
If you substitute dried for fresh herbs, use half the amount.

The Supporting Columns

I HAVE called this chapter *The Supporting Columns* because, to my mind, the recipes included are exactly that – without them, there would be no base upon which to build the amazingly varied, multi-flavoured and textured mosaic which makes up Italian cuisine. These recipes are as basic as making a béchamel or white sauce, creating the perfect stock, or frying an onion correctly when preparing risotto! The more proficient cooks can probably skip most of the chapter, although by following the instructions I have given you, you should not only be able to cook proficiently, but also as a born and bred Italian! It is also important to remember that, in order to cook like an Italian, you must have to hand the basic store-cupboard ingredients of an average Italian kitchen. Also, your own kitchen should ideally contain a few basic Italian implements. So, in order to set the scene, let me first give you a list of the store-cupboard ingredients normally housed in my own kitchen.

ANCHOVIES

Anchovies are used in many Italian dishes. I like to use salted anchovies for flavouring sauces and anchovies canned in oil for use whole. Salted anchovies are available in delicatessens.

PECORINO AND PARMIGIANO OR GRANA PADANO CHEESES

These are absolutely vital to a huge variety of Italian recipes, especially pasta and risotto. This type of hard grating cheese keeps well for a long time. Pecorino is a ewes' milk cheese and has a distinctive peppery taste. Parmigiano and Grana Padano are very similar, but still distinctively different (see *Italian Cheeses* page 299) but both are used chiefly for grating and are milder than Pecorino.

DRIED RED CHILLI PEPPERS

Hanging in bunches from your kitchen ceiling, these not only look very pretty, they are also vital in many Italian dishes. They give a marvellously strong, piquant spiciness to many recipes.

HERBS AND SPICES

If you can, always use fresh herbs, although a few freeze-dried herbs actually work better in some dishes. A good example of this is oregano, which only really develops its full pungency when it is carefully dried. Remember that the flavour of herbs does change when they are dried and that you will generally need less of the dried herb in terms of quantity. As far as spices are concerned, whole nutmegs which can be grated as necessary taste much better than the ready-grated variety. Freshly milled black peppercorns are important, and then some cinnamon, cloves and juniper.

DRIED PORCINI MUSHROOMS

You only need to use a small amount of funghi porcini, once reconstituted, to impart a really rich, woody flavour to a dish, so although they are expensive, try to build up a small store of them. They are available in large supermarkets and delicatessens and keep very well in a tightly closed screw-top jar.

OLIVES, OLIVE PASTE, CAPERS AND SUN-DRIED TOMATOES

Though perhaps best kept in the fridge once opened, these are also ingredients which can give an otherwise ordinary dish a very distinctive Italian accent. Olive paste is delicious when spread on bread which has been lightly toasted then rubbed with a garlic clove. To my mind, capers preserved in salt have much more flavour and a better texture than those tiny balls preserved in brine or vinegar. They are available at delicatessens. Also part of this category and available in large supermarkets or delicatessens are sun-dried tomatoes preserved in olive oil. They are available dried, but you need to store them covered in olive oil for some time until they are ready to use. They are also sold as a spreadable smooth paste.

EXTRA VIRGIN OR VIRGIN OLIVE OIL

This will lift any dish you cook and give it that special Mediterranean glow. For cooking purposes, make sure you buy an olive oil with a relatively mild flavour. Stronger flavoured oils are best used for dressing salads.

DRIED DURUM WHEAT PASTA

As you become more expert at cooking Italian recipes, you will discover which shapes of pasta best suit the various sauces. For example, pesto generally marries a long thin ribbon of pasta such as bavette or linguine better than something short and stubby such as eliche. There are no hard and fast rules, but some combinations make much better sense than others. However, in the end, the decision is always down to personal preference.

PULSES

Dried and canned pulses form the healthy basis of many an Italian meal. Green or continental lentils cook relatively quickly and are full of flavour. They tend to be much more authentic than the bright orange variety. Borlotti beans, cannellini beans and chick peas are all very good standbys. The general rule of thumb is: use dried if you have time to soak and pre-boil them, otherwise opt for the canned version.

POLENTA FLOUR

In order to discover what polenta is all about, you need to try making it at home. The old-fashioned version will require fifty minutes' worth of solid stirring. The new quick-cook varieties only take five minutes and are quite passable, although not as good, to my mind. In either case, remember that it is what you put with the polenta that really counts.

ARBORIO RICE

It is very important that you find a supplier of arborio rice for making risottos; either your local supermarket or delicatessen. Long-grain or short-grain rice of other types just won't give you the same creamy texture which makes risotto so special.

PASSATA AND CANNED TOMATOES

Passata is quite simply canned tomatoes which have been sieved for you, so you buy them in a deliciously smooth, seed-free purée in a carton, bottle or can. If Passata is hard to find, simply sieve some canned tomatoes, which you will need for your store-cupboard in any case. For extra density of flavour and texture, it is also a good idea to keep some tomato purée.

WINE VINEGAR AND BALSAMIC VINEGAR

Both of these give salads and other recipes a very authentic touch. Good Italian wine vinegar tends to be extremely sharp and piquant. The treacly, dense flavour of the balsamic vinegar tends to be an acquired taste. Like most acquired tastes, however, once found it is usually hard to lose.

EQUIPMENT

As far as equipment is concerned, you will need a big enough saucepan to cook pasta comfortably. A 3 litre (5¹/₄ pint) pot is usually about right. A big, preferably metal, colander with feet or a stand underneath is useful for draining pasta and also cleaning vegetables successfully. A fairly shallow, heavy-based saucepan is important for making risotto, as is a deep heavy-based and heavy-sided saucepan for casseroles and stews. A good selection of chopping boards is a must, plus a good, heavy, sharp knife, a rocking chopper, *mezzaluna*, and a medium-sized good quality pestle and mortar. Finally, I also think that food processors are an excellent invention and that for luxury, everybody should own an ice-cream maker!

For me, all the above tips have been simply basic facts of the kitchen ever since I began to cook at the age of five, back home in Tuscany!

La Salsa di Pomodoro
Raw Tomato Sauce

Made only with raw tomatoes, preferably fresh and very ripe,
this is a bottled sauce which keeps very well in a cool dark place
throughout the winter. As a child I can remember endless afternoons
spent sitting in the garden preparing vast mountains of
tomatoes and swapping stories with friends and neighbours who
had gathered to take part in this annual event.
Although nowadays fridges and freezers make these winter preparations
rather obsolete, there is still nothing quite like the flavour of fresh
tomato sauce to warm up a bitter cold February.
Once the bottles are open, they must be kept in the fridge.
If you are using Champagne bottles, you will need a proper corking tool.
You can also use strong screw-top jars, in which case tighten the lids
then undo them by one quarter turn before boiling.
Tighten them completely after boiling.

MAKES 6 CHAMPAGNE BOTTLES OR KILNER JARS

5 kg (11 lb) fresh ripe tomatoes

Blanch the tomatoes in boiling water for 1 minute. Remove them with a slotted spoon and peel them quickly. Push them through a food mill or chop them with a sharp knife. Wash the bottles or jars very carefully and drain them completely. Fill each one with tomato, but only as far as the start of the neck. Pour a little of the remaining liquid into each bottle or jar but be sure to leave a small air gap. If you are using Champagne bottles, boil the corks until soft and sterilised, then dry them and cork all the bottles firmly using an appropriate corking tool. Tie each bottle up firmly using thick string. Go over the cork and under the bottle in a cross movement. This is to prevent the corks flying off during the boiling process. If you are using kilner jars, seal them with new sealing rings and the spring clips. Wrap each bottle or jar in newspaper or rags and stand them upright in a large saucepan filled with cold water up to the neck of the bottles. Bring the water to the boil and boil steadily for 1 hour. Be sure to boil the bottles as soon as possible after filling because the tomato will start to ferment very quickly.

Il Sugo di Pomodoro
Plain Tomato
Sauce

This is a cooked tomato sauce,
the most basic and classic of all the Italian sauces.
For extra special flavour, use the tomato sauce from
the previous recipe and you will get the full,
luscious taste of an Italian summer!

SERVES 6

1 kg (2 lb) fresh tomatoes,
skinned and quartered or canned tomatoes,
drained and quartered
or
equivalent Salsa di Pomodoro (page 12)
1 small onion, peeled and quartered
1 carrot, quartered
1 stick celery, quartered
1 large sprig fresh parsley
7 leaves fresh basil
3 tablespoons olive oil
salt

Put all the ingredients except the salt into a saucepan. Cover and bring to the boil then simmer for 30 minutes. Remove the lid and continue to simmer for about 20 minutes until most of the liquid has evaporated.

Remove from the heat and push through a food mill or sieve. Season to taste with salt and re-heat to serve.

La Besciamella
Béchamel
Sauce

A simple béchamel sauce forms the basis of many recipes.
By reducing or increasing the amount of milk used,
you get a thicker or thinner sauce.
To this basic sauce you can add cheese,
mustard or various other ingredients to
make much more elaborate sauces.

MAKES 600 ML (1 PINT)

50 g (2 oz) unsalted butter
50 g (2 oz) plain white flour
600 ml (1 pint) milk, cold
salt
freshly grated nutmeg

Melt the butter until foaming then add the flour and stir together quickly. Add the cold milk and whisk together over a low heat for about 20 minutes until the sauce is thickened and no longer has a floury aftertaste. Season to taste with salt and freshly grated nutmeg.

Salsa Bruna
Brown Sauce

This is a very basic brown sauce to which mushrooms, truffles, madeira, red wine or other ingredients are added according to specific recipes.

MAKES ABOUT 600 ML (1 PINT)

50 g (2 oz) unsalted butter
50 g (2 oz) lean prosciutto crudo, chopped
1 carrot, finely chopped
1 stick celery, finely chopped
1 large sprig fresh parsley, chopped
4-5 parsley stalks
25 g (1 oz) dried funghi porcini,
soaked in warm water for 20 minutes
$^{1}/_{2}$ clove
4–5 black peppercorns, lightly crushed
$^{1}/_{2}$ bay leaf
salt
$^{1}/_{2}$ wine glass dry white wine
600 ml (1 pint) water or meat stock
1 teaspoon beef extract or 1 beef stock cube
1 teaspoon cornflour
2 tablespoons marsala
freshly ground black pepper

Melt about one-third of the butter and fry the prosciutto gently for about 5 minutes. Add the carrot, celery, parsley and parsley stalks and cook for about 8 minutes until soft. Drain the mushrooms, chop them coarsely and add them to the pan with the clove, peppercorns, bay leaf and a pinch of salt. Cover and simmer for about 15 minutes. Stir in one-third of the wine and wait for it to evaporate before adding half of what remains. Wait for this to evaporate before adding the remainder. Stir in the water or stock and the beef extract or stock cube. Bring to the boil, cover and simmer gently for 30 minutes. Remove from the heat and push through a food mill or sieve then return to the saucepan. Blend together the cornflour and marsala and stir this into the mixture. Return to the heat and heat through until thickened, stirring constantly, then remove from the heat. Chop the remaining butter into small pieces and stir it into the sauce with a wooden spoon. Re-heat as required to serve.

Salsa Chiara Vellutata
Clear Velvet Sauce

*To this basic sauce you can add mushrooms,
eggs, tomatoes and other ingredients
according to specific recipes.
The sauce can also be made for
fish recipes using fish stock.*

MAKES ABOUT 600 ML (1 PINT)

30 g (1¹/₂ oz) unsalted butter
30 g (1¹/₂ oz) plain white flour
750 ml (1¹/₄ pints) clear chicken or
vegetable broth (made without tomato)
2 tablespoons finely chopped fresh parsley

Melt the butter in a large saucepan until foaming, add the flour and stir together until smooth and completely lump free. Cook over a very low heat for about 10 minutes until a golden yellow colour, stirring continuously. Stir in half the stock, bring to the boil and add the parsley. Continue to simmer the sauce for about 45 minutes, stirring in the remaining stock a spoonful at a time. Remove from the heat and use as required, re-heating as necessary.

Fave con Pecorino e Prosciutto

SEE PAGE 42

(Overleaf) Insalata di Carciofi Crudi

SEE PAGE 43

Spiedini di Polenta e Funghi

SEE PAGE 53

La Maionese Veloce
Simple Mayonnaise

This is a very easy recipe for making a mayonnaise for which you need to use a food processor or liquidiser. If you use olive oil for making mayonnaise, make sure you use one with a very light flavour.

SERVES 6

2 egg yolks
250 ml (8 fl oz) light olive or sunflower oil
juice of 1/2 lemon
or 2 tablespoons white wine vinegar
salt
freshly ground black pepper

Put the egg yolks in a liquidiser or food processor with a blade attachment. Process the egg yolks until pale yellow and well blended, then add the oil in a very thin and steady stream, keeping the motor running. Gradually the sauce will thicken and become amalgamated. Stop the motor to check the consistency.

Only when you are happy that the texture is as you want it should you add the lemon juice or wine vinegar and season to taste with salt and pepper.

La Maionese Classica
Classic Mayonnaise

---

*There is a great deal of satisfaction to be drawn from making
your own mayonnaise by hand, although I must warn you that
it does involve a lot of energy and time and there are
quite a few things that can go horribly wrong!
This basic sauce can be made more elaborate by
the addition of anchovies, garlic,
herbs and other ingredients for specific recipes.*

SERVES 6

2 egg yolks
1 tablespoon white wine vinegar
or lemon juice
salt
white pepper (optional)
200 ml (7 fl oz) light olive or sunflower oil

This sauce depends on three factors to turn out correctly: the eggs, bowl and oil must all be at blood temperature; the oil must be added one drop at a time; and you must respect the proportion of eggs to oil – for each egg you will need 100 ml ($3^{1}/_{2}$ fl oz) of oil, no more and no less.

Put the egg yolks into a bowl with the wine vinegar or lemon juice and a pinch of salt. Add the white pepper, if using. Begin to stir the egg yolks with a wooden spoon, always stirring in the same direction and not spreading them out too much. Now begin to add the oil one drop at a time, continuing to stir in a smooth and even rhythm. When about 2 tablespoons of the oil have been absorbed, the sauce may thicken too much to make stirring easy. If this happens, add a few more drops of wine vinegar or lemon juice to return the texture to an easy stirring mixture. Then begin to pour the oil in a steady stream, still stirring constantly. The stream must be as fine as possible. If the sauce thickens up too much again before it has absorbed all the oil, add a few drops of wine vinegar or lemon juice. The finished sauce should be thick enough to hold up the weight of the spoon on its surface.

Brodo di Carne
Meat Broth

Used an enormous amount in many different aspects of Italian cuisine all over the country, il Brodo, *the broth, is one of the most important ingredients for anybody who wishes to prepare Italian dishes at their best.*
You cannot make perfect risotto without good broth, and it is also an essential ingredient for many soups. To a lesser extent, it is required in stews, casseroles and sauces and for basting or thinning purposes.
Broth differs from stock, to my mind, in so far as there is a more complicated and careful procedure which must be followed with broth, whereas stock is simply a question of throwing a few oddments into a saucepan of water in order to create a flavoursome liquid.

MAKES ABOUT 3 LITRES (5¹/₄ PINTS)

3 litres (5¹/₄ pints) water
salt
600 g (1 lb 5 oz) whatever meat you have chosen:
beef, lamb, veal or pork
1 clove
1 onion, peeled
1 large carrot, quartered
1 stick celery
2 small tomatoes
1 sprig fresh flat-leaf parsley

The preparation of meat broth is absolutely fundamental, but you must select your cut of meat with great care in order for the finished effect to come out as it should. Neck, breast, shin, skirt or end of rump are all good cuts. You need something which is fairly meaty and gristly rather than being too fatty. Calculate 100 g (4 oz) of meat and 500 ml (17 fl oz) of water per person. The vegetables and remaining ingredients are simply there to add flavour.

Measure the water into a large saucepan and add salt to taste. Lay the meat in the water and place it over a very low heat. Bring it to the boil as slowly as possible so that the flavour from the meat is released very gradually. When the broth begins to boil, press the clove into the onion and add it to the pan with the remaining ingredients. Cover and continue to simmer the broth very very gently for at least $3^1/2$ hours. It will not be necessary to skim off the broth if you begin with cold salted water, if you choose a good cut of meat and if you cook it slowly.

Transfer the meat to another container, cover it with a little broth to prevent it from drying out and put it aside. It can be minced later and used for making fillings, meatballs, pies or other dishes. Let the broth cool then skim the fat from the surface with a slotted spoon. Pour the broth through muslin into a clean container to remove all impurities and use as required.

For chicken broth, calculate 100 g (4 oz) of chicken per person to 500 ml (17 fl oz) of cold water and proceed in exactly the same way. Where possible, use a boiling fowl.

For fish broth, use 100 g (4 oz) of large fish heads and plenty of bones, skin, tails and fins to 500 ml (17 fl oz) of water and proceed exactly as above.

Brodo Vegetale
Vegetable
Broth

*This has always been considered a very light and
easily digestible broth,
good for invalids, children and elderly people.
It is also very cheap and easy to make and can be
flavoured with a herb of your choice.*

MAKES ABOUT 2 LITRES (3^1/$_2$ PINTS)

2 litres (3^1/$_2$ pints) water
2 cloves
3 onions, peeled
5 medium-sized potatoes, peeled
2 large carrots
1 small head celery
4 small tomatoes
salt

Measure the water into a large saucepan. Press the cloves into one of the onions and add all the ingredients to the pan, seasoning with salt to taste. Bring to the boil very slowly, cover and simmer as gently as possible for about 2 hours. Strain the finished broth and use the vegetables for another dish if you wish. Cool and use as required.

Soffritto di Verdura
Vegetable Soffritto

In Italian cooking, most soups, sauces and risottos,
as well as casseroles, stews and pot roasts,
are started off with some kind of a soffritto or battuto.

MAKES A BASE SAUCE FOR A DISH TO SERVE 6

1 onion, peeled and finely chopped
2 cloves garlic, peeled and finely chopped
1 carrot, finely chopped
1 large stick celery with leaves, finely chopped
4 tablespoons olive or sunflower oil

Put all the ingredients into a saucepan together and heat gently over a medium heat, stirring constantly.

Fry carefully for about 10 to 15 minutes until the vegetables are soft but not coloured. Add other ingredients and use as required.

Soffritto all'Aglio
Soffritto with Garlic

This is a very strong-tasting sauce or casserole base
which should be used with care.
It gives a casserole, stew or sauce a basic garlic flavour
which can then develop further as the dish cooks.

MAKES A BASE SAUCE FOR A DISH TO SERVE 6

4 cloves garlic, peeled and finely chopped
3 salted anchovies, boned, rinsed and dried
1 sprig fresh celery leaves, finely chopped
3 tablespoons olive or sunflower oil

Put all the ingredients into a saucepan and fry very gently over a low heat, using a fork to mash the anchovies to a smooth brown purée.

Fry gently for about 15 minutes until the garlic is soft and the texture is smooth and evenly amalgamated.

Soffritto d'Aglio e Peperoncino
Chilli and Garlic Soffritto

This is simply a way of flavouring olive oil for addition to a recipe.
You can make it more or less potent according to your requirements.
By omitting the garlic, you will have a much cheaper version of
the ready-made chilli oil which is on sale
in supermarkets and delicatessens.

MAKES A BASE SAUCE FOR A DISH TO SERVE 6

$^1/_2$–2 dried red chilli peppers
2–5 cloves garlic, peeled or unpeeled
1 large wine glass olive oil

If you want it to have a really strong impact, rub the chilli peppers between your palms to release the oils. Please wash your hands carefully after doing this, as it will be very unpleasant if you inadvertently touch your lips or eyes whilst they are still saturated in chilli. If you leave the garlic unpeeled it will impart a less strong flavour than if you peel it.

Heat the chilli peppers, garlic and oil together until warm. Let the oil become flavoured without burning for a maximum of 5 minutes, then strain the oil, discard the chilli and garlic and use the oil as required.

Soffritto di Cipolla
Onion Soffritto

*This is essential for the preparation of most risottos and
certain sauces, soups and stews.
Although it appears so simple, it is the careful preparation of
these basics which will make the difference between success and failure.
Imagine how disappointing it would be to waste expensive ingredients which
follow on later in the recipe, just because you have failed to get the first bit right!
Red onions will generally add a sweeter, rounder basis of
flavour to the dish, but remember they will be purple in colour when cooked.
Remember also that more gutsy flavours will generally suit an
olive or sunflower oil base, whereas more sophisticated dishes,
especially those to which cream is to be added later,
must use onion fried in butter.*

MAKES A BASE SAUCE FOR A DISH TO SERVE 6

1 medium to large onion, peeled
2 tablespoons unsalted butter
or
4 tablespoons olive or sunflower oil

Slice the onion then chop it finely and evenly or quarter it and process it in a
food processor until chopped but not liquefied. Fry the onion gently with the
butter or oil in a heavy-based pan for 10 to 15 minutes until the onion is soft
and translucent but not coloured. Stir frequently with a wooden spoon which
is kept exclusively for this purpose. This is because it will absorb the flavour
of the onion and frying butter or oil and will thus affect the flavour of other
recipes. Add other ingredients as indicated in the recipe when the onion is
thoroughly cooked and not before.

Remember that if you allow the onion to brown it will develop a sweetish,
nutty taste and this will carry through the rest of the recipe, so if this is not
what you want to achieve you might have to throw it away and start again.

The more delicate the dish, the more carefully and lightly the onion needs
to be cooked.

Battuto
alla Romana
Roman
Battuto

You can make double the quantity of this sort of battuto and keep it in a firmly closed screw-top jar in the fridge to use as required.
If you make it in a food processor it is easier to make a larger quantity.

MAKES A BASE SAUCE FOR A DISH TO SERVE 6

50 g (2 oz) pork fat or ham fat
3 cloves garlic, peeled
2 soft sprigs fresh rosemary
1 salted anchovy, boned, rinsed and dried
salt
freshly ground black pepper
dry white wine

Using a pestle and mortar, blend the fat with the garlic to create a relatively smooth paste. Add the rosemary and anchovy and season to taste with salt and pepper. Continue to amalgamate the ingredients, using a little white wine to help blend them together.

Antipasti

THIS IS PROBABLY the most typical aspect of any Italian meal. The Ancient Romans called this light first course *gustum*, and in those days left-overs would often be enjoyed as breakfast. All kinds of ingredients can be used to make these dishes, and they can be served hot or cold.

One of the best things about this course is that if you want to, you can put it together with no cooking at all. A trip to your local supermarket, delicatessen or specialist food store could yield an excellent array of goodies for a delicious antipasto.

There is a huge selection of cured meat, for example, which you can either ask the shopkeeper to slice for you or buy in packets neatly pre-sliced. On the whole, the pre-sliced varieties tend not to be as good as the freshly sliced selection.

If I were preparing an antipasto selection of this type, I would have a few slices of two or three different varieties of salami as a base. For example, Salame Milano, Salame Felino and Salame Finnocchiona. Then I would add a little Coppa, some prosciutto crudo and a little mortadella. For extra authenticity and flavour as well as garnish, I would then add some olives – again choosing more than one variety – some sun-dried tomatoes steeped in olive oil, and perhaps a few slivers of cheese such as Pecorino or Provolone. I might even include some mushrooms, aubergines, artichoke hearts or other vegetables preserved in oil, *sott'olii*, and a few of the very sharp and tangy Italian pickles, *sott'aceti*. To round off the dish, I would make sure that there was plenty of bread on the table with which to savour the various different flavours and textures of my selection.

This is only my selection, of course, but it gives you an idea of the variety of products which are now widely available. I am certain that once you have tried and tasted sufficiently to discover your own favourites, you'll be able to come up with many other combinations.

An antipasto can be simply a tiny portion of the whole meal, or it can be a meal in itself. How much you decide to serve depends on the circumstances of the situation. Traditionally, the antipasto would have been the course which set the gastric juices flowing for all that was to follow, but nowadays – eating habits being so much more relaxed – you don't have to limit your imagination or your desires in any way! If you are serving it as an anteprandium course, make sure you select ingredients which won't clash or be repeated with the other courses. For example, if you serve Parma ham with figs as your antipasto, it would be better to avoid a pasta dish with ham as your first course, or a dessert with figs. I was always taught never to repeat the same colour or flavour twice when constructing the menu for any meal. This is a fairly easy guideline to follow, and you can decide how rigidly you wish to follow that rule depending upon the event itself.

Tomatoes, especially in the combination of an Insalata Caprese, a tomato and Mozzarella salad, are a very popular part of the antipasto course. To my mind, there is nothing sadder than a pale, watery winter tomato being served up in mid-January. Tomatoes are in their prime when they have soaked up the heat of the sun and therefore should be reserved for the summer months. There is no comparison between a miserable winter specimen and a rich, luscious, sweet, red jewel.

Sun-dried tomatoes can and do provide an alternative to the misery of fresh winter tomatoes. They are widely available and you can buy them in jars preserved in olive oil, or you can buy them dried and leathery, in which case you can put them in jars with whatever herbs you like and cover them in olive oil until they are softened and chewy. They do tend to be quite expensive, however, and I like to regard them as a special treat. Also, although they are very fashionable at the moment, they are undoubtedly an acquired taste which may not be to everyone's liking.

They can also be puréed or bought as a paste which can then be spread on to lightly toasted bread. I like the combination of sun-dried tomatoes with Mozzarella and fresh basil, provided that the Mozzarella is moist and fresh and the basil is as pungently perfumed as possible.

Mozzarella di Bufala is the rarest and most expensive type of Mozzarella as it is made with water buffalo milk, an animal which is a lot less common than a cow! However, ordinary cows' milk does make extremely good Mozzarella, provided it is really fresh. It must have plenty of whey surrounding the cheese to prevent it from drying out and becoming horribly rubbery. When this happens, it affects the flavour just as much as the texture. Good Mozzarella is best eaten fresh; as soon as it begins to dry out, use it in a dish which requires cooking.

Canned tuna fish is another very good standby for creating simple antipasto dishes. The most classic is a salad of flaked, canned tuna mixed with boiled borlotti or cannellini beans, thinly sliced red onions and a good sharp oil and vinegar dressing. Left to steep for a couple of hours so that the beans absorb all the flavours, then stirred once more with plenty of freshly chopped parsley just before serving, this can be a dish fit for Umberto di Savoia.

In Italy, there are still some shops which buy tuna in enormous industrial-sized cans and then sell it by weight. I don't quite know how, but this always seems to taste so much better than the small supermarket cans. Try it for yourself the next time you are self-catering in Italy.

BUYING FRESH PRODUCE

Whatever you are buying from the supermarket or delicatessen, always make sure that the various elements are as fresh as possible. Hard, leathery cured meats are obviously old. Anything which smells musty or looks as though it has been sitting there for longer than you would consider sensible should also be left behind. Whole salami can be gently squeezed to test for age and value for money. They should be soft and easy to indent with your fingertips and the floury exterior should be fairly brilliant white. Prosciutto goes darker as it ages, which is fine, within reason, if you need to use it for cooking, but it will not be very nice eaten as it is.

PREPARING MUSSELS

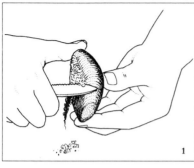 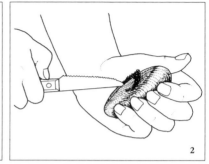

The mussels should feel very heavy when you hold them in your hand and be tightly closed. Any broken or slightly open mussels must be thrown away along with any which feel light or smell peculiar. Next rinse the mussels very thoroughly to get rid of all the surface dirt. Then scrape off all the barnacles and weeds with a sharp serrated knife and a scrubbing-brush (1). Extract the little brown beard at the side with the use of a small knife and a sharp upward jerk (2). After all this, rinse the mussels again very carefully in several changes of fresh water and then they will be ready to cook.

COOKING MUSSELS

Another very popular and extremely light antipasto dish is a plate of mussels. The essential thing here is that the mussels must be extremely fresh and very carefully cleaned and prepared (see above). The simplest way to cook mussels is to put them in a wide shallow pan with some crushed garlic, lemon, parsley and a large glass of dry white wine. Put a lid on the pan and place over the heat for about 5 to 7 minutes, shaking the pan occasionally to help distribute the heat and open up all the mussels. Any mussels which have not opened up after this time must be discarded. *Never* force open a mussel with the intention of actually eating it.

As you can see, they require a fair amount of work, but are well worth all the effort in the end.

PREPARING ARTICHOKES

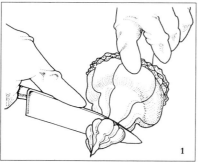 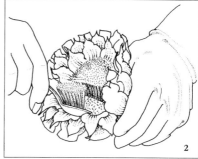

While preparing artichokes, it is probably a good idea to wear rubber gloves as the juice will stain your hands. Be ruthless in removing all the exterior leaves right down to the pale green, tender interior. Cut the top so that you get a flat appearance and lose all the sharp tips of the remaining leaves (1). Prise open the leaves to expose the hairy choke in the centre. Scoop this out with a teaspoon or your fingers (2). Peel the stalk and cut away the harder woody end. Leave the remaining soft length of stalk on the artichoke. The finished vegetable should look like a rather thick flower. Drop the artichokes into a basin containing water and lemon to prevent them going black.

PREPARING ARTICHOKES

Artichokes are another popular vegetable for creating a wide variety of Italian dishes. They, too, require a fair amount of preparation (see above). Choose firm, fresh artichokes which feel heavy with juice. Shrivelled outer leaves or a bruised appearance are to be avoided at all costs.

Prosciutto Crudo con...
Cured Ham with...

*I have decided to open with what has to be the most well known and
classic of all the Italian range of antipasti.
Prosciutto crudo is wrongly called Parma ham by the majority of British consumers.
Although it is true that arguably the best cured raw ham, prosciutto crudo,
comes from the area of Parma because the climatic conditions are so perfect there,
prosciutto crudo is, in fact, prepared in various parts of the country.
The three most famous types of prosciutto crudo are Prosciutto di Parma,
Prosciutto San Daniele and Prosciutto di Carpegna.
Although the best quality prosciutto crudo need not be accompanied by anything at all,
it has become customary to serve it with melon or figs.
Here are a few tips for the serving of this delightful speciality.*

SERVES 6 (GENEROUSLY)

500 g (1 lb 2 oz) prosciutto crudo, very thinly sliced

If you buy prosciutto crudo from a shop where they will slice it for you, please
buy it as near as possible to the time when you are going to serve it. If you buy
it ready sliced in a packet, unwrap it about 20 minutes before you serve it so
as to allow the flavour to develop once the ham is in contact with the air.
If you buy a whole or a joint of prosciutto and slice it yourself with a knife,
remember that you will not be able to achieve the same sort of slices as those
you would get with a slicer. I have made good friends with my local butcher
who slices my prosciutto for me whenever I am fortunate enough to receive
a piece which needs expert attention.

Now as to what to serve with the prosciutto: cold, dry white wine or light
red wine; good quality Italian bread and some unsalted butter; a few olives. If
you are going to serve melon with prosciutto crudo, wait until melon is in
season and you'll be sure of buying a good, sweet, sun-ripened melon which
comes from an area not too far away from where the ham was cured! The
same principle applies to figs. When neither figs nor melon are in season,
prosciutto can be served with ripe pears. I have also eaten excellent prosciutto
served with mangoes or kiwi fruit, but the basic thing to remember is that if
the prosciutto is of good quality it need not be served with any fruit. I do
recommend that you find a good supplier where you can be sure that the
quality will be consistently good and where the ham will be expertly sliced to
air-mail paper thinness! For hot prosciutto recipes, read on!

Minestra di Fagioli e Fontina

SEE PAGE 72

Risotto alle Verdure Miste

SEE PAGE 81

La Caprese
Caprese Salad

*Probably the second most popular of all the Italian antipasti,
this salad has been much maligned and
betrayed since its original conception.
Here it is, as created on Capri!
The best Mozzarella to use is Mozzarella di Bufala,
but it is expensive and not always easy to find.*

SERVES 6

4 large marmande or
beefsteak tomatoes (not too ripe)
a handful of fresh basil leaves
2 large Mozzarella cheeses or
4 smaller ones
salt
olive oil

Slice the tomatoes evenly and arrange them on a serving platter. Place a basil
leaf on each tomato slice; the amount of basil used is entirely up to personal
preference. Cut the Mozzarellas into slices the same size as the tomato slices
and lay one slice of Mozzarella on each tomato. Sprinkle with salt to taste
then pour a little oil to taste over the top. Serve at once or chill for no longer
than 30 minutes.

This is one way of serving the salad, although some people dispute that
this is the way it was first invented and simply serve cubed cheese, sliced
tomatoes, basil leaves, salt and pepper tossed in a bowl with olive oil.

Insalata di Fagioli e Tonno
Bean and Tuna Salad

*For this deliciously simple classic,
it is best to use freshly cooked borlotti beans,
although dried or canned beans will be fine.*

SERVES 6

350 g (12 oz) canned tuna in brine,
drained and flaked
1 red onion, peeled and thinly sliced
2 heaped tablespoons chopped,
fresh flat-leaf parsley
500 g (1 lb 2 oz) cooked borlotti beans
salt
freshly ground black pepper
olive oil
1 lettuce, shredded

Mix together the tuna, onion, parsley and beans. Season to taste with salt and plenty of pepper then dress with as much oil as you like. Bear in mind that both the tuna and the beans will absorb quite a lot of oil. Chill until required and adjust the seasoning and oil to taste just before serving. Serve on a bed of lettuce leaves on individual plates.

Cozze alla Maionese
Mussels with Mayonnaise

This is a marvellous way to serve these delectable shellfish.
If you are in a big hurry, you can use bought mayonnaise and
stir the other ingredients into it, otherwise make your own according to
the recipes on pages 17 or 18.
Please remember to buy really fresh mussels from a good source and
clean them carefully before you cook them (see page 30).

SERVES 6

60 live mussels, scrubbed and bearded
1 large onion, peeled and chopped
10 parsley stalks
1 teaspoon very coarsely ground black pepper
1 wine glass dry white wine
2 tablespoons very finely chopped onion
1 tablespoon double cream
6 tablespoons very thick mayonnaise
juice of 1/2 lemon
1/2 teaspoon French mustard
1 tablespoon chopped fresh parsley

Place the mussels in a wide shallow pan with the onion, parsley stalks and pepper, cover and place the saucepan over a low heat for about 5 minutes, shaking the pan from time to time to help distribute the heat and open up all the mussels. Remove from the heat and discard any that have not opened. Remove and discard the empty shells and pile the full shells on a serving platter. Let the liquid in the saucepan settle for a while.

When the sediment has settled, strain the liquid from the mussels through muslin and set it aside. Put the wine in another saucepan, bring it to the boil and leave it to simmer until it has reduced to one-third of the original quantity. Add 5 tablespoons of the strained cooking liquid and continue to boil until it has reduced to about 1 wine glass full. Stir in the chopped onion and cream and leave to cool. Stir this mixture into the mayonnaise with the lemon juice, mustard and parsley, pour the sauce over the mussels and serve at once or chill until required.

Zucchine Crude con Maionese
Raw Courgettes with Mayonnaise

This is a really delicious and original antipasto dish.
If you combine it with one or two other
dishes from this section of the book,
you can create an entire meal that will be light and fresh
— perfect for a hot summer's day.

SERVES 6

3 large courgettes
2 tablespoons white wine vinegar
salt
2 egg yolks
juice of $1/2$ lemon
200 ml (7 fl oz) light olive oil
$1/2$ teaspoon very hot mustard

Slice the courgettes very finely using a sharp knife; they need to be like tooth-picks. Lay them in a dish and sprinkle with vinegar and salt. Set aside for 2 to 3 hours, stirring occasionally.

Meanwhile, mix together the egg yolks, lemon juice and a pinch of salt. Begin to stir the egg yolks with a wooden spoon, always stirring in the same direction and not spreading them out too much. Add the oil one drop at a time, continuing to stir in a smooth and even rhythm. If the sauce becomes too thick to stir, add a few more drops of lemon juice to return it to an easy stirring mixture. Pour in the oil in a fine steady stream, stirring constantly, until you have a smooth thick mayonnaise. Stir in the mustard.

Drain the courgettes carefully and squeeze them in your hands to extract the moisture. Mix the mayonnaise and courgettes together and serve at once or chill until required. Serve with plenty of crusty Italian bread and a dish of sliced salame.

Crostini all'Aringa
Crostini with Smoked Herring

Crostini have become increasingly popular in Britain.
They are ideal to serve as snacks with a pre-prandial drink,
or as a quick solution to mid-afternoon hunger pangs.
Basically, they consist of toasted bread with a topping.
This recipe has a definitely northern Italian indulgence about it,
but is wonderful with the sharp Italian pickles and
some icy white Pinot Grigio.

SERVES 6

400 g (14 oz) smoked herring fillets
milk
1 eating apple, peeled, cored and cubed
1 onion, peeled and coarsely chopped
salt and freshly ground black pepper
2–3 tablespoons olive oil
1 tablespoon white wine vinegar
12 small slices ciabatta bread, toasted

Place the herring fillets in a bowl and just cover with milk. Leave to soak for at least 6 hours.

Drain the fish thoroughly and put it in the food processor with the apple and onion and season to taste with salt and pepper. Process until smooth, adding oil and vinegar to taste. Spread on toasted ciabatta bread and serve with a dish of Italian pickled vegetables.

Olive Nere in Insalata
Black Olive Salad

This is a very strong-tasting antipasto,
excellent with a dish of cured meats or
strongly flavoured hard cheese
and plenty of Italian bread.
The best olives for this dish are the slightly dried-out
variety with a wrinkled skin.

SERVES 6

600 g (1 lb 5 oz) black olives
1 large orange
$1/2$ large lemon
2 cloves garlic, peeled and lightly crushed
a handful of dried wild fennel or
fresh summer savoury, chopped
olive oil
salt
freshly ground black pepper

Place the olives in a bowl, cover them with warm water and leave them to soak for 5 minutes. Drain and dry the olives, remove the stones and place the olives in a salad bowl. Pare the rind off the orange and the half lemon and cut it carefully into thin strips.

Add the strips of rind to the olives. Stir in the herbs and then add oil to taste, making sure everything is thoroughly soaked. Mix well and season to taste with salt and pepper. Leave to stand for about 1 hour before serving.

Antipasto d'Arance
Antipasto of Oranges

Very unusual but none the less delicious,
this dish is typical of southern Italy.
It looks most impressive if you use a combination of
blood oranges with ordinary oranges.
You can garnish the dish with sprigs of
flat-leaf parsley to finish it off.

SERVES 6

5 large oranges
150 g (5 oz) canned anchovy fillets, drained
1/2 wine glass olive oil
salt

Wash the oranges carefully and slice them very thinly with their skin into neat rounds. Arrange all the slices on a serving platter. Arrange the anchovy fillets on top of the oranges then sprinkle with oil and salt to taste. Serve at once or chill until required.

Insalata di Parmigiano e Funghi
Parmesan and Mushroom Salad

There is one particular trattoria in Rome, very near the Rai,
that makes this salad particularly well.
It is one of my favourite salads and I like to try making it with
a combination of different mushrooms like shiitake,
oyster or brown cap as well as the more traditional champignons.
Whichever mushrooms you select, make sure they are tasty
before you make the salad.

SERVES 6

450 g (1 lb) Parmesan cheese
450 g (1 lb) button mushrooms, thinly sliced
juice of $1/2$ lemon
2 tablespoons chopped fresh flat-leaf parsley
olive oil
salt
freshly ground black pepper

Shave flakes of Parmesan off the wedge and cover the surface of six individual plates with cheese. Scatter the mushrooms on top so as almost to cover the cheese. Sprinkle each plate with lemon juice, parsley and oil to taste and season to taste with salt and pepper. Leave to stand for 15 minutes before serving.

Insalata di Riso con Fontina
Rice Salad with Fontina

*This is a deliciously filling rice salad,
perfect for picnics or al fresco summer lunches.
Fontina cheese, with its distinctive flavour,
gives the salad a very special punch.
If you can't find Fontina, use very mature Cheddar.*

SERVES 6

400 g (14 oz) cooked long grain rice
200 g (7 oz) Fontina cheese, cubed
100 g (4 oz) prosciutto (cooked ham), cubed
100 g (4 oz) mortadella, cubed
200 g (7 oz) pickled Italian vegetables
250 g (9 oz) cooked mixed vegetables, cubed
100 g (4 oz) cooked cold chicken, cubed
juice of $1/2$ lemon
olive oil
salt
freshly ground black pepper

Mix the rice with the Fontina, prosciutto, mortadella, pickles, vegetables and chicken. Stir it all together and dress it generously with lemon juice, oil and salt and pepper to taste. Leave to stand for about 1 hour before serving.

Fave con Pecorino e Prosciutto

Broad Beans with Pecorino and Prosciutto

*All the flavours of these ingredients combine to make
a really mouth-watering traditional antipasto,
just right to get everyone in the mood for the feast to follow.
Traditionally, Pecorino has always been eaten with broad beans as
they both come into the peak of their season at the same time.
The chilli variety of Pecorino cheese is the best one to use and
the dish is also delicious with cubes of mortadella.*

SERVES 6

300 g (11 oz) shelled very young, tender broad beans
300 g (11 oz) Pecorino cheese, grated or cubed
300 g (11 oz) prosciutto crudo, cubed
olive oil
a few drops of lemon juice
salt
freshly ground black pepper

Arrange the beans, Pecorino and ham in three separate piles on a serving platter. Drizzle a little oil over each pile, sprinkle with lemon juice and season to taste with salt and pepper.

Serve at once with plenty of crusty bread and white wine.

Insalata di Carciofi Crudi
Raw Artichoke Salad

Raw artichokes have a flavour that is quite different from that of cooked artichokes. It is best to choose those which are young and tender for this salad.

SERVES 6

6 globe artichokes
juice of 2 lemons
salt
freshly ground black pepper
olive oil
12 thin slices prosciutto crudo

Peel off the hard outer leaves of each artichoke right down to the soft centre. Cut into quarters, remove the hairy choke in the centre and drop the quarters into a basin of cold water with half the lemon juice. This will prevent them from going black. When all the quarters have been prepared, remove them one at a time from the basin of water and slice them very thinly with a sharp knife. Put them all in a serving bowl and pour over the remaining lemon juice. Season to taste with salt and pepper and dress with as much oil as you like. Leave to stand until required.

To serve the antipasto, lay 2 slices of prosciutto on each of the 6 plates. Toss the salad again and cover the prosciutto with the salad.

Stuzzicarelli
Roman
Antipasto

This is a very simple Roman dish designed to be enjoyed with
several litres of cool Frascati...
preferably whilst lounging under a pine tree!

SERVES 6

300 g (11 oz) unsalted butter,
chilled and hard
300 g (11 oz) good-quality anchovies preserved in
olive oil, drained
200 g (7 oz) sweet black and
green olives, stoned
2 loaves ciabatta bread, sliced

Take the butter out of the fridge about 20 minutes before you wish to serve the meal. Using a butter curler or cheese slicer, cut it into fine flakes. Serve the butter with the anchovies, olives and bread. The idea is to lay butter thickly on the bread then to lay a couple of anchovy fillets on top and bite into the bread. Alternate bites of bread with olives to get the authentic flavour of the dish!

Bruschetta al Pomodoro
Garlic Toast with Tomato

A delicious barbecue dish,
this is perfect to munch on while you wait for the sausages to grill.
Bruschetta grilled on a barbecue always tastes so much better!

SERVES 6

6 large slices ciabatta bread or
other crusty bread
2 cloves garlic, peeled
3 marmande or beefsteak tomatoes, sliced
a few leaves fresh basil, chopped
salt
freshly ground black pepper
olive oil

Toast the slices of bread until their surfaces are hard and crisp. Rub the surfaces with the garlic until the juice is absorbed into the bread. Rub the slices of tomato over the bread and squash them down with a fork to moisten the bread as much as possible. Scatter the basil leaves on top of the tomatoes and season to taste with salt and pepper. Drizzle oil to taste all over the dish and leave to stand for about 10 minutes before serving.

Bresaola all'Olio
Bresaola
with Olive Oil

Bresaola is cured beef fillet.
It is one of the classiest of all the cured meats and
certainly one of the most delectable.
It is available sliced and vacuum-packed at most large supermarkets,
but by far the best Bresaola is bought at specialised
delicatessens and it is sliced for you.
Buy it as near as possible to the time you wish to serve it and
follow these simple rules to make the most of this wonderful delicacy.

SERVES 6

500 g (1 lb 2 oz) freshly sliced Bresaola
juice of 1 lemon
5 tablespoons olive oil
6 sprigs rocket
1 onion, peeled and very thinly sliced (optional)
freshly ground black pepper

Arrange the Bresaola evenly in a single layer on 6 individual plates. Sprinkle each portion with lemon juice then with oil and scatter the rocket on top. Some people add onion to this dish, but in my opinion it is best to leave out the rocket if you decide to use the onion. Cover the meat completely with a very thin layer of onion, then drizzle a little more oil on top. Finish off with a generous grinding of black pepper and serve.

Insalata di Mare
Seafood Salad

*This is my own version of this classic summer dish.
If you can, use raw prawns and blanch them in boiling water for
about 5 minutes until tender to get that special sweet flavour.
If you buy fresh squid, refer to page 227 for
information on how to prepare it.*

SERVES 6

300 g (11 oz) fresh or frozen squid, cleaned,
trimmed and cut into rings
salt
5 small potatoes, peeled
6 cooked crab claws or 4 small lobster tails
250 g (9 oz) cooked, peeled prawns
3 tablespoons chopped fresh parsley
juice of $1/2$ lemon
6 tablespoons olive oil
freshly ground black pepper

Place the squid in a saucepan of salted water, bring to the boil and simmer
for about 25 minutes or until tender. Drain the squid and tip it into a serving
bowl. Boil the potatoes until tender then cool and cube them and place in the
bowl. Remove the shell from the crab claws or lobster tails, slice the meat
into neat pieces and add it to the bowl with the prawns. Mix everything
together well. Sprinkle over the parsley and lemon juice and mix again. Pour
on the oil and toss together then season to taste with salt and pepper. Serve
at once.

If you like, you can add about 6 tablespoons of cooked or canned drained
cannellini beans with the cubed potatoes.

La Bagna Cauda
Hot Anchovy Dip
for Vegetables

*There are many different versions of this classic Piedmontese
dip but this is the one I like best.
A fondue set (without the forks) is a very useful item for serving this dish.
You can serve it with any vegetables of your choice and it is a dish where
baby vegetables can be used to their best advantage.
Choose only the youngest and most sweet and tender vegetables and
vary the selection according to your preferences and mood.
Vegetables can include:
raw artichokes (pull off one leaf at a time, dip and eat);
strips of raw carrot, celery, courgettes or red and yellow peppers;
small florets of very tender broccoli or cauliflower;
firm young spinach leaves; radishes or asparagus.*

SERVES 6 TO 8

200 ml (7 fl oz) light olive oil
1 tablespoon unsalted butter
3 cloves garlic, peeled and very finely chopped
12 salted anchovies, boned, rinsed,
dried and chopped

Heat the oil and butter together in a small saucepan. As soon as the butter is
foaming, stir in the garlic and cook for about 2 minutes. Add the anchovies
and cook, stirring, until the anchovies have completely disintegrated and
amalgamated into the oil. Serve at once with lots of raw vegetables.

Cozze alla Parmigiana
Grilled Mussels with Parmesan Cheese

The unusual Italian combination of fish and cheese works extremely well with this light, lemony dish. The mussels must be very fresh and well cleaned (see page 30).

SERVES 6

36 large live mussels, scrubbed and bearded
$1/2$ lemon
50 g (2 oz) Parmesan cheese, freshly grated
1 tablespoon fine fresh white breadcrumbs
40 g ($1^1/2$ oz) unsalted butter
salt
freshly ground black pepper

Pre-heat the oven to gas mark 9, 240°C (475°F). Place the mussels in a wide shallow pan with the lemon, cover and place over a medium heat for about 5 minutes, shaking the pan from time to time to help distribute the heat and open up all the mussels. Remove from the heat and discard any that have not opened (you may like to put in a few extra just in case!).

Remove one shell from each mussel and place the full shells in a shallow ovenproof dish. Mix together the Parmesan and breadcrumbs and sprinkle over the mussels. Place a knob of butter on top of each one and season to taste with salt and pepper. Bake at the top of the oven for about 4 minutes and serve at once.

Crostini di Mozzarella e Alici

Mozzarella and Anchovies on Toasted Ciabatta Bread

*The classic combination of the strongly flavoured anchovies with
the delicate, pure, clean taste of Mozzarella really comes into
its own in this delightfully simple dish.
You can add capers or strips of sun-dried tomatoes for
extra texture and flavour, and it is delicious with strips of
prosciutto crudo instead of anchovies for a change.
You can use diagonal slices of baguette if you can't find ciabatta.*

SERVES 6

12 thick slices Mozzarella
12 small slices ciabatta bread
24 anchovy fillets in oil, drained, rinsed and dried
freshly ground black pepper

Cut the Mozzarella slices as near as possible to the same size as the bread. Lay the Mozzarella on top of the bread and place under a hot grill for about 2 minutes. When the Mozzarella is just soft, press the anchovy fillets on top of the cheese and return them to the grill.

Grill for about 3 minutes until the cheese is runny and serve at once.

Bruschetta al Pomodoro e Olive
Toasted Garlic Bread with
Tomatoes and Olives

*This open sandwich encapsulates all the flavours of
a Mediterranean summer!
In Italy, I make up several of these before I go to
the beach so that while I'm out, all the juices can seep into
the bread for a really scrummy lunch.*

SERVES 6

6 large slices or 12 small slices ciabatta bread
2 cloves garlic, peeled
4 tablespoons olive oil
8 ripe tomatoes
10 black olives, stoned
a large pinch of dried oregano
1 tablespoon salted capers, rinsed, drained and chopped
salt
freshly ground black pepper

Grill the bread on both sides until the surfaces are rough and pale golden. Rub the bread with one of the cloves of garlic and set it aside. Put the other clove of garlic into a saucepan with the oil and fry gently for about 3 minutes until the garlic is golden brown, then remove the garlic from the pan. Add the tomatoes, cover and simmer for about 10 minutes until the tomatoes are falling apart and pulpy. Remove from the heat and push the cooked tomatoes through a sieve. Return the tomato sauce to the heat and bring to a gentle simmer. Stir in the olives, oregano and capers and heat through for a few minutes then remove from the heat and season to taste with salt and pepper. Spoon the hot tomato sauce over the garlic bread and serve at once.

Crostini di Polenta con Gorgonzola
Toasted Polenta with Gorgonzola

*I love the flavour combination of these two ingredients,
but if blue cheese is not to your liking,
use Brie, Camembert or Fontina as alternatives.
This dish tastes lovely with a green salad with plenty of
rocket and a balsamic vinegar dressing.*

SERVES 6

1 litre (1³/₄ pints) cold water
salt
250 g (9 oz) quick-cook polenta
200 g (7 oz) Gorgonzola cheese, sliced
5 tablespoons chopped walnuts
freshly ground black pepper

Bring the salted water to the boil in a large saucepan. Sprinkle in the polenta with one hand so that it falls into the water like fine rain, whisking constantly to prevent lumps. Continue in this way for about 5 minutes until the mixture begins to thicken then use a wooden spoon to stir constantly as the polenta cooks. You will know it is ready when it comes away easily from the sides of the pan. If you use ordinary polenta, it will take at least 30 minutes. Turn out and cool until completely solid. This can be done well in advance.

When you wish to serve, slice the polenta into neat strips and arrange them on a grill. Toast on one side until lightly browned, then turn the slices over and cover each one with Gorgonzola. Return to the grill and toast for about 5 minutes until the cheese is runny. Arrange on a warm serving platter, scatter with the walnuts and season to taste with pepper. Serve at once.

Spiedini di Polenta
e Funghi
Grilled Polenta and
Mushroom Kebabs

Here you can indulge your passion for mushrooms
and use more than one variety –
shiitake, oyster, champignon or even field mushrooms –
to make the dish even more imaginative and flavoursome.
I like to serve this with a fresh tomato salad.

SERVES 6

400 g (14 oz) cooked polenta (see page 138)
250 g (9 oz) back bacon, thickly sliced
250 g (9 oz) Mozzarella cheese
40 g (1½ oz) unsalted butter
250 g (9 oz) brown cap mushroom caps
2 tablespoons olive oil
3 tablespoons dried breadcrumbs
salt
freshly ground black pepper

Pre-heat the oven to gas mark 5, 190°C (375°F). Slice the polenta thickly and grill it lightly on both sides then cut it into chunky squares. Grill the bacon lightly and cut it into similar-sized squares. Cut the Mozzarella into similar-sized chunks. Melt the butter in a saucepan and toss the mushroom caps lightly for a few minutes until just soft.

Thread the polenta, bacon, Mozzarella and mushrooms alternately on to kebab skewers. Lay the kebabs in an oiled ovenproof dish, sprinkle with breadcrumbs and season to taste with salt and pepper. Bake in the oven for about 8 minutes then serve at once.

Olive all'Ascolana
Fried Olives

*Ascolane olives make perfect nibbles for serving with
pre-prandial drinks as they stimulate the appetite without filling you up.
Try serving some deep-fried olives alongside various other kinds of
olives without the breadcrumbs: olive di Gaeta,
marinated green olives, stuffed black olives and so on.*

SERVES 6

60 large green olives, stoned
2 tablespoons olive oil
250 g (9 oz) mixed minced meat
(pork, veal, beef, ham, chicken livers etc.)
5 eggs
8 tablespoons fresh breadcrumbs
a large pinch of freshly grated nutmeg
salt
freshly ground black pepper
olive oil for deep-frying
1 lemon, cut into wedges

Rinse and dry the olives. Heat the oil and fry the meat for 2 or 3 minutes until browned then remove from the heat. Mix in 3 of the eggs and 6 tablespoons of breadcrumbs and season to taste with nutmeg, salt and pepper. Stuff the olives with the filling. Beat the remaining eggs and roll the stuffed olives in the egg, then in the remaining breadcrumbs. Heat the oil until a small cube of bread dropped in it sizzles instantly. Deep-fry the olives for a few minutes until crisp and golden brown, then drain on kitchen paper. Any remaining filling can be rolled into small balls then coated in egg and breadcrumbs and fried in the same oil. Serve hot with lemon wedges.

Polenta Fritte con Cipolle
Polenta with Fried Onions

This is a very wholesome, filling dish.
It's a perfect way of using up left-over polenta.
You can also add a sprinkling of chives to garnish the dish.
My brother sometimes adds dried red chilli peppers to
the olive oil before he fries the onions so
as to give the dish extra spice.

SERVES 6

4 red onions, peeled and thinly sliced
4 tablespoons olive oil
salt
12 small slices cooked polenta (see page 138)
8 tablespoons sunflower oil
12 finger-sized slices of Fontina cheese
freshly ground black pepper

Fry the onions with the oil over a low heat for about 8 minutes until soft. Remove them from the heat, season to taste with salt and keep them warm. Meanwhile, grill the polenta on one side. Turn the slices over and lay a sliver of cheese on top of each slice of polenta. Grill again for about 4 minutes until the cheese is bubbling. Arrange the polenta on 6 warmed plates and cover and surround with the hot onions. Serve at once.

Arancini di Riso
Rice Oranges

*If you have some left-over risotto, you can use that to
make these marvellous and extremely filling snacks.
They originally come from Sicily but are now made all over southern Italy.
They are perfect for a quick lunch, especially with a fresh green salad.*

SERVES 6

75 g (3 oz) unsalted butter
1 large onion, peeled and finely chopped
120 g (4¹/₂ oz) minced veal or beef
100 g (4 oz) chicken livers, chopped
salt and freshly ground black pepper
100 g (4 oz) shelled fresh peas or frozen petits pois
300 g (11 oz) long-grain rice
1.5 litres (2¹/₂ pints) chicken broth
4 eggs, beaten
75 g (3 oz) Pecorino or Parmesan cheese, freshly grated
2 hard-boiled eggs, sliced
9 tablespoons dried breadcrumbs
olive oil for deep-frying

Melt half the butter and fry the onion for about 5 minutes until soft then add
the minced meat and fry for a further 5 minutes. Season to taste with salt and
pepper, add the chicken livers and fry for a further 4 minutes. Add the peas
and cook for a further 5 or 6 minutes. You should now have a very thick
mixture. Meanwhile, place the rice in a saucepan, just cover with broth, bring
to the boil and simmer gently until the liquid is absorbed. Add some more
stock and simmer until it is absorbed then continue to cook in this way for
about 20 minutes until the rice is tender but still firm. Remove from the heat
and mix in the remaining butter, 2 eggs and the Pecorino or Parmesan. When
the rice is cool enough, take handfuls of the rice and roll it firmly between
your hands to make balls similar in size and shape to satsumas. Make a hole in
the centre of each ball and put a little hard-boiled egg and a spoonful of the
filling into the hole. Press the hole closed lightly and then roll each ball in
beaten egg and breadcrumbs. Heat the oil until a small cube of bread dropped
into it sizzles instantly. Fry the rice balls in the oil for about 5 minutes until
crisp and golden. Drain carefully on kitchen paper and serve warm.

Crocchettine di Riso
Rice Fritters

*I like to make these for children's parties because
they taste really special even though they are so simple.
Be sure to serve them piping hot.
For a sweet version, replace the cheese with the
same amount of caster sugar and
dust with icing sugar once drained.*

SERVES 6

400 g (14 oz) long-grain rice
1 litre (1³/₄ pints) water
40 g (1¹/₂ oz) unsalted butter
3 eggs, beaten
50 g (2 oz) Parmesan cheese, freshly grated
a large pinch of freshly grated nutmeg
salt
freshly ground black pepper
4 tablespoons plain white flour
5 tablespoons dried breadcrumbs
light olive oil for deep-frying

Place the rice, water and butter in a saucepan, bring to the boil and simmer
until the rice has absorbed almost all the water. Drain it and mix in 2 of the
eggs and the Parmesan and season to taste with nutmeg, salt and pepper. Roll
this mixture into small balls about the size of walnuts then coat each ball
lightly in flour, then egg and then breadcrumbs. Heat the oil and deep-fry the
rice fritters for about 5 minutes until crisp and golden. Serve at once.

Pomodori al Forno
Baked Tomatoes

These tomatoes are wonderful eaten either hot or cold.
You can cook peppers in exactly the same way but
they may need a little more liquid.
Ideal for a light lunch, they can be prepared all year round
now that big marmande tomatoes are available everywhere.

SERVES 6

6 large firm ripe tomatoes
200 g (7 oz) long-grain rice
salt
8 tablespoons olive oil
2 cloves garlic, peeled and crushed
8 leaves fresh basil, chopped
a large pinch of dried oregano
freshly ground black pepper
2 medium-sized potatoes, peeled and
cut into 12 slices

Pre-heat the oven to gas mark 4, 180°C (350°F). Cut the tomatoes in half horizontally and scoop out and reserve the insides. Turn the tomato shells upside down on a board to drain while you prepare the filling.

Meanwhile, boil the rice in salted water for about 8 minutes until tender but still firm then drain it thoroughly. Heat half the oil and fry the garlic until golden then remove the garlic. Push the tomato flesh through a sieve and add the pulp to the garlic-flavoured oil. Stir in the basil and oregano, season to taste with salt and pepper and simmer for about 5 minutes, stirring occasionally. Stir the sauce into the drained rice and fill each tomato half with the mixture. Lay a slice of potato on top of each tomato half. This acts as a lid to keep the rice moist and help it to cook. Oil a shallow ovenproof dish with the remaining oil and arrange the tomatoes in the dish. Bake in the oven for about 30 minutes and serve hot or cold, removing the potato first if you wish.

Peperoni con la Mozzarella
Peppers with Mozzarella

*This dish looks very pretty if you
choose peppers of different colours.
You can now buy orange, purple and white peppers as
well as the more classic green, red and yellow.
In fact, they all taste the same, so what is most
important is that they should be juicy and fleshy.*

SERVES 6

1 large firm red pepper
1 large firm green pepper
1 large firm yellow pepper
3 tablespoons olive oil
salt
freshly ground black pepper
24 thin flat slices of Mozzarella cheese
24 leaves fresh basil

Push a fork into the stalk base of each pepper and hold the peppers over a naked flame, turning them around so as to blister the skin all over and blacken the surface very thoroughly. Put the peppers in a plastic bag and leave aside to sweat for about 10 minutes. Remove them from the bag and rub the skin off each pepper using a piece of kitchen paper. Halve the peppers, remove the seeds and membranes then cut each pepper into 8 flat wide strips. Arrange the pepper slices on a grill and brush them lightly with oil.

Season to taste with salt and pepper then lay a slice of Mozzarella on top of each one. Drizzle a little more oil on top and finish off with a couple of basil leaves on each one. Grill for just 2 or 3 minutes until the Mozzarella softens and begins to run. Serve at once.

Melanzane alla Giudia

Aubergines in the Jewish Style

There are several recipes from Jewish cuisine linked to the traditions of the old ghetto in the centre of Rome. This is a delightful recipe for preparing aubergines as a warm side dish to be served with cheese or cured meat.

SERVES 6

3 large or 4 smaller aubergines, cubed
salt
5 tablespoons olive oil
3 cloves garlic, peeled and lightly crushed
freshly ground black pepper
a handful of chopped fresh parsley

Put the cubed aubergines in a colander and sprinkle generously with salt. Cover with a plate with a weight on top and leave in the sink for about 2 hours to drain out the bitter juices.

Rinse and dry the aubergines very thoroughly. Heat the oil and garlic in a frying pan for about 3 minutes until the garlic goes brown, then discard the garlic. Place the aubergines in the flavoured oil and cook them, uncovered, for 15 minutes. Cover the pan and cook for a further 10 minutes, stirring occasionally, until the aubergines are soft and cooked through. Remove from the heat and season to taste with salt and pepper. Transfer to a warmed serving dish, sprinkle with parsley and serve hot or cold with thinly sliced prosciutto crudo.

Giardinetto al Gratin
Mixed
Grilled Vegetables

*This is a very tasty version of
the popular dish of grilled vegetables.
You can also use courgettes for the dish if you like.*

SERVES 6

6 aubergines, halved lengthways
100 g (4 oz) Parmesan cheese, freshly grated
100 g (4 oz) fresh breadcrumbs
100 g (4 oz) chopped fresh parsley
3 cloves garlic, peeled and finely chopped
salt
6 large firm ripe tomatoes,
halved and juice reserved
6 firm peppers, halved and de-seeded
8 tablespoons olive oil

Put the aubergines in a colander and sprinkle generously with salt. Cover with a plate with a weight on top and leave in the sink for about 2 hours to drain out the bitter juices.

Pre-heat the oven to gas mark 4, 180°C (350°F). Rinse and dry the aubergines very thoroughly. Using a very sharp knife, make about 4 incisions in the flesh of each aubergine half almost all the way through to the skin but without going through it. Mix together the Parmesan, breadcrumbs, parsley and garlic and season to taste with salt. Use this mixture to fill and cover all the halved vegetables. Press down quite firmly to make sure the filling mixture sticks securely. Oil a large shallow ovenproof dish and arrange all the vegetables in it without them overlapping. Sprinkle with the remaining oil and the reserved tomato juice and bake in the oven for about 45 minutes. Serve warm with plenty of crusty bread.

Barchette di Zucchine al Formaggio
Courgette Boats with Cheese

I love the delicate flavour of this dish,
although you can use a stronger cheese in order to
give the dish more of a punchy taste.
It is delicious served with a carrot and celery salad.

SERVES 6

12 courgettes
salt
8 tablespoons olive oil
4 tablespoons passata
5 leaves fresh basil, chopped
freshly ground black pepper
200 g (7 oz) Bel Paese cheese,
cut into tiny cubes
3 eggs, beaten
2 tablespoons fresh breadcrumbs

Pre-heat the oven to gas mark 4, 180°C (350°F). Blanch the courgettes in boiling salted water for about 2 minutes then drain and leave to cool. Cut them in quarters lengthways and scoop out the interior to make little boats. Put the courgette pulp into a saucepan with 1 tablespoon of oil and the passata. Simmer gently for about 5 minutes, stirring occasionally, then add the basil leaves and season to taste with salt and pepper. Pour this mixture into a bowl and mix in the Bel Paese, eggs and breadcrumbs. Use the mixture to fill the courgette boats and arrange them in an oiled ovenproof dish. Pour over the remaining oil and bake in the oven for about 30 minutes.

Soups

IN ITALIAN PEASANT COOKERY, soup is probably the most important meal of the day. Even a big family can be fed quite substantially on a basic broth made with a few bones, some simple vegetables and a few chunks of stale bread. This is soup at its most simple, seen as a way of filling hungry bellies when very little was available and the icy winter winds were biting. For this reason, even nowadays you will find many recipes for Italian soup which instruct you to line the soup bowls or tureen with a layer of sliced bread, sometimes toasted or stale and sometimes rubbed with garlic, over which the hot soup is poured. This is reminiscent of the time when the bread in the soup provided the bulk, and it still makes for an extremely filling soup.

On the whole, and largely owing to their cultural background, it would be fair to say that most Italian soups are virtually a meal in themselves. Top of this list must be the hugely filling and multi-coloured Minestrone with its many vegetables, beans and pasta. At the other end of the spectrum is the Zuppa di Pesce with all the different kinds of shellfish and fish flavoured with garlic, tomato and white wine. In between there are lots of delicious combinations of vegetables and pulses with either rice or pasta which make marvellously satisfying soups. There are some soups which are much lighter in their content and would therefore be suitable as a first course to be followed by a main course and a dessert. These are soups which do not include rice, pasta, pulses or bread and which are considerably more sophisticated. I hope that I have given you a reasonably balanced collection of both types of soup in this chapter. Of course, there is never anything to stop you leaving out the rice, pasta, pulses or bread to make a less substantial soup or, on the other hand, adding a handful of rice or pasta to a light soup to make it more filling.

It has always been preferred to serve soup in the evening in Italy. Traditionally, the larger meal eaten at lunch time could be slept off during a siesta. Now that siestas are less popular and, in line with the rest of Europe, Italians are grabbing a sandwich for lunch, the evening meal has become more important. With these guidelines, soup should therefore be moved to the lunch time slot, as it is simple and quick to prepare – or at least to re-heat – and provides a nourishing and wholesome meal. In my own household, I have to provide lunch for four adults every lunch time. After many experiments, I make enormous soups twice a week during the cold Norfolk winters, always with pulses, pasta or rice to make them really filling. This means less time spent in the kitchen in preparing the food and a lot less clearing up to do. In the evening, when I have more time, I can opt for more variety.

There is a whole range of light and easily digestible soups which are designed for consumption by small children, invalids or elderly people who all need to be well nourished as simply and pleasantly as possible. Of these, La Stracciatella is a very good example. This is one of those soups which uses *brodo*, carefully made broth, as its basis. In all cases where broth is used, whether it is made with chicken or meat, make sure that it is richly flavoured with a luxuriously tantalising smell. I always like to serve my soup from a central tureen so that everybody can help themselves to some more if they wish. This works particularly well if you have a soup without a bread base. Soups that are poured over bread may be best served in individual bowls so that each person gets their own slice of bread.

In Italian, soup is sometimes called *zuppa* and sometimes called *minestra*. I wish I could give you a simple way of knowing which name refers to which kind of soup, but unfortunately there doesn't seem to be a hard-and-fast rule! I can't even say that in one part of the country they call it *zuppa* and in another they call it *minestra* because there are just too many exceptions!

However and whenever you eat your soup, I hope very much that you will enjoy it!

Zuppa di Lenticchie

SEE PAGE 74

Risotto con Gamberetti

SEE PAGE 84

La Stracciatella
Roman Egg
and Cheese Soup

*The most classic of all the Roman soups with
its origins planted firmly in the cuisine of Apicius,
this makes a nourishing and light meal if
you are feeling as though it is 'the morning after'.*

SERVES 6

6 eggs
50 g (2 oz) Parmesan cheese, freshly grated
a large pinch of freshly grated nutmeg
1 teaspoon grated lemon rind
1 tablespoon dried breadcrumbs
salt
freshly ground black pepper
1.5 litres (2^1/$_2$ pints) chicken broth

Beat the eggs very thoroughly with the Parmesan, nutmeg, lemon rind and
breadcrumbs and season to taste with salt and pepper. Bring the broth to the
boil very slowly so as not to lose any of the flavour. When it is boiling, pour
in the egg mixture and whisk constantly until it cooks and thickens.

Be careful not to allow the mixture to go lumpy. Serve at once.

Minestrone
Minestrone

*The name means 'big soup' and that is
just what it is meant to be.
You can omit the pasta or rice for a much less filling soup.*

SERVES 6

250 g (9 oz) dried borlotti or cannellini beans,
soaked overnight in cold water
3 tablespoons olive oil
1 onion, peeled and finely chopped
1 clove garlic, peeled and finely chopped
3 sticks celery, finely chopped
500 g (1 lb 2 oz) fresh spinach, chopped
2 courgettes, cut into tiny cubes
2 carrots, finely chopped
2 medium potatoes, peeled and quartered
2 small tomatoes, skinned, de-seeded and chopped
1.5 litres (2^1/$_2$ pints) water
200 g (7 oz) long-grain rice or small pasta
salt
freshly ground black pepper
75 g (3 oz) Parmesan cheese, freshly grated

Drain and rinse the beans, put them in a saucepan with fresh water, bring to the boil and boil rapidly for 5 minutes then drain.

Meanwhile, put the oil into a large saucepan with the onion and garlic and fry very gently for about 8 minutes until soft but not browned. Add the celery, spinach, courgettes, carrots, potatoes and tomatoes, stir it all together and cook for about 10 minutes until heated through and softened. Add the water, bring to the boil, cover and simmer very gently for about 1 hour. Add the beans, cover and simmer for a further 1 hour until the beans are completely soft. Add the rice or pasta and boil for about 7 minutes until tender. Season to taste with salt and pepper and serve hot or leave to cool a little and serve at room temperature. Serve with plenty of freshly grated Parmesan.

Zuppa di Cipolle e Vino

Onion and Wine Soup

This one is a real winter warmer.
My mother used to make this soup for
us children when we had colds.
You can use red wine if you prefer.

SERVES 6

1.5 kg (3 lb 4 oz) onions, peeled and thickly sliced
3 tablespoons olive oil
100 g (4 oz) unsalted butter
600 ml (1 pint) dry white wine
600 ml (1 pint) chicken stock
3 cloves
a pinch of salt
a pinch of white pepper
5 slices white bread, cubed
2 cloves garlic, peeled and crushed
25 g (1 oz) Parmesan cheese, freshly grated

Put the onions, oil and half the butter in a large deep saucepan and fry for about 8 minutes until soft. Add the wine and simmer for a few minutes until reduced to three-quarters of the original quantity. Add the stock and bring back to the boil. Season to taste with the cloves, salt and white pepper, cover and simmer for about 40 minutes.

Meanwhile, heat the remaining butter and fry the bread cubes and garlic for about 5 minutes until crisp and brown. Discard the garlic and put the fried garlic bread in the bottom of 6 soup bowls. Pour over the hot soup, sprinkle with Parmesan and serve at once.

Pappa al Pomodoro
Tuscan
Tomato Soup

*This simple old-fashioned soup requires really sweet,
ripe, juicy tomatoes if it is to taste as it should.
Add as much basil as you like to finish off the soup with
a pungent summery flavour.
It tastes wonderful either hot, cold, warm or re-heated.*

SERVES 6

1.5 litres (2^1/$_2$ pints) vegetable, chicken
or meat broth
1 onion, peeled and chopped
1.2 kg (2 lb 12 oz) very ripe,
soft tomatoes, coarsely chopped
8 tablespoons olive oil
400 g (14 oz) stale bread,
crusts removed and thinly sliced
3 cloves garlic, peeled and crushed
a handful of fresh basil leaves, chopped
salt
freshly ground black pepper

Heat the broth slowly in a large saucepan. Meanwhile, put the onion, tomatoes and half the oil in a separate pan and fry together over a gentle heat for about 10 minutes until soft. Push the mixture through a food mill or sieve and add it to the hot broth.

Add the bread, garlic and basil and season to taste with salt and pepper. Cover and simmer gently for about 45 minutes until thick and creamy, stirring occasionally. Stir in the remaining oil and serve at once.

Zuppa di Finocchi
Fennel Soup

*Fennel has marvellously refreshing and digestive qualities.
If you want to, you can use other herbs as well as
the parsley and you can serve freshly grated Parmesan separately for
people to add to their own portion.*

SERVES 6

8–10 small fennel bulbs
6 tablespoons olive oil
3 cloves garlic, peeled and finely chopped
6 tablespoons chopped fresh parsley
salt
freshly ground black pepper
1.5 litres (2^1/$_2$ pints) chicken or meat broth

Remove all the hard exterior part of the fennel bulbs and slice them thinly. Put the fennel, oil, garlic and parsley in a saucepan and fry gently for about 10 minutes until soft. Season generously with salt and pepper and add the broth. Bring to the boil, stir well, cover and simmer for about 45 minutes until the fennel is soft and falling apart. Serve warm with plenty of bread.

Minestra di Fagioli con Riso e Verdura
Bean and Rice Vegetable Soup

This is a soup containing lots of different ingredients and flavours which all blend together beautifully to make a rich and tasty dish for supper or lunch. If you wish to use dried beans for the soup, they should be soaked overnight in cold water then boiled in fresh water for 5 minutes before you start.

SERVES 6

75 g (3 oz) ham fat, preferably from prosciutto crudo
2 cloves garlic, peeled and finely chopped
300 g (11 oz) fresh spinach, coarsely chopped
$^1/_2$ savoy cabbage, coarsely shredded
250 g (9 oz) chopped mixed vegetables:
carrot, courgette, potato, celery, tomato, onion
2 strips belly pork, finely cubed
5 tablespoons passata
300 g (11 oz) canned cannellini beans, drained
900 ml (1$^1/_2$ pints) meat or chicken broth or vegetable stock
salt
freshly ground black pepper
225 g (8 oz) long-grain rice
50 g (2 oz) Parmesan cheese, freshly grated

Fry the ham fat with the garlic in a large saucepan for about 4 minutes until the garlic is soft then remove from the heat. In a separate saucepan, steam the spinach and cabbage together with no extra water for a few minutes until just wilted and soft. Drain and squeeze dry, then transfer to the saucepan containing the garlic and return to the heat. Stir thoroughly then add the mixed vegetables and pork and cook for 5 minutes. Stir in the passata, beans and broth or stock and season to taste with salt and pepper. Bring to the boil, cover and simmer for about 1 hour until all the vegetables and beans are soft and pulpy. Add the rice, return to the boil and simmer for about 10 minutes until the rice is tender. Remove from the heat, stir in the Parmesan and serve at once. In summer time, this soup is often served cold.

Minestra di Zucchine
Courgette Soup

*I adore this light and nourishing soup with its intense
herby taste and dense, sweet flavour of onions.
It is especially good with Pecorino cheese to finish it off.*

SERVES 6

2 large onions, finely chopped
5 tablespoons olive oil
6 large courgettes, cubed
a small bunch of fresh herbs tied
together with cook's string:
basil, bay leaf, thyme, rosemary
750 ml (1¼ pints) chicken stock
2 eggs, beaten
salt
freshly ground black pepper
50 g (2 oz) Parmesan or Pecorino cheese,
freshly grated

Fry the onions with the oil in a large saucepan for about 5 minutes until the onions are transparent. Stir in the courgettes then the herbs. Add the stock and bring to the boil, cover and simmer for about 30 minutes until the courgettes are pulpy. Remove from the heat and take out the herbs. Stir in the eggs and whisk them through the soup and season to taste with salt and pepper. Serve at once with freshly grated Parmesan or Pecorino.

Minestra di Fagioli e Fontina
Bean and Fontina Soup

A really simple but rich bean soup,
finished off with the delicious taste of Fontina cheese,
this should be served with bread to go with the melted cheese.
If Fontina is unavailable,
you can use Camembert or Brie instead.

Serves 6

400 g (14 oz) canned cannellini beans,
drained, or dried beans soaked overnight in cold water
1 large onion, peeled and finely chopped
4 tablespoons olive oil
600 ml (1 pint) milk
salt
freshly ground black pepper
200 g (7 oz) Fontina cheese, cubed

If you are using dried beans, boil them in fresh water for 30 minutes or until completely soft. Then push them through a food mill or sieve to make a purée. Canned beans can simply be puréed without cooking. Fry the onion with the oil in a large saucepan for about 8 minutes until the onion is soft and golden brown. Stir in the bean purée and heat through. Add the milk and bring to the boil, cover and simmer gently for about 30 minutes, stirring frequently. Season to taste with salt and pepper and stir in the cheese. Simmer gently for a few minutes until the cheese is soft and just beginning to melt without liquefying. Serve at once.

Zuppa di Ceci
Chick Pea Soup

*The humble chick pea has been part of
the Mediterranean diet for many centuries.
I always find it seems to marry best with the intense flavour of
rosemary so I have included it in this delightfully simple soup.*

SERVES 6

400 g (14 oz) dried chick peas,
soaked overnight in cold water with
a pinch of bicarbonate of soda
100 g (4 oz) unsalted butter
2 onions, peeled and chopped
1 carrot, chopped
1 large stick celery, chopped
3 sprigs fresh rosemary
150 g (5 oz) pancetta, chopped
salt
freshly ground black pepper
6 thin slices ciabatta bread, cubed

Drain the soaked chick peas and transfer them to a large clean saucepan.
Cover with plenty of cold water, bring to the boil and simmer for about 40
minutes until completely tender. Meanwhile, melt half the butter and fry the
onions, carrot, celery, rosemary and pancetta for about 5 minutes until soft.
Drain the chick peas, reserving the cooking water.

Add the chick peas to the saucepan, season to taste with salt and pepper
and gradually dilute the soup with the cooking water. Bring to the boil, cover
and simmer gently for about 30 minutes, adding liquid as necessary until the
soup is thick and amalgamated. Heat the remaining butter and fry the bread
for a few minutes until crisp. Scatter over the soup to serve.

Zuppa di Lenticchie
Lentil Soup

*Including chestnuts in the ingredients makes this a
lentil soup with a difference.
The addition of all the herbs gives it an amazingly fresh finish.*

SERVES 6

300 g (11 oz) brown lentils,
soaked overnight in cold water
1 litre ($1^3/_4$ pints) water
3 bay leaves
3 tablespoons olive oil
4 rashers back bacon or pancetta,
rinded and finely chopped
1 sprig fresh marjoram, chopped
1 sprig fresh thyme, chopped
1 small sprig fresh rosemary, chopped
1 large sprig fresh basil, chopped
20 chestnuts, roasted or boiled,
peeled and coarsely chopped
salt

Drain the lentils and place them in a saucepan with the water and bay leaves.
Bring to the boil, cover and simmer for about 40 minutes until tender.
Meanwhile, fry the oil, bacon or pancetta and herbs in a large saucepan over
a low heat for about 5 minutes. Stir in the chestnuts and simmer over a low
heat for about 5 minutes. Stir in the cooked lentils and season to taste with
salt. Simmer very gently for about 30 minutes, adding a little more water if
necessary. Serve very hot.

Zuppa Pavese
Soup of Pavia

The story behind this soup is that it was first made for
Francis I of France as he wandered lost in the vicinity of Pavia.
The peasant woman who made it for him created it out of
the few simple ingredients she had available.
Since its origins, it has become one of the classic soups and
is well known and appreciated all over the world.

SERVES 6

3 tablespoons unsalted butter
6 slices coarse Italian bread
6 eggs
salt
1.25 litres (2¹/₄ pints) good-quality rich meat or
chicken broth or stock, boiling hot

Heat half the butter and fry the bread lightly on both sides. Add the remaining butter, break the eggs into the pan and fry them until just firm. Sprinkle the egg whites with salt and arrange the fried bread and eggs in the bottom of 6 soup plates. Pour the boiling hot broth on and around them and serve at once.

Pasta Reale
Royal Pasta

*This is a classic — typical dinner-party food of the type my parents
used to serve to their guests when I was a child.
The broth really does have to be of absolute top quality.*

SERVES 6

150 ml (5 fl oz) cold water
100 g (4 oz) unsalted butter
100 g (4 oz) plain white flour
3 eggs
salt
freshly ground black pepper
1.5 litres (2¹/2 pints) good-quality broth
or stock, boiling hot

Pre-heat the oven to gas mark 4, 180°C (350°F). Heat the water in a small saucepan. When it reaches boiling point, add the butter and stir until amalgamated. Remove from the heat, tip in the flour and stir vigorously until you have a smooth lump-free mixture. Return to the heat and stir for a few minutes until the mixture comes away from the sides of the pan and makes a popping sound. Remove from the heat and leave to cool slightly.

Stir in the eggs one at a time, being absolutely sure that each egg has been blended into the mixture before you add the next. Season generously with salt and pepper. Place the mixture in an icing bag with a wide nozzle and make neat rows of pastry in tidy lumps on a greased baking sheet. Bake in the oven for about 12 minutes until golden brown and puffy. Leave to cool on a wire rack for 2 minutes then transfer them to a soup tureen. Pour the boiling hot broth or stock over the baked choux balls and serve at once.

Risotto

RISOTTO is one of my favourite dishes. The most important ingredient is, of course, the rice. It is absolutely no good trying to make this marvellously creamy, sumptuous dish with long-grain or pudding rice. Only risotto rice is suitable and fortunately it is now widely available.

Ideally, the very best variety of rice with which to make risotto is a very large-grained type called carnaroli. The larger grains make absorption of flavour much better and improve the texture of the finished dish. However, it is almost impossible to get hold of even in Italy, and it is incredibly expensive. Arborio is the next best type of rice, although a pure arborio is now extremely rare. Risotto rice is a generic term for a type of rice which is suitable for making risotto.

What makes a real risotto so special is that it can be so varied. Once you have the right type of rice, a little butter, chopped onion and some well flavoured stock, you can then create the most delicious dish – only your imagination could possibly restrict you. Mushrooms, seafood, meat sauces, all kinds of vegetables, even fruit such as strawberries and cherries can be made into the most superb combinations.

I have some very special and very fond memories about risotto because it was the first thing I ever learned to make. I was a very tiny girl, only three or four, and I had to stand on a big chair next to my friend as he made it. Beppino comes from Vicenza and used to be a chef at one of the top restaurants in Milan, so you could say that he had risotto in his blood, as both those areas are famous for producing excellent risottos. With immense patience, he would explain to me just how to stir the grains as he poured in the hot stock. He would teach me how much it needs to stick on the bottom of the pot and how the surface had to ripple like the sea touched by gentle breezes. *Deve fare l'onda*, he would say. *Guarda l'onda, se no non é risotto.* 'It must make a wave. Watch the wave or else it isn't risotto.' He also taught me that anything from a humble courgette to an exotic wild mushroom can turn a simple risotto into something really quite amazing, the sort of everlasting flavour impression which you can recall at any time.

I will never be able to cook or eat risotto again without remembering that kitchen, that chair and my friend Beppino.

MAKING RISOTTO

The basic method of making risotto is always the same, all that changes are the extra ingredients. To make a basic risotto, you need to have the stock, *brodo*, standing by and very hot, and you need a fairly deep saucepan with a solid base and two handles. Fry a little onion, or in some· cases garlic, in the pan with some butter or oil. As soon as the onion or garlic is soft and well cooked (*soffritto*) without browning, you can add all the rice in one go. Stir the rice around very thoroughly to coat it in the flavours and to toast it lightly on all sides. Then begin to add the hot stock, stirring after each addition.

Remember to add the stock a little at a time and to let the grains absorb the liquid before adding more stock. The risotto will take 20 minutes to make from when you add the rice to the saucepan. It is important to stir all the time and to have the stock constantly hot so that the risotto never drops in temperature during the cooking time. If you keep to these basic rules, you'll produce a perfect and very Italian risotto no matter what else you add to the rice as flavouring. To make a perfect *soffritto* and *brodo*, refer to chapter one, pages 19, 22, 23 and 24.

Risotto alla Milanese
Milanese Risotto

*The most classic and best loved of all the risottos,
it can be as pale yellow or bright ochre as you like,
depending on whether you add more or less saffron.
Traditionally, it is always made with powdered saffron,
although you can steep threads in warm water if you prefer.
You can omit the bone marrow if you can't get hold of it,
but it is a traditional ingredient.*

SERVES 6

1/2 onion, peeled and finely sliced
75 g (3 oz) unsalted butter
1 large tablespoon fresh beef marrow
500 g (1 lb 2 oz) risotto rice
1.75 litres (3 pints) chicken stock,
kept just below boiling point
1/2 teaspoon powdered saffron
salt
freshly ground black pepper
75 g (3 oz) Parmesan cheese, freshly grated

Soak the onion in cold water for about 20 minutes. Drain it carefully, pat it dry and chop it finely. Melt half the butter and all the beef marrow in a heavy-based saucepan and fry the onion for about 5 minutes until soft and transparent, stirring frequently. Add all the rice in one go and stir it around until it is toasted and covered with onion and butter. Then add the first ladleful of stock. Stir until the stock has been absorbed, then add some more. Always add small amounts and always wait for the rice to absorb the stock before you add any more. After about 10 minutes, the rice will be half cooked. Add the saffron with some stock and season to taste with salt and pepper. Continue stirring and adding stock for a further 10 minutes until the rice is swollen but still firm in the middle. Stir in the remaining butter and the Parmesan, remove from the heat, cover and leave to stand for about 3 minutes. Transfer the risotto to a warmed serving platter or warmed individual plates and serve at once.

Risotto alle Erbe
Mixed Herb Risotto

*What is really important about this dish is that
there should be as wide a variety of herbs as possible,
although you should be careful only to add small quantities of
the strong-tasting herbs.
You can add a little cream at the end if you want to
give it a really rich finish.*

SERVES 6

1 small onion, peeled and quartered
a large handful of pungent fresh herbs:
parsley, basil, oregano, thyme, rosemary,
summer savory, sorrel
75 g (3 oz) unsalted butter
500 g (1 lb 2 oz) risotto rice
1.75 litres (3 pints) chicken or
vegetable stock, kept just below boiling point
75 g (3 oz) Parmesan cheese, freshly grated
salt
freshly ground black pepper
$1^1/_2$ tablespoons chopped fresh parsley

Chop the onion and herbs together. Melt half the butter and fry the onion and herbs for about 5 minutes until the onion is soft. Add all the rice in one go and stir it around until it is heated through and shining. Then add the first ladleful of stock. Stir until the stock has been absorbed, then add some more. Always add small amounts and always wait for the rice to absorb the stock before you add any more. Continue in this way for about 20 minutes until the rice is swollen but still firm in the middle. Stir in the remaining butter and the Parmesan and season to taste with salt and pepper. Stir it all thoroughly, remove from the heat, cover and leave to stand for 3 minutes.

Transfer to a warmed serving platter or warmed individual plates, sprinkle with parsley and serve at once.

Risotto d'Asparagi

SEE PAGE 85

(Overleaf) Cannelloni con Ricotta e Spinaci

SEE PAGE 130

Spaghetti allo Scoglio

SEE PAGE 94

Risotto alle Verdure Miste
Mixed Vegetable Risotto

*My friend Alvaro Maccione makes a wonderful version of
this risotto at his restaurant la Famiglia.
It is delightfully fresh and light; ideal for vegetarians.*

SERVES 6

75 g (3 oz) unsalted butter
1 onion, peeled and chopped
1 carrot, finely chopped
1 courgette, peeled and finely chopped
1 stick celery, finely chopped
4 tablespoons shelled fresh peas
1 cos lettuce heart, shredded
1 plum tomato, skinned, de-seeded and chopped
500 g (1 lb 2 oz) risotto rice
1.75 litres (3 pints) vegetable stock,
kept just below boiling point
salt
freshly ground black pepper
75 g (3 oz) Parmesan cheese, freshly grated

Melt the butter in a large heavy-based saucepan and fry the vegetables gently for about 5 minutes until soft. Add all the rice in one go and stir it around until it is heated through and shining. Then add the first ladleful of stock. Stir until the stock has been absorbed, then add some more.

Always add small amounts and always wait for the rice to absorb the stock before you add any more. Continue in this way for about 20 minutes until the rice is swollen but still firm in the middle. Season to taste with salt and pepper and stir in the Parmesan. Remove from the heat, cover and leave to stand for about 3 minutes. Transfer to a warmed serving platter or warmed individual plates and serve at once.

Risotto al Pollo e Pisellini
Risotto with Chicken and Peas

This is one of my children's favourite risottos.
It is a very good way of using up left-over chicken.

SERVES 6

75 g (3 oz) unsalted butter
1/2 onion, peeled and chopped
250 g (9 oz) cooked chicken, coarsely chopped
250 g (9 oz) shelled fresh peas or frozen petits pois
500 g (1 lb 2 oz) risotto rice
1.75 litres (3 pints) chicken stock,
kept just below boiling point
75 g (3 oz) Parmesan cheese, freshly grated
salt
freshly ground black pepper

Melt half the butter and fry the onion for about 5 minutes until soft and transparent. Add the chicken and peas and stir carefully over a low heat for about 5 minutes. Add all the rice in one go and stir it around until it is heated through and shining. Then add the first ladleful of stock. Stir until the stock has been absorbed, then add some more. Always add small amounts and always wait for the rice to absorb the stock before you add any more. Continue in this way for about 20 minutes until the rice is swollen but still firm in the middle.

This risotto is traditionally served quite liquid and runny. Stir in the remaining butter and three-quarters of the Parmesan and season to taste with salt and pepper. Remove from the heat, cover and leave to stand for about 3 minutes. Transfer to a warmed serving platter, sprinkle with the remaining Parmesan and serve at once.

Risotto con le Cozze
Risotto with Mussels

A deliciously fishy risotto,
this should be made with a fish stock with a good rich flavour
and mussels which are as fresh as possible.
Remember to clean and prepare them carefully (see page 30).

SERVES 6

1 kg (2 lb) live mussels, scrubbed and bearded
3 tablespoons olive oil
1 large clove garlic, peeled and lightly crushed
75 g (3 oz) unsalted butter
1 small onion, peeled and finely chopped
500 g (1 lb 2 oz) risotto rice
1.75 litres (3 pints) fish stock, kept just below boiling point
salt
freshly ground black pepper

Place the mussels in a wide shallow pan with the oil and garlic, cover and place over a medium heat for about 5 minutes, shaking the pan from time to time to help distribute the heat and open up all the mussels. Remove from the heat and discard any mussels that have not opened. Strain the cooking liquid into a clean bowl, remove the mussels from their shells and discard the shells. Melt half the butter and fry the onion for about 8 minutes until soft and lightly browned.

Add the rice all in one go and stir it around until it is heated through and shining. Then add the first ladleful of stock. Stir until the stock has been absorbed, then add some more. Always add small amounts and always wait for the rice to absorb the stock before you add any more. Continue in this way for about 15 minutes then add the mussels and their cooking liquid. Stir carefully and continue cooking for a further 5 minutes until the rice is swollen but still firm in the middle. Stir in the remaining butter and add a little salt and plenty of pepper.

Remove from the heat, cover and leave to stand for about 3 minutes. Transfer to a warmed serving platter and serve at once.

Risotto con Gamberetti
Risotto with Prawns

Raw prawns are essential for this dish as they give it extra sweetness and fishy flavour. Order them in advance from your fishmonger who should be able to get them for you if he has enough notice. It makes a marvellous dinner or luncheon-party dish.

SERVES 6

750 g (1 lb 10 oz) raw prawns
1 small onion, peeled and finely chopped
1 clove garlic, peeled and finely chopped
1 small carrot, finely chopped
$1/2$ stick celery, chopped
4 tablespoons olive oil
4 tablespoons dry white wine
1 litre ($1^3/4$ pints) cold water
salt and freshly ground black pepper
2 tablespoons unsalted butter
1 shallot, peeled and thinly sliced
2 tablespoons brandy
1 tablespoon tomato purée
500 g (1 lb 2 oz) risotto rice
50 g (2 oz) Parmesan cheese, freshly grated

Remove the heads and legs from the prawns, extract the tails and set them aside. Put all the shells and heads into a saucepan with the onion, garlic, carrot, celery and 3 tablespoons of oil and fry gently for about 5 minutes. Add the wine and boil off the alcohol for 2 minutes then add the water and season to taste with salt and pepper. Bring to the boil, cover and leave to simmer gently. In a separate saucepan, heat the remaining oil with the butter and fry the shallot very gently for about 5 minutes. Add the prawn tails and cook for 5 minutes. Pour on the brandy and boil off the alcohol for 2 minutes. Stir in the tomato purée. Add the rice all in one go and stir it around until it is heated through and shining. Then add the first ladleful of stock from the prawn shells. Stir until the stock has been absorbed, then add more. Always add small amounts and always wait for the rice to absorb the stock before you add any more. Continue this for about 20 minutes until the rice is swollen but still firm in the middle. Stir in the remaining butter and the Parmesan. Remove from the heat, cover and leave to stand for about 3 minutes. Transfer to a warmed serving platter and serve at once.

Risotto d'Asparagi
Asparagus Risotto

*The delicate flavours of fresh asparagus and shallots really come
into their own in this delightful risotto.
Make sure you use good quality stock to complement the other ingredients.*

SERVES 6

500 g (1 lb 2 oz) fresh asparagus
salt
75 g (3 oz) unsalted butter
2 large shallots, peeled and chopped
500 g (1 lb 2 oz) risotto rice
chicken or vegetable stock
50 g (2 oz) Parmesan cheese, freshly grated
1 tablespoon chopped fresh parsley
freshly ground black pepper

Boil the asparagus with a large pinch of salt for about 6 minutes until just
tender. Drain, reserving the cooking liquid, and leave to cool. Melt half the
butter and fry the shallots for about 5 minutes until soft and transparent. Cut
the asparagus into small pieces. If the end of the asparagus stalk is very
tough, scrape out the inside with a knife and discard the rest. Add the
asparagus to the shallots and cook very gently for about 2 minutes. Add the
rice all in one go and stir it around until it is heated through and shining.
Then add the first ladleful of asparagus cooking liquid. Stir until the liquid has
been absorbed, then add some more.

Always add small amounts and always wait for the rice to absorb the liquid
before you add any more. When you run out of the cooking liquid, begin to
add the stock. Continue in this way for about 20 minutes until the rice is
swollen but still firm in the middle. Stir in the Parmesan and parsley and
season to taste with pepper. Remove from the heat, cover and leave to stand
for about 3 minutes. Transfer to a warmed serving platter and serve at once.

Pasta

TRADITIONALLY, *pasta asciutta*, in other words pasta with a sauce which is tossed together in a bowl as opposed to pasta in a baked dish or pasta as part of a soup, is served after the antipasto and before the main course. The level of richness of the pasta dish will, of course, affect what is served as an antipasto and what follows as a main dish. However, nowadays our appetites are getting smaller and our demands for big long meals are much rarer, so very often a dish of pasta, perhaps served with a salad, constitutes an entire meal. This is, in fact, an extremely healthy way of eating. Pasta contains many valuable vitamins and nutrients and, contrary to what many people think, it isn't actually fattening. The sauce which you put on the pasta will make up the extra naughty calories.

Interestingly, the very laborious to make, rich and luxurious baked pasta dishes like lasagne and cannelloni were all dishes which were originally created for special occasions. Nobody in their right mind would set about making these rather complicated and expensive dishes for everyday family consumption; they were reserved for baptisms, confirmations and wedding banquets, not to mentions saints' days and funerals. Yet nowadays, these are the dishes which most often crop up in the convenience food section of your average supermarket. True, they are almost unrecognisable when you compare them with the original concept, but they are still based on dishes which were about as far removed from the whole idea of fast food as you can get. It is a shame that these dishes of celebration should end up as deep-frozen slabs in neat cardboard boxes.

Pasta divides into four very separate categories even before you think about cooking it. Fresh commercially made pasta is made with flour and water and may have eggs added to the dough. Fresh commercially made pasta which contains eggs, *pasta all'uovo*, can also be bought dried as tagliatelle, lasagne, cannelloni and so on. Home-made fresh pasta is almost always made with flour and eggs. Durum wheat factory-made pasta such as spaghetti, maccheroni, penne, eliche and so on is by far the most commonly used type of pasta. In my experience, unless fresh pasta is made particularly well you would be better off sticking to the durum wheat factory-made variety.

One of the questions I am often asked is what sauce to put with what shape of pasta. There are so many different shapes of pasta available on the market (at the last count somebody gave me the official figure as being 620), this issue can become extremely confusing! I can only say that this decision is largely down to trial and error. Certain shapes marry certain sauces much better than others. The general rule of thumb is that delicately flavoured, light sauces go best with delicate pasta shapes, whether they be ribbon-shaped or short. The more rich, chunky sauces, particularly those which contain meat or game, tend to sit better with bigger, chunkier pasta shapes. But there are simply no hard-and-fast rules. I have grown up eating specific sauces on specific shapes, so I feel quite disorientated when I am served a dish of pasta which is very different from what I was expecting! But one must always be flexible and as pasta becomes more and more of an international phenomenon, the sauces and various combinations become more adventurous and exotic.

However, there is one very specific combination which would completely floor an Italian and cause utter outrage in a real trattoria. You must never, under any circumstances, sprinkle Parmesan or any other kind of cheese on a pasta sauce which contains fish of any description; from the humblest anchovy purée to the freshest silver sardine. *Niente formaggio con il pesce!*

MAKING PASTA

To make pasta, put all the flour in a pile on a work surface and plunge your fist into the centre to make a hole. Break the eggs into the hole and add a pinch of salt. Using your fingers, beat the eggs roughly into the flour. Then use your hands to begin to knead everything together.

Remember you are not making pastry, this is not the moment for a delicate, minimalistic approach! Knead the flour and eggs together until you have a really smooth, pliable ball of dough. Now comes the hard part! Roll out the dough as thinly as possible with a strong, long rolling pin then fold it in half and roll it all out again. Continue to do this over and over again until your dough is really elastic, smooth and shiny. It should cool considerably as you work it. There are two ways in which you will know that it is ready to cut into the desired shape. The rolling pin will make a neat snap as it rolls over the fold, indicating that the tension in the dough is at the right point. The sheet of dough will feel exactly like a brand-new, wrung-out, damp chamois leather.

GNOCCHI

The final word of this introduction must be reserved for the humble gnocco, or gnocchi in the plural. To understand gnocchi you must first know that the word roughly translates as 'lumps', thus removing any sophistication which you may attempt to give it. Gnocchi answer the question of when is pasta not really pasta because they can be made with flour and water to become *strozzapreti*, or priest-stranglers; potato and flour, *gnocchi di patate*; semolina and milk, *gnocchi di semolino*; spinach, flour, egg and cheese, *gnocchi di spinaci*; and pumpkin, *gnocchi di zucca*.

Thereafter you move into the whole area of *knödel* in the more northerly areas of the country, for when does a gnocco cease being a lump and become a dumpling? What I am really trying to say is that there is nothing very complicated about gnocchi and that the real thing, whatever it is made with, must not be mistaken for the dried durum wheat pasta shape called gnocchi which is supposed to look like a real potato gnocco. Confused? The only way to sort out the muddle is to cook your way through the recipes!

Spaghettini al Burro e Limone
Spaghettini with Butter and Lemon

You can add some chopped fresh herbs to this light lunch dish if you wish.

SERVES 6

500 g (1 lb 2 oz) spaghettini
salt
75 g (3 oz) unsalted butter
grated rind of 1 lemon
75 g (3 oz) Parmesan cheese, freshly grated
freshly ground black pepper

Bring a large saucepan of salted water to a rolling boil, toss in the spaghettini and give it one good stir. Cover the pan and bring the water back to the boil. Remove the lid and cook the spaghettini until *al dente*; brands vary but 5 minutes should be about right. Drain the spaghettini thoroughly then return it to the warm empty saucepan. Add the butter, lemon rind and Parmesan and season to taste with pepper. Toss everything together very quickly and thoroughly. Transfer to a warmed serving bowl and serve at once.

Spaghettini con Pomodoro e Mozzarella
Spaghettini with Tomatoes and Mozzarella

*Definitely best when made with fresh, ripe, juicy tomatoes,
this is a pasta dish for hot summer days.
Fresh herbs are essential.*

SERVES 4–6

a large handful of fresh basil
a large handful of fresh parsley
2 cloves garlic, peeled
$1/4$ dried red chilli pepper
65 g ($2^1/2$ oz) unsalted butter
400 g (14 oz) canned tomatoes, de-seeded and
chopped or equivalent fresh, very ripe tomatoes, skinned
salt
freshly ground black pepper
500 g (1 lb 2 oz) spaghettini
250 g (9 oz) Mozzarella cheese, cubed

Chop or process the basil, parsley, garlic and chilli together until finely chopped. Melt the butter in a heavy-based saucepan, add the herb mixture and fry for about 7 minutes. Stir in the tomatoes and season to taste with salt and pepper. Simmer for about 10 minutes then remove from the heat.

Meanwhile, bring a large saucepan of salted water to a rolling boil, toss in the spaghettini and give it one good stir. Cover the pan and bring the water back to the boil. Remove the lid and cook until *al dente*; brands vary but 5 minutes should be about right. Drain the spaghettini thoroughly and transfer it to the warm empty saucepan. Pour over the sauce, toss together thoroughly over a low heat. Add the Mozzarella and toss again to melt the cheese slightly. Transfer to a warmed serving bowl and serve at once.

Spaghetti alla Carbonara
Spaghetti Carbonara

A very simple and classic pasta dish,
this works best with spaghetti although you can use
any other pasta shape if you prefer.

SERVES 6

8 rashers pancetta or streaky bacon
4 eggs, thoroughly beaten
40 g (1 1/2 oz) Parmesan cheese, freshly grated
sea salt
freshly ground black pepper (optional)
2 tablespoons double cream (optional)
500 g (1 lb 2 oz) spaghetti

Lay the pancetta or bacon on a grill and place under a medium heat until cooked through. Beat the eggs with the Parmesan, a pinch of salt, plenty of pepper, if using, and the cream, if using. Remove the pancetta or bacon from the grill, cut off and reserve the fat and cut the bacon into small pieces with scissors. Put both aside in a warm place. Meanwhile, bring a large saucepan of salted water to a rolling boil, toss in the spaghetti and give it one good stir. Add a large pinch of coarse sea salt, cover the pan and bring the water back to the boil. Remove the lid and give it another good stir. Cook until *al dente*; brands vary but 7 minutes should be about right.

Meanwhile, re-heat the bacon with its fat very slowly in a small frying pan. Drain the spaghetti thoroughly then return it to the warm empty saucepan. Pour over the beaten eggs and toss together very thoroughly. Add the sizzling hot bacon, which by now should be very crispy, and serve at once.

Spaghetti Aglio e Olio

Spaghetti with Oil and Garlic

As a change, you can make Spaghetti Aglio, Olio e Peperoncino simply by adding some dried red chilli peppers to the recipe, or you can use Olio Santo, olive oil in which peppers have been steeped, or half ordinary oil and half Olio Santo. This is a very good hangover cure, especially if eaten before going to sleep! Cheese is never served with this pasta dish, but you can scatter a little chopped fresh parsley over the finished dish if you wish.

SERVES 6

500 g (1 lb 2 oz) spaghetti
salt
300 ml (^{1}/$_2$ pint) olive oil
2–5 cloves garlic, peeled and lightly crushed

Bring a large saucepan of salted water to a rolling boil, toss in the spaghetti and give it one good stir. Cover the pan and bring the water back to the boil. Remove the lid and cook the spaghetti until *al dente*; brands vary but 7 minutes should be about right.

Meanwhile, gently heat the oil and garlic together until the garlic is dark brown. Drain the spaghetti thoroughly then return it to the warm empty saucepan. Pour the oil over the spaghetti, toss together and serve at once.

Spaghetti al Pomodoro
Spaghetti
with Tomato Sauce

*A real classic, very easy to make and
packed with flavour and goodness,
you can serve this with grated Parmesan offered separately.
You can also use La Salsa di Pomodoro (page 12) or
Il Sugo di Pomodoro (page 13) to dress spaghetti.*

SERVES 6

5 tablespoons olive or vegetable oil or
3 tablespoons unsalted butter or 3 tablespoons water
1 small onion, peeled and finely chopped
1 clove garlic, peeled and finely chopped
1 small carrot, finely chopped
1 stick celery, finely chopped
400 g (14 oz) canned tomatoes,
drained and de-seeded, if desired
salt
freshly ground black pepper
500 g (1 lb 2 oz) spaghetti
50 g (2 oz) Parmesan cheese, freshly grated

Put 3 tablespoons of oil, 2 tablespoons of butter or 3 tablespoons of water in a saucepan and add the onion, garlic, carrot and celery. Cook the vegetables gently for about 5 minutes until soft. Stir in the tomatoes and season to taste with salt and pepper. Bring to the boil, cover and simmer gently for about 45 minutes until the tomatoes have completely fallen apart.

Bring a large saucepan of salted water to a rolling boil, toss in the spaghetti and give it one good stir. Cover the pan and bring the water back to the boil. Remove the lid and cook until *al dente*; brands vary but 7 minutes should be about right. Drain the spaghetti thoroughly then return it to the warm empty saucepan. Pour over the sauce and add the remaining oil or butter. Toss everything together and serve with freshly grated Parmesan.

Spaghetti allo Scoglio
Spaghetti
with Seafood Sauce

For this recipe, it is important that you have as
wide a variety of seafood as possible and that
it should all be very fresh and well cleaned (see page 225).
You can use pre-cooked seafood,
but in this case it will need less than half the time to cook.
If you overcook it, you'll end up with a horribly rubbery texture.

SERVES 6

6 tablespoons olive oil
2 cloves garlic, peeled and very finely chopped
1 kg (2 lb) mixed live shellfish such as
clams, mussels, cockles etc., including shells, scrubbed
250 g (9 oz) raw peeled prawns
salt
freshly ground black pepper
1 tumbler dry white wine
3 tablespoons tomato purée
500 g (1 lb 2 oz) spaghetti
3 tablespoons chopped fresh parsley

Fry the oil and garlic for about 10 minutes. Add the shellfish and stir very thoroughly. Cover the pan and leave over a medium heat for about 5 minutes, shaking the pan from time to time to help distribute the heat and open up all the shellfish. Discard any shellfish that have not opened. Add the prawns and stir again. Season to taste with salt and pepper. Pour on the wine and boil off the alcohol for about 2 minutes. Stir in the tomato purée, cover and leave to simmer. Bring a large saucepan of salted water to a rolling boil, toss in the spaghetti and give it one good stir. Cover the pan and bring the water back to the boil. Remove the lid and cook until *al dente*; brands vary but 7 minutes should be about right. Drain the spaghetti thoroughly and transfer it to a warmed serving bowl. Pour over the sauce, toss together thoroughly and sprinkle with parsley before serving.

Spaghetti alle Vongole
Spaghetti
with Clam Sauce

*The live clams which you buy in their shells in Britain
tend to be very sandy. To avoid that thoroughly unpleasant
feeling of having grit squeaking between the teeth,
it is imperative that you soak the clams in several
changes of water to try to get rid of all the sand.
Boiled clams preserved in brine are not suitable for this dish.*

SERVES 4

1.5 kg (3 lb 4 oz) live clams, soaked and scrubbed
7 tablespoons olive oil
3 cloves garlic, peeled and chopped
$1/4$ teaspoon crushed dried red chilli pepper
400 g (14 oz) spaghetti
salt
freshly ground black pepper
4 tablespoons chopped fresh parsley

Drain and rinse the clams and place them in a wide shallow pan with 2 tablespoons of olive oil and 1 clove of garlic. Cover and place over a high heat for about 8 minutes, shaking the pan from time to time to help distribute the heat and open up all the clams. Discard any clams that have not opened. Drain the clams and strain and reserve the liquid. Heat the remaining oil with the remaining garlic and the chilli and fry gently for 5 minutes. Add the opened clams and mix together quickly, then add the strained liquid, season to taste with salt and pepper and stir again. Remove from the heat and cover. Meanwhile, bring a large saucepan of salted water to a rolling boil, toss in the spaghetti and give it one good stir. Cover the pan and bring the water back to the boil.

Remove the lid and cook until *al dente*; brands vary but 7 minutes should be about right. Drain the spaghetti thoroughly and return it to the warm empty saucepan. Pour over the clams and toss together. Transfer to a warmed serving bowl, sprinkle with the parsley and serve at once.

Spaghetti con Funghi e Piselli
Spaghetti with Peas and Mushrooms

*A marvellous lunch or supper dish,
very creamy and tasty;
you can use oyster mushrooms as
a substitute for the funghi porcini if you prefer.*

SERVES 4

275 g (10 oz) shelled fresh peas or frozen petits pois
75 g (3 oz) unsalted butter
2 tablespoons water
salt
freshly ground black pepper
100 g (4 oz) dried funghi porcini,
soaked in warm water for 20 minutes then drained
400 g (14 oz) spaghetti
175 ml (6 fl oz) single cream
120 g (4^1/$_2$ oz) Parmesan cheese, freshly grated

Place the peas in a heavy-based saucepan with half the butter and the water and simmer over a low heat for about 10 minutes until tender. Season to taste with salt and pepper and set aside. Melt the remaining butter and toss the mushrooms for a few minutes until softened. Season to taste with salt and pepper and set aside. Meanwhile, bring a large saucepan of salted water to a rolling boil, toss in the spaghetti and give it one good stir. Cover the pan and bring the water back to the boil. Remove the lid and cook until *al dente*; brands vary but 7 minutes should be about right. Heat the cream until just below boiling point and re-heat the peas and mushrooms. Drain the spaghetti thoroughly and return it to the warm empty saucepan.

Add the peas, mushrooms and cream and toss together thoroughly. Add half the Parmesan and toss again. Transfer to a warmed serving bowl, sprinkle with the remaining Parmesan and serve at once.

Maccheroni al Sugo di Salsicce

SEE PAGE 104

Pappardelle alla Lepre

SEE PAGE 116

Spaghetti alla Menta con il Maiale
Spaghetti with Mint and Pork

*Ideal for an easy lunch,
do make sure that you use pork loin that is tender and cut into
really small cubes for this simple spaghetti dish.
Fresh mint is also essential as
the flavour will develop beautifully with the heat.*

SERVES 4

75 g (3 oz) unsalted butter
2 large cloves garlic, peeled and thinly sliced
200 g (7 oz) pork loin, cubed
1 tablespoon plain white flour
3 tablespoons dry white wine
3 tablespoons water
a handful of fresh mint leaves, finely chopped
salt
freshly ground black pepper
400 g (14 oz) spaghetti

Melt the butter in a heavy-based saucepan over a low heat with the garlic. Toss the meat cubes in the flour. Add them to the butter and brown them all over. Pour on the wine and boil off the alcohol for about 1 minute. Add the water, cover and simmer gently for about 30 minutes until the meat is tender. Add the mint and season to taste with salt and pepper. Stir together well, cover, remove from the heat and keep warm. Bring a large saucepan of salted water to a rolling boil, toss in the spaghetti and give it one good stir. Cover the pan and bring the water back to the boil. Remove the lid and cook until *al dente*; brands vary but 7 minutes should be about right. Drain the spaghetti thoroughly and return it to the warm empty saucepan. Pour over the sauce and toss together thoroughly. Transfer to a warmed serving bowl and serve at once.

Bucatini all'Amatriciana
Bucatini with Bacon and Tomato Sauce

*A traditional sauce which really needs
Italian bacon to make it taste as it should,
although any good quality,
strongly flavoured bacon will work quite well.
It is essential to serve this with freshly grated Pecorino in
order to give the dish the maximum amount of pungency.*

SERVES 6

1 tablespoon olive oil
150 g (5 oz) guanciale, thick-cut pancetta or
very strongly flavoured, peppery bacon, cubed
1 large dried red chilli pepper, de-seeded and broken into pieces
400 g (14 oz) canned tomatoes,
drained and de-seeded if desired
salt
freshly ground black pepper
500 g (1 lb 2 oz) bucatini
75 g (3 oz) Pecorino cheese, grated

Heat the oil gently with the guanciale, pancetta or bacon and the chilli pepper in a heavy-based saucepan until the fat begins to run freely. Add the tomatoes and stir to break them up with a fork then season to taste with salt and pepper.

Bring to the boil, cover and simmer gently for about 30 minutes. (Some people prefer to remove the meat at this point and return it to the sauce at the very end to prevent it going soggy.) Bring a large saucepan of salted water to a rolling boil, toss in the bucatini and give it one good stir. Cover the pan and bring the water back to the boil. Remove the lid and cook until *al dente*; brands vary but 8 minutes should be about right. Drain the bucatini thoroughly and return it to the warm empty saucepan. Add half the sauce and toss together thoroughly. Arrange on a warmed serving platter and cover with the remaining sauce. Sprinkle with the Pecorino and serve at once.

Bucatini alla Puttanesca
Bucatini with Anchovy, Garlic and Tomato Sauce

Very easy to make and perfect for a quick lunch,
this is a strongly flavoured,
pungent sauce with lots of different textures and tastes.

SERVES 4

4 canned anchovy fillets in oil, drained
4 tablespoons milk
3 cloves garlic, peeled and chopped
3 tablespoons olive oil
50 g (2 oz) unsalted butter
150 g (5 oz) stoned black olives, chopped
1¹/₄ tablespoons salted capers, rinsed, dried and chopped
2 tablespoons chopped fresh parsley
250 g (9 oz) canned tomatoes, drained and coarsely chopped
salt
freshly ground black pepper
400 g (14 oz) bucatini

Soak the anchovies in the milk for about 30 minutes then drain, rinse and chop them. Put the anchovies in a heavy-based saucepan with the garlic, oil, butter, olives, capers and parsley and fry gently for about 10 minutes, stirring frequently. Add the tomatoes, season to taste with salt and pepper and simmer for a further 15 minutes.

Meanwhile, bring a large saucepan of salted water to a rolling boil, toss in the bucatini and give it one good stir. Cover the pan and bring the water back to the boil. Remove the lid and cook until *al dente*; brands vary but 8 minutes should be about right. Drain the bucatini thoroughly and transfer it to a warmed serving bowl. Pour over the sauce, toss everything together thoroughly and serve at once.

Penne all'Arrabbiata
Fiery Penne

Vary the amount of chilli in this quick and easy dish according to your guests' personal tastes. Grated cheese is never served with this dish.

SERVES 4

3 cloves garlic, peeled and finely chopped
1–3 dried red chilli peppers or
1–3 teaspoons crushed dried red chilli peppers
8 tablespoons olive oil
350 ml (12 fl oz) passata
salt
freshly ground black pepper
400 g (14 oz) penne
4 tablespoons chopped fresh parsley

Heat the garlic, chilli peppers and oil together over a very low heat for about 8 minutes until the garlic becomes very dark and the oil begins to smoke. Stir in the passata and season to taste with salt and pepper. Simmer very gently for about 10 minutes.

Meanwhile, bring a large saucepan of salted water to a rolling boil, toss in the penne and give it one good stir. Cover the pan and bring the water back to the boil. Remove the lid and cook until *al dente*; brands vary but 10 minutes should be about right. Drain the penne thoroughly and return it to the warm empty saucepan. Pour over the sauce and toss together thoroughly. Add half the parsley and toss again. Transfer to a warmed serving bowl, sprinkle with the remaining parsley and serve at once.

Penne Primavera
Springtime
Penne

*A delicious combination of
pasta with vegetables and minced beef,
this makes a good lunch time dish with plenty of
different textures and flavours.*

SERVES 6

1 small onion, peeled and finely chopped
1 carrot, finely chopped
1 stick celery, finely chopped
120 ml (4 fl oz) olive oil
300 g (11 oz) coarsely minced beef
salt
freshly ground black pepper
175 ml (6 fl oz) beef stock
150 g (5 oz) sliced, grilled peppers or canned peppers
200 g (7 oz) shelled fresh peas or frozen petits pois
300 g (11 oz) canned tomatoes, chopped
500 g (1 lb 2 oz) penne

Fry the onion, carrot and celery gently with the oil for about 5 minutes until soft. Add the beef and fry until browned all over. Season to taste with salt and pepper and cook for a further 10 minutes, gradually adding a little stock. Stir in the peppers and peas and bring to a bubbling simmer. Stir in the tomatoes, bring to a simmer, cover and simmer for a further 40 minutes. Check the seasoning and add a little more beef stock if necessary.

Bring a large saucepan of salted water to a rolling boil, toss in the penne and give it one good stir. Cover the pan and bring the water back to the boil. Remove the lid and cook until *al dente*; brands vary but 10 minutes should be about right. Drain the penne thoroughly and return it to the warm empty saucepan. Pour over half the sauce and toss together thoroughly. Transfer to a warmed serving bowl, cover with the remaining sauce and serve at once.

Penne al Salame
Penne
with Salame

*Make sure you use good quality Italian salami,
such as Milano or Napoletano, for this dish.
If you like the flavour of fennel seeds you can opt
for the delectable Finnocchiona.*

SERVES 4

150 g (5 oz) salame, thickly sliced and coarsely chopped
50 g (2 oz) unsalted butter
2 tablespoons sunflower oil
2 small sprigs fresh rosemary
5 tablespoons dry red or white wine
2 large eggs, beaten
1 tablespoon natural yoghurt
50 g (2 oz) Parmesan, Groviera or
Pecorino cheese, freshly grated
salt
freshly ground black pepper
400 g (14 oz) penne
1 tablespoon chopped fresh parsley

Fry the salame very gently with the butter, oil and rosemary until the fat from the salame is running freely. Add the wine and boil off the alcohol for about 2 minutes. Remove from the heat and don't cook it for any longer or the salame will toughen. Beat the eggs with the yoghurt, cheese and a pinch each of salt and pepper.

Meanwhile, bring a large saucepan of salted water to a rolling boil, toss in the penne and give it one good stir. Cover the pan and bring the water back to the boil. Remove the lid and cook until *al dente*; brands vary but 10 minutes should be about right. Drain the penne thoroughly and return it to the warm empty saucepan. Pour over the eggs and mix together quickly so that the heat from the pasta lightly cooks the eggs. Add the salame and toss again. Transfer to a warmed serving bowl, sprinkle with the parsley and serve at once.

Rigatoni con Prosciutto e Olive

Rigatoni with Ham and Olives

Choose black olives with lots of flavour which are really juicy. For variety, use smoked ham (speck) instead of Parma ham to change the flavour.

SERVES 4

5 tablespoons extra virgin olive oil
8 paper-thin slices Parma ham, sliced into
very thin strips
2 shallots, peeled and minutely chopped
1 clove garlic, peeled and finely chopped
20 black olives, stoned and chopped
400 g (14 oz) rigatoni
2 tablespoons chopped fresh parsley
salt
freshly ground black pepper

Heat the oil gently with the prosciutto, shallot and garlic for about 10 minutes. Stir in the olives. Meanwhile, bring a large saucepan of salted water to a rolling boil, toss in the rigatoni and give it one good stir. Cover the pan and bring the water back to the boil. Remove the lid and cook until *al dente*; brands vary but 10 minutes should be about right. Drain the rigatoni thoroughly and return it to the warm empty saucepan. Pour over the ham and olive sauce and toss together thoroughly.

You may like to add a little extra oil if it appears to be too dry. Transfer to a warmed serving bowl, sprinkle with the parsley, season to taste with salt and pepper and serve at once.

Maccheroni al Sugo di Salsicce
Maccheroni
with Sausage Sauce

*This is a family favourite in my household. Make sure you use proper
Italian sausages to create the really intense flavour which typifies the sauce.*

SERVES 4

1 onion, peeled and chopped
1 clove garlic, peeled and chopped
1 carrot, chopped
1 stick celery, chopped
3 tablespoons olive oil
4 Italian sausages, skinned
1 Italian sausage, unskinned
$^1/_2$ tumbler dry red wine
500 g (1 lb 2 oz) passata
salt
freshly ground black pepper
400 g (14 oz) maccheroni
75 g (3 oz) Parmesan cheese, freshly grated

Fry the onion, garlic, carrot and celery in the oil for about 5 minutes. Prick
the sausage skin in several places then add all the sausages to the pan and stir
thoroughly until the sausage meat is browned all over and the fat is running
freely. Pour in the wine and boil off the alcohol for about 2 minutes. Stir in
the passata and season to taste with salt and pepper, but be careful as the
sausages will probably be very peppery and salty. Bring to the boil, cover and
simmer gently for about 1$^1/_2$ hours, stirring frequently.

Bring a large saucepan of salted water to a rolling boil, toss in the
maccheroni and give it one good stir. Cover the pan and bring the water back
to the boil. Remove the lid and cook until *al dente*; brands vary but 14
minutes should be about right. Drain the maccheroni thoroughly and return it
to the warm empty saucepan. Pour over the sauce and toss together
thoroughly. Transfer to a warmed serving bowl and serve at once. The guest
of honour gets the whole sausage! Offer the Parmesan separately.

Maccheroni al Sugo Napoletano
Maccheroni with Neapolitan Sauce

This is a meaty, rich sauce, very different from the kind of speedy tomato sauces that are normally prepared in Naples. It will make a big difference if you buy beef shin and mince it yourself rather than using ready-minced beef.

SERVES 4–5

65 g (2¹/₂ oz) ham fat, finely chopped
4 tablespoons olive oil
1 onion, peeled and finely chopped
1 large clove garlic, peeled and finely chopped
1 carrot, chopped
1 stick celery, finely chopped
300 g (11 oz) beef shin, coarsely minced
1 large wine glass dry red wine
a large pinch of dried marjoram
¹/₂ teaspoon freshly grated nutmeg
salt and freshly ground black pepper
400 g (14 oz) canned tomatoes, sieved or chopped
400 g (14 oz) maccheroni
75 g (3 oz) Parmesan cheese, freshly grated

Put the ham fat and oil in a saucepan and fry over a low heat for about 10 minutes until the fat has almost dissolved into the oil. Add the onion, garlic, carrot and celery and fry gently for about 10 minutes until the vegetables are completely soft. Add the meat and stir it thoroughly to brown it all over. Pour on the wine and boil off the alcohol for about 2 minutes. Add the marjoram and nutmeg and season to taste with salt and pepper. Stir in the tomatoes, cover loosely and simmer for about 2 hours, adding a little water occasionally if the sauce appears to be drying out.

Bring a large saucepan of salted water to a rolling boil, toss in the maccheroni and give it one good stir. Cover the pan and bring the water back to the boil. Remove the lid and cook until *al dente*; brands vary but 5 minutes should be about right. Drain the maccheroni thoroughly and return it to the warm empty saucepan. Pour over the sauce and toss together thoroughly. Add half the Parmesan and toss again. Transfer to a warmed serving bowl, sprinkle with the remaining Parmesan and serve at once.

Maccheroni ai Quatro Formaggi
Maccheroni with Four Cheeses

*It is very important that you choose cheeses that all have
different tastes so that they
blend together to create a smooth-textured sauce with lots of flavour.
It makes an ideal family supper dish.*

SERVES 4

50 g (2 oz) unsalted butter
1/2 tablespoon plain white flour
250 ml (8 fl oz) milk
50 g (2 oz) Mozzarella cheese, diced
50 g (2 oz) Groviera cheese, diced
50 g (2 oz) Fontina cheese, diced
50 g (2 oz) Edam cheese, diced
salt
freshly ground black pepper
400 g (14 oz) maccheroni
50 g (2 oz) Parmesan cheese, freshly grated

Melt half the butter in a saucepan until foaming. Stir in the flour vigorously to make a smooth roux. Add the milk and whisk constantly over a low heat for about 15 minutes until the sauce thickens slightly and no longer tastes floury. Add all the cheeses except the Parmesan and stir until everything has melted. Season to taste with salt and pepper, put aside and keep warm.

Meanwhile, bring a large saucepan of salted water to a rolling boil, toss in the maccheroni and give it one good stir. Cover the pan and bring the water back to the boil. Remove the lid and cook until *al dente*; brands vary but 14 minutes should be about right. Drain the maccheroni thoroughly and return it to the warm empty saucepan. Add the remaining butter and toss together. Pour over half the sauce and toss again. Transfer to a warmed serving bowl, pour over the remaining sauce, sprinkle with the Parmesan and serve at once.

Ruote
alla Ricotta
Pasta Wheels
with Ricotta

*A very simple, delicately flavoured dish,
ideal for children.
I like to serve this in summer as a lunch time treat.*

SERVES 4

300 g (11 oz) Ricotta cheese
1 shallot, finely chopped
1 tender stick celery, finely chopped
3–4 tablespoons milk
salt
freshly ground black pepper
400 g (14 oz) ruote or other pasta shapes
50 g (2 oz) unsalted butter
50 g (2 oz) Parmesan cheese,
freshly grated (optional)
3 teaspoons chopped fresh parsley or chives

Mash the Ricotta with the shallot and celery, adding the milk gradually to make a smooth creamy paste. Season to taste with salt and pepper.

Meanwhile, bring a large saucepan of salted water to a rolling boil, toss the ruote into the water and give it one good stir. Cover the pan and bring the water back to the boil. Remove the lid and cook until *al dente*; brands vary but 8 minutes should be about right. Drain the pasta, but not too thoroughly, and return it to the warm empty saucepan. Add the butter and toss together thoroughly then add the Ricotta sauce and toss again. Add the Parmesan and toss again only if you want a stronger cheese flavour.

Transfer to a warmed serving bowl, sprinkle with the parsley or chives and serve at once.

Pasta con i Broccoli
Pasta
with Broccoli

A classic of Roman cuisine,
you can make this even more spicy if you use
some chilli oil instead of ordinary oil,
or reduce or leave out the chilli peppers if you
prefer a milder flavour.

SERVES 6

120 ml (4 fl oz) olive oil
2 dried red chilli peppers
2 large cloves garlic, peeled and lightly crushed
6 large salted anchovies, boned, rinsed,
dried and finely chopped
500 g (1 lb 2 oz) pasta shapes
600 g (1 lb 5 oz) broccoli florets
salt and freshly ground black pepper

Heat the oil in a small heavy-based saucepan with the chilli and garlic for about 10 minutes until the garlic and chilli have turned brown. Remove them from the oil and discard them. Stir in the anchovies and continue to stir until you have created a smooth brown purée. Remove from the heat and keep warm.

Meanwhile, bring a large saucepan of salted water to a rolling boil, toss in the pasta and broccoli and give them one good stir. Cover the pan and bring the water back to the boil. Remove the lid and cook until the pasta is *al dente* and the broccoli is tender; 8 minutes should be about right. Drain the pasta and broccoli thoroughly and return them to the warm empty saucepan. Pour over the anchovy sauce and toss together thoroughly. Season to taste with salt and pepper, transfer to a warmed serving bowl and serve at once.

Chiocciole con Noci e Mascarpone
Chiocciole Pasta with Walnuts and Mascarpone

*I really like the combination of creamy Mascarpone
with crunchy walnuts.
If Mascarpone is unavailable,
use a fresh and rich cream cheese instead.*

SERVES 4

400 g (14 oz) chiocciole
40 g (1¹/₂ oz) unsalted butter, melted
100 g (4 oz) Mascarpone cheese, mashed
15 walnuts, shelled, peeled and coarsely chopped
salt
freshly ground black pepper
75 g (3 oz) Parmesan cheese, freshly grated

Bring a large saucepan of salted water to a rolling boil, toss in the chiocciole and give it one good stir. Cover the pan and bring the water back to the boil. Remove the lid and cook until *al dente*; brands vary but 10 minutes should be about right. Drain the chiocciole thoroughly and return it to the warm empty saucepan. Pour over the melted butter and toss together thoroughly. Add the Mascarpone and walnuts and toss again. Season with a little salt and pepper. Add half the Parmesan and toss again. Transfer to a warmed serving bowl, sprinkle with the remaining Parmesan and serve at once.

Lasagnette alla Lucchese
Lasagnette with Veal Sauce

This is a very filling and meaty dish, perfect for a family supper. If you don't want to use veal, substitute very lean beef or strips of pork loin instead.

SERVES 4

100 g (4 oz) unsalted butter
1 large red onion, peeled and finely chopped
1 large carrot, finely chopped
1 large stick celery, finely chopped
3 tablespoons chopped fresh parsley
3 small sprigs fresh thyme
500 g (1 lb 2 oz) tender, lean beef or
veal, sliced into finger-thick strips
2 tablespoons plain white flour
6 tablespoons dry white wine
500 g (1 lb 2 oz) passata
salt
freshly ground black pepper
250 ml (8 fl oz) beef stock
400 g (14 oz) durum wheat lasagnette
50 g (2 oz) Parmesan cheese, freshly grated

Melt half the butter in a heavy-based saucepan and fry the onion, carrot, celery, parsley and thyme over a low heat for about 5 minutes. Toss the meat in the flour, add it to the pan and fry until browned on both sides. Add the wine and boil off the alcohol for about 2 minutes. Stir in the passata and season to taste with salt and pepper. Add the stock, bring to the boil, cover and simmer for about 1 1/2 hours until the sauce is well reduced.

Bring a large saucepan of salted water to a rolling boil, toss in the lasagnette and give it one good stir. Cover the pan and bring the water back to the boil. Remove the lid and cook until *al dente*; brands vary but 10 minutes should be about right. Drain the lasagnette thoroughly and return it to the warm empty saucepan. Add the remaining butter and the Parmesan and toss together thoroughly. Arrange a layer of pasta on a warmed serving platter, cover with the sauce and repeat until you have used up all the ingredients. Serve at once.

Vermicelli con Peperoni e Melanzane
Vermicelli with Peppers and Aubergines

*It is important that you use juicy peppers and
firm aubergines for this dish.
You can add as much basil as you like,
just make sure it is fresh and not dried.*

SERVES 4

1 small onion, peeled and chopped
3 cloves garlic, peeled and chopped
4 tablespoons olive oil
1 large aubergine, peeled and cubed
2 large peppers, de-seeded and cubed
250 g (9 oz) passata
salt
freshly ground black pepper
6 leaves fresh basil, torn into small pieces
400 g (14 oz) vermicelli

Fry the garlic and onion in the oil for about 5 minutes until soft. Add the aubergine and pepper and cook for about 8 minutes. Stir in the passata and season to taste with salt and pepper. Cover loosely and simmer for about 20 minutes, stirring frequently. Stir in the basil, cover and remove from the heat. Leave to one side so that the flavour of the basil develops in the heat of the sauce.

Bring a large saucepan of salted water to a rolling boil, toss in the vermicelli and give it one good stir. Cover the pan and bring the water back to the boil. Remove the lid and cook until *al dente*; brands vary but 5 minutes should be about right. Drain the vermicelli thoroughly and return it to the warm empty saucepan. Pour over the sauce and toss together thoroughly. Transfer to a warmed serving bowl and serve at once.

Bavette
con le Fave Fresche
Bavette with
Fresh Broad Beans

*Use fresh broad beans because the flavour will simply not be
the same with dried, canned or frozen beans.
The white onions are also important because they have
a milder flavour than the brown-skinned variety.
You could use red onions instead of white if you
can't find them in the local supermarket.*

SERVES 4

1.5 kg (3 lb 4 oz) fresh, young, tender broad beans
4 tablespoons extra virgin olive oil
2 white onions, peeled and finely chopped
3–4 tablespoons chicken stock
salt
freshly ground black pepper
400 g (14 oz) bavette
3 tablespoons unsalted butter or extra virgin olive oil
75 g (3 oz) Parmesan cheese, freshly grated

Remove all the beans from their pods and gently peel off the inner skin. Heat
the oil in a heavy-based saucepan with the onions and fry together gently for
about 10 minutes. Add the broad beans and stock and season to taste with
salt and pepper. Bring to the boil, cover and simmer for about 20 minutes
until the beans are soft. Purée the beans in a food processor.

Bring a large saucepan of salted water to a rolling boil, toss in the bavette
and give it one good stir. Cover the pan and bring the water back to the boil.
Remove the lid and cook until *al dente*; brands vary but 7 minutes should be
about right. Drain the bavette thoroughly and return it to the warm empty saucepan. Pour over the puréed beans and toss together thoroughly. Add the butter
or oil and toss again. Add half the Parmesan, toss again and transfer to a warmed
serving bowl. Sprinkle with the remaining Parmesan and serve at once.

Tagliatelle al Ragù Bolognese
Tagliatelle with Bolognese Sauce

*This is the quick everyday version; real Bolognese sauce contains a
minimum of twenty-two ingredients and takes at least seven hours to cook.
This is as authentic as you can get in less time and with less expenditure!
However, there is a very important point which I feel should be made.
In Bologna they never eat this kind of sauce on spaghetti.
Spaghetti Bolognese is an English invention!
In Bologna, or indeed anywhere else in Italy, this chunky red,
rich meaty wonder would be served on tagliatelle,
maccheroni or maybe lasagnette ... but never spaghetti!*

SERVES 6

1 onion, peeled and chopped
1 clove garlic, peeled and chopped
1 large carrot, chopped
1 large stick celery, chopped
4 tablespoons olive or vegetable oil or
2 tablespoons unsalted butter or
3 tablespoons water or wine
400 g (14 oz) minced beef
2 slices prosciutto crudo, finely chopped
400 g (14 oz) canned tomatoes, drained and
de-seeded if desired
2 tablespoons tomato purée
salt
freshly ground black pepper
500 g (1 lb 2 oz) tagliatelle
75 g (3 oz) Parmesan cheese, freshly grated

Fry the onion, garlic, carrot and celery in the oil, butter, water or wine for about 10 minutes until soft and cooked through. Add the beef and prosciutto and fry until well browned but still soft. Stir in the tomatoes and tomato purée and season to taste with salt and pepper. Bring to the boil, cover and simmer gently for about 2 hours, stirring occasionally.

Bring a large saucepan of salted water to a rolling boil, toss in the tagliatelle and give it one good stir. Cover the pan and bring the water back to the boil. Remove the lid and cook until *al dente*; brands vary but 5 minutes should be about right for dried pasta or 3 minutes for fresh. Drain the tagliatelle thoroughly then return it to the warm empty sauce-pan. Pour over half the sauce and toss together then transfer to a warmed serving bowl. Cover with the remaining sauce and serve with the Parmesan.

Tagliatelle al Prosciutto
Tagliatelle with Ham and Cream

For this dish you will need good quality, fresh tagliatelle.
You can buy it ready-made from one of the many shops or supermarkets which supply
fresh pasta, but the recipe will be especially good if you make the pasta yourself.

SERVES 4

400 g (14 oz) plain white flour
4 eggs
a pinch of salt
1 egg yolk
250 ml (8 fl oz) single cream
100 g (4 oz) prosciutto crudo, finely chopped
a pinch of freshly grated nutmeg
salt
freshly ground black pepper
75 g (3 oz) Parmesan cheese, freshly grated
50 g (2 oz) unsalted butter

If you are making your own pasta, you should do this first. Pile the flour on to a work surface and plunge your fist into the centre to make a hole. Break the eggs into the hole and add the salt. Using your fingers, beat the eggs roughly into the flour then use your hands to knead everything together thoroughly until you have a smooth pliable ball of dough. Roll out the dough as thinly as possible then fold it in half and roll it out again. Continue to do this until the dough is elastic, smooth and shiny and the rolling pin snaps as it rolls over the fold. Roll it out again then fold the pasta up on itself and slice it neatly into 7 mm (1/4 in) strips with a very sharp knife. Bring a large saucepan of salted water to a rolling boil, toss in the tagliatelle and give it one good stir. Cover the pan and bring the water back to the boil. Remove the lid and cook until *al dente*; 3 minutes should be about right. Meanwhile, whisk together all the other ingredients except the butter in a small bowl. Drain the tagliatelle thoroughly then return it to the warm empty saucepan. Add the butter and toss together then pour over the cream sauce. Toss again, transfer to a warmed serving bowl and serve at once.

Pappardelle alla Lepre
Pappardelle with Hare Sauce

*You should begin to prepare this marvellously rich and
gamey dish the day before because
the hare needs to marinate overnight.
You can also make it with wild rabbit or venison.*

SERVES 8

500 ml (17 fl oz) dry red wine
1 large onion, peeled and quartered
1 stick celery, quartered
5–6 black peppercorns
a pinch of dried thyme
2 bay leaves
1.5 kg (3 lb 4 oz) hare, jointed into 8
5 tablespoons olive oil
8 rashers streaky bacon or pancetta, chopped
1 pinch of freshly grated nutmeg
salt
freshly ground black pepper
250 ml (8 fl oz) beef or game stock
750 g (1 lb 10 oz) plain white flour
6 eggs
a pinch of salt
75 g (3 oz) unsalted butter

Put the wine, onion, celery, peppercorns, thyme and bay leaves into a bowl.
Place the hare in the marinade, submerge it thoroughly and cover the bowl
with cling film. Leave to stand in a cool place for about 12 hours.

Drain the hare joints thoroughly and strain the marinade into a second
bowl. Put the oil and bacon or pancetta into a heavy-based saucepan and fry

together gently until all the fat from the bacon runs. Lay the hare joints in the saucepan and brown them all over. Season to taste with nutmeg, salt and pepper. Simmer gently for about $1^1/2$ hours, adding the marinade and stock alternately so that the meat is kept moist all the time. Remove from the heat and put to one side.

Pile the flour on to a work surface and plunge your fist into the centre to make a hole. Break the eggs into the hole and add the salt. Using your fingers, beat the eggs roughly into the flour then use your hands to knead everything together thoroughly until you have a smooth pliable ball of dough. Roll out the dough as thinly as possible then fold it in half and roll it out again. Continue to do this until the dough is elastic, smooth and shiny and the rolling pin snaps as it rolls over the fold. Cut the pasta into strips about as wide as a man's thumb and as long as you feel is practical for the size of your pot!

Re-heat the hare in its sauce until bubbling hot and bring a large saucepan of salted water to a rolling boil. Remove the hare joints, set aside and keep warm. Toss the pappardelle into the boiling water and give it one good stir. Cover the pan and bring the water back to the boil. Remove the lid and cook until *al dente*; 3 minutes should be about right. Drain the pappardelle thoroughly then return it to the warm empty saucepan. Add the butter and toss together then add the hot sauce and toss again. Arrange a portion of pappardelle in each of 8 warmed soup plates and place a joint of hare on top of each portion. Serve at once.

Maltagliati all'Anatra
Maltagliati with Duck Sauce

*I like to use wild duck for this very special dish as
it gives a lot of extra flavour.
The pine kernels add extra crunch and
a lovely resinous taste.*

SERVES 6

1 large onion, peeled and finely chopped
4 tablespoons olive oil
1 young duckling, jointed into 6
1 large wine glass dry white wine
1 sprig fresh rosemary
1 sprig fresh sage
1 bay leaf
a small handful of pine kernels
salt
freshly ground black pepper
500 g (1 lb 2 oz) passata
600 g (1 lb 5 oz) plain white flour
6 eggs
75 g (3 oz) unsalted butter

Fry the onion lightly in the oil for about 5 minutes until soft. Lay the duckling in the onion and brown it carefully all over. Add the wine and boil off the alcohol for about 2 minutes. Add the herbs and pine kernels and season to taste with salt and pepper. Stir in the passata thoroughly and bring to the boil. Cover and simmer gently for about 2 hours. If the sauce appears to be drying out, add a little more wine or water or stock.

Pile the flour on to a work surface and plunge your fist into the centre to make a hole. Break the eggs into the hole. Using your fingers, beat the eggs roughly into the flour then use your hands to knead everything together thoroughly until you have a smooth pliable ball of dough. Roll out the dough as thinly as possible then fold it in half and roll it out again. Continue to do this until the dough is elastic, smooth and shiny and the rolling pin snaps as it rolls over the fold. Roll out the dough once more then roll it up on itself. Cut across the roll on the bias, first across one corner, then across the other. With the third cut, slice the roll straight across to give it a straight edge once more. The maltagliati will open out into a rough shape, each one about 1 cm ($^1/_2$ inch) wide at the most. The name means 'badly cut' which is precisely what they should look like!

Remove the duck joints from the sauce, put them aside and keep them warm. Bring a large saucepan of salted water to a rolling boil, toss in the pasta and give it one good stir. Cover the pan and bring the water back to the boil. Remove the lid and cook until *al dente*; 3 minutes should be about right. Drain the pasta thoroughly and return it to the warm empty saucepan. Add the butter and toss together thoroughly. Pour over the warm sauce and toss again.

Arrange the pasta in 6 warmed soup plates and place a duck joint in the centre of each one. Serve at once.

Trenette
al Pesto
Trenette with
Pesto Sauce

For this recipe you'll need a huge amount of fresh basil.
It is an ideal dish to make whilst on holiday in Italy
where basil is easily available in gigantic bunches.
The basic principle for pesto started out with the premise that you
need to pound together fresh basil and garlic and use the
resulting paste to dress some hand-made strips of pasta.
This very simple recipe has evolved and continues to
evolve into a myriad of different versions.
Bearing in mind that I have already mentioned the original recipe,
I feel quite within my rights to give you my own personalised
version for the sauce, as not one of my Liguarian friends has
yet agreed on a common recipe and they all continue to
propose their own versions as the only true possibility.
However, I feel bound to mention one or two points concerned with this
much-discussed sauce. First of all,
most cooks add either pine kernels or walnuts,
whereas I like to have both.
Secondly, many cooks in Genova add curd to
their sauce to make it more creamy.
I sometimes use Greek yoghurt as a substitute and have
received no complaints thus far!
Many cooks tell me that you should actually serve pesto with
equal parts of trenette, cubed boiled potatoes and green beans.
This is delicious and certainly makes a wonderfully
filling yet fresh summer dish.

SERVES 4–5

400 g (14 oz) plain white flour
2 eggs
2 tablespoons chopped fresh basil or borage
salt
water
30–50 leaves fresh basil
3 cloves garlic, peeled
a handful of pine kernels
2 tablespoons chopped walnuts
8 tablespoons light olive oil
50 g (2 oz) Parmesan cheese, freshly grated
4 tablespoons Greek yoghurt (optional)
4 tablespoons chopped green olives (optional)
freshly ground black pepper

Pile the flour on to a work surface and plunge your fist into the centre to make a hole. Break the eggs into the hole and add the basil or borage and a pinch of salt. Using your fingers, beat the eggs roughly into the flour then use your hands to knead everything together thoroughly, adding just enough water to make a smooth pliable ball of dough. Roll out the dough as thinly as possible then fold it in half and roll it out again. Continue to do this until the dough is elastic, smooth and shiny and the rolling pin snaps as it rolls over the fold. Roll out the dough again then roll it up on itself and cut it into ribbons.

Bring a large saucepan of salted water to a rolling boil, toss in the trenette and bring the water back to the boil. Remove the lid and cook until *al dente*; 3 minutes should be about right.

Meanwhile, pound the basil and garlic together to a smooth paste and stir in the pine kernels, walnuts, oil, Parmesan, and yoghurt and olives, if using. Season to taste with salt and pepper. Drain the trenette thoroughly then return it to the warm empty saucepan. Add the sauce and toss together thoroughly then transfer to a warmed serving bowl and serve at once.

Lasagne
al Forno
Baked Lasagne

This is a simple version of this classic special occasion dish.
The more complicated version contains all kinds
of other ingredients such as peas,
slivers of truffle and thin slices of Parma ham.
To serve 6 people, you will need about
40 lasagne sheets of 7 x 10 cm (3 x 4 in).

SERVES 6

1 onion, peeled and finely chopped
1 carrot, finely chopped
1 stick celery, chopped
3 tablespoons olive or sunflower oil
300 g (11 oz) coarsely minced beef or veal
4 tablespoons red wine
500 g (1 lb 2 oz) passata
salt
freshly ground black pepper
50 g (2 oz) unsalted butter
50 g (2 oz) plain white flour
600 ml (1 pint) milk
120 g (4¹/₂ oz) Parmesan cheese, freshly grated
a pinch of freshly grated nutmeg
2 teaspoons melted butter
550 g (1 lb 4 oz) strong plain white flour
6 eggs

Make the sauces first. Fry the onion, carrot and celery together in the oil for about 5 minutes, stirring frequently. Add the beef or veal and mix thoroughly until the meat is browned. Add the wine and boil off the alcohol for about 2 minutes. Add the passata and season to taste with salt and pepper. Stir and cover loosely. Simmer for about 1 hour; the longer the better.

Melt the butter in a small saucepan until foaming. Mix in the flour very quickly to blend thoroughly. Whisk in the milk and continue whisking or stirring while it comes to the boil. Simmer for about 15 minutes until the sauce no longer tastes of raw flour. Add half the Parmesan and season to taste with nutmeg, salt and pepper. Cover the top with a very thin layer of melted butter to prevent a skin forming. Remove from the heat and set aside until required.

Then make the pasta. Pile the flour on to a work surface and plunge your fist into the centre to make a hole. Break the eggs into the hole and add a pinch of salt. Using your fingers, beat the eggs roughly into the flour then use your hands to knead everything together thoroughly until you have a smooth pliable ball of dough. Roll out the dough as thinly as possible then fold it in half and roll it out again. Continue to do this until the dough is elastic, smooth and shiny and the rolling pin snaps as it rolls over the fold. Roll it out again and cut it into 40 even-sized rectangles about 7 x 10 cm (3 x 4 in).

Clear plenty of space and cover your largest work surface with a large damp cloth. Bring a large saucepan of salted water to the boil, toss 5 lasagne sheets into the water at a time and simmer for about 5 minutes then scoop them out of the pot and lay them on the wet cloth without overlapping.

Meanwhile, pre-heat the oven to gas mark 5, 190°C (375°F). Arrange the meat sauce, pasta, cheese sauce and Parmesan cheese in layers in a large ovenproof dish, finishing with a layer of cheese sauce sprinkled with Parmesan. Bake in the oven for about 30 minutes until bubbling and golden on top. Leave to rest for about 5 minutes before serving.

Tortellini alla Bolognese
Tortellini in the Bolognese Style

This should make 300 tortellini if you
can make them small enough,
but considerably fewer if you do not have decades
of experience in this field!

SERVES 6

2 tablespoons unsalted butter
100 g (4 oz) pork loin, diced
50 g (2 oz) trimmed veal, diced
50 g (2 oz) mortadella, diced
100 g (4 oz) turkey breast, diced
50 g (2 oz) prosciutto crudo, diced
2 egg yolks
225 g (8 oz) Parmesan cheese, freshly grated
a pinch of freshly grated nutmeg
salt and freshly ground black pepper
500 g (1 lb 2 oz) strong plain white flour
Ragu Bolognese (page 113)

Melt the butter in a saucepan and cook all the meat for about 10 minutes, stirring frequently to brown it all over. Remove it from the heat and process it for about 40 seconds to reduce it to a fairly smooth mixture. Add the egg yolks and half the Parmesan and season to taste with nutmeg, salt and pepper. Process all this to make a smoothly amalgamated mixture. Set aside until required.

Pile the flour on to a work surface and plunge your fist into the centre to make a hole. Break the eggs into the hole and add a pinch of salt. Using your fingers, beat the eggs roughly into the flour then use your hands to knead everything together thoroughly until you have a smooth pliable ball of dough. Roll out the dough as thinly as possible then fold it in half and roll it out again. Continue to do this until the dough is elastic, smooth and shiny and the rolling pin snaps as it rolls over the fold.

When you make the tortellini, you will need to work fast to prevent the dough from drying out. I recommend that you either enlist a team of assistants (you could always run a competition to see who can make the smallest tortellino!) or roll out your dough in small sections, keeping the bulk swathed in a damp tea cloth while you work on the section which is rolled out. Roll out the dough again as thinly as possible and cut it into small squares. Put a tiny amount of filling in the centre of each square. Fold it in half to make a triangle. Wrap this triangle around your little or index finger and fold the two corners back and around the finger to overlap and make a closed circle. Bend the third, upturned triangle backwards and slip the tortellino off your finger.

When they are all formed and looking like Venus' belly buttons in neat rows, cover them with a slightly moist tea cloth and bring a large saucepan of salted water to the boil. Toss in the tortellini and cook for about 7 minutes (taste one to check) until they are puffy and tender. If they are all different sizes they will cook at different speeds, so do bear this in mind when you are making them. The longer they are left to stand around the dryer they will become and the longer they will take to cook.

Meanwhile, heat the Bolognese sauce. Drain the tortellini thoroughly and transfer them to a warmed serving bowl. Pour over the hot sauce and toss gently to avoid splitting the tortellini.

Sprinkle with half the remaining Parmesan and toss again. Sprinkle with the remaining Parmesan and serve at once.

Ravioli
alla Genovese
Ravioli
with a Meat
and Spinach Filling

It is important that the dough used for
making ravioli should have as few eggs as possible so you
need to have a higher proportion of water than eggs.
This is because you already have a
fairly rich filling and also you need to have a
pasta pocket which will cook very quickly.

SERVES 6

500 g (1 lb 2 oz) lean beef, cubed
1 onion, peeled and chopped
3 cloves garlic, peeled and chopped
3 tablespoons olive oil
1 tiny sprig fresh rosemary
4 tablespoons dry red wine
1.75 kg (4 lb) canned tomatoes, chopped
salt
freshly ground black pepper
500 g (1 lb 2 oz) cooked spinach
(about as much as a large orange)
2 Italian sausages
4 eggs
100 g (4 oz) Parmesan cheese, freshly grated
500 g (1 lb 2 oz) plain white flour
120 ml (4 fl oz) water

Make the sauce first. Fry the beef, half the onion and 2 cloves of garlic in the oil, stirring until the meat is well browned. Add the rosemary and wine and simmer together for about 10 minutes. Add the tomatoes and season to taste with salt and pepper. Bring to the boil, cover and simmer for at least 2 hours.

Next make the filling. Remove the meat from the sauce with a slotted spoon and mince it finely with the cooked spinach and the remaining onion and garlic. Grill the sausages for about 10 minutes, remove the skin and crumble them into the filling mixture. Stir in 2 eggs, season to taste with salt and pepper then stir in half the Parmesan. Set aside until required.

Put the flour on to a work surface and plunge your fist into the centre to make a hole. Break the remaining eggs into the hole and add a pinch of salt. Using your fingers, beat the eggs roughly into the flour, adding just enough water very gradually to make a smooth dough. Use your hands to knead everything together thoroughly until you have a smooth pliable ball of dough. Roll out the dough as thinly as possible then fold it in half and roll it out again. Continue to do this until the dough is elastic, smooth and shiny and the rolling pin snaps as it rolls over the fold. Roll out the dough again and cut it into even-sized rectangles about 4 x 9 cm ($1^1/_2$ x $3^1/_2$ in) with a pastry wheel. Put a small quantity of filling on one half of each rectangle. Fold it in half and press tightly closed with the prongs of a fork. Bring a very large saucepan of salted water to a rolling boil, toss in the ravioli and cook for about 3 minutes until tender and puffy.

You will need a really big saucepan or you will have to cook them in batches. Drain the ravioli carefully and transfer to a warmed serving platter. Cover with the hot sauce, sprinkle the remaining Parmesan and serve at once.

Gnocchi di Spinaci
Spinach
Gnocchi

I cannot pretend to you that this is an easy dish to make.
You really will need to be very careful that you don't end up
with hard green rubbery lumps.
The secret is to handle the dough as little as possible.

SERVES 6

1.25 kg (3 lb) spinach, steamed
2 eggs, beaten
2 egg yolks
2 tablespoons single cream
150 g (5 oz) stale bread, soaked in enough milk to cover
150 g (5 oz) Parmesan cheese, freshly grated
a large pinch of freshly grated nutmeg
salt
freshly ground black pepper
3–5 tablespoons plain white flour
100 g (4 oz) unsalted butter, melted

Squeeze as much water as possible out of the spinach with your hands. Push through a sieve or purée briefly in a food processor. Mix in the eggs, egg yolks and cream. Sqeeze the bread as dry as possible and mix that into the spinach with half the Parmesan. Season to taste with nutmeg, salt and pepper. Bring a large saucepan of salted water to the boil. Using your fingers with a very light touch, make small dumplings out of the spinach mixture, using the minimum amount of flour to prevent them sticking. Be very miserly with the flour or you will end up with rubbery gnocchi. Slip them carefully in small batches into the boiling water and cook them for no more than 2 minutes, just until they float to the surface. Remove from the saucepan with a slotted spoon and arrange on a warmed serving dish. Continue until they are all cooked. Pour over the melted butter, sprinkle with the remaining Parmesan and serve at once.

Gnocchi di Semolino

SEE PAGE 129

Pizza con Funghi e Mozzarella

SEE PAGE 143

Bollito con Patate

SEE PAGE 160

Pizzette

SEE PAGE 149

Gnocchi di Semolino
Semolina
Gnocchi

*My children adore this dish and it is the only
form in which they will eat semolina!
If you like, you can add a sachet of saffron powder to
the semolina in order to give it a bright
yellow colour and a more exotic flavour.*

SERVES 6

1 litre (1 ³/₄ pints) milk
250 g (9 oz) semolina
2 egg yolks
100 g (4 oz) Parmesan cheese, freshly grated
100 g (4 oz) unsalted butter
a pinch of ground cinnamon
salt
freshly ground black pepper

Pre-heat the oven to gas mark 7, 220°C (425°F). Bring the milk to the boil in a large saucepan. Sprinkle in the semolina with one hand so that it falls into the water like fine rain, whisking constantly to prevent lumps. Continue in this way until the mixture begins to thicken then use a wooden spoon to stir constantly for about 10 minutes as the semolina cooks. You know it is ready when it comes away from the bottom of the pan and forms a smooth thick ball.

Remove from the heat. Stir in the egg yolks, half the Parmesan and half the butter and season to taste with cinnamon, salt and pepper. Dampen a work surface lightly with cold water and tip out the semolina. Spread it out flat with a wide-bladed knife dipped in cold water until it is about 1 cm (¹/₂ in) thick.

Using a pastry cutter or upturned glass, cut the semolina into even-sized circles. Use some of the remaining butter to grease a shallow ovenproof dish. Arrange a layer of gnocchi on the bottom, cover with a little Parmesan and a few dots of butter. Repeat until all the ingredients have been used up. Melt any remaining butter and trickle it over the top. Bake in the oven for about 15 minutes before serving.

Cannelloni con Ricotta e Spinaci
Cannelloni with Ricotta and Spinach

This is a very light dish, perfect for lunch or supper.
As with the previous recipe,
you can use dried ready-made cannelloni if you wish.

SERVES 6

200 g (7 oz) Ricotta cheese
250 g (9 oz) cooked spinach
50 g (2 oz) Parmesan cheese, freshly grated
a pinch of freshly grated nutmeg
salt
freshly ground black pepper
400 g (14 oz) plain white flour
4 eggs
75 g (3 oz) unsalted butter
450 ml (15 fl oz) milk

Mash the Ricotta with a fork. Squeeze the spinach as dry as possible and then chop it finely with a rocking chopper or a heavy knife. Mix together the Ricotta and spinach, add half the Parmesan and season to taste with nutmeg, salt and pepper.

Reserve 2 tablespoons of flour. Pile the remaining flour on to a work surface and plunge your fist into the centre to make a hole. Break the eggs into the hole and add a pinch of salt. Using your fingers, beat the eggs roughly into the flour then use your hands to knead everything together thoroughly until you have a smooth pliable ball of dough. Roll out the dough as thinly as possible then fold it in half and roll it out again.

Continue to do this until the dough is elastic, smooth and shiny and the rolling pin snaps as it rolls over the fold. Roll out the dough again and cut it into 10 cm (4 in) squares.

Pre-heat the oven to gas mark 6, 200°C (400°F). Bring a large saucepan of salted water to a rolling boil, toss in the pasta and cook in batches of 5 for 2 minutes. Lay the cooked pasta on a work surface without overlapping. Put a spoonful of the Ricotta filling in the centre of each square and roll the squares up to close them. Use one-third of the butter to grease an ovenproof dish large enough to take all the cannelloni in one layer. Arrange them in the dish. Melt the remaining butter until foaming, stir in the reserved flour and cook for about 2 minutes. Whisk in the milk, bring to the boil and cook for about 15 minutes until smooth and thick. Stir in half the remaining Parmesan and pour this sauce over the cannelloni.

Sprinkle with the remaining Parmesan and bake in the oven for about 15 minutes until bubbling and browned on top. Leave to rest for about 5 minutes before serving.

Cannelloni Ripieni di Carne
Cannelloni with a Meat Filling

You could use ready-made cannelloni for this dish,
the kind that requires no pre-cooking,
but it will be really special if you use fresh pasta.
It is very much a recipe for a special occasion.

SERVES 6

100 g (4 oz) unsalted butter
1 onion, peeled and chopped
1 carrot, finely chopped
1 stick celery, finely chopped
5 sprigs fresh parsley, chopped
a handful of dried funghi porcini,
soaked in warm water for 20 minutes
800 g (1 lb 12 oz) lean beef, cubed
$1/2$ tumbler marsala
4 tablespoons tomato purée
900 ml ($1^1/2$ pints) warm water
salt
freshly ground black pepper
5 slices prosciutto crudo
100 g (4 oz) Parmesan cheese, freshly grated
300 g (11 oz) plain white flour
3 large eggs
1 teaspoon olive oil

Melt half the butter in a large saucepan with the onion, carrot, celery and parsley and fry together carefully and gently for about 6 minutes until soft. Drain the mushrooms and squeeze out as much water as possible. Chop them coarsely and add them to the vegetables. Add the beef and seal it thoroughly on all sides. Add the marsala and boil off the alcohol for about 2 minutes. Dilute the tomato purée in the warm water and stir this into the pan. Season to taste with salt and pepper, bring to the boil, cover and simmer for about 1 hour.

Remove the meat from the sauce and mince it with the prosciutto crudo and about 2 tablespoons of Parmesan. Season if necessary.

Pile the flour on to a work surface and plunge your fist into the centre to make a hole. Break the eggs into the hole and add a pinch of salt and the oil. Using your fingers, beat the eggs roughly into the flour then use your hands to knead everything together thoroughly until you have a smooth pliable ball of dough. Roll out the dough as thinly as possible then fold it in half and roll it out again. Continue to do this until the dough is elastic, smooth and shiny and the rolling pin snaps as it rolls over the fold. Roll out the dough again and cut it into 10 cm (4 in) squares.

Pre-heat the oven to gas mark 6, 200°C (400°F). Bring a large saucepan of salted water to a rolling boil, toss in the pasta and cook in batches of 5 for just 2 minutes. Scoop them out with a slotted spoon and lay them on a work surface without overlapping. Spoon a little of the minced beef mixture into the centre of each one and roll them up tightly on themselves. Use half of the remaining butter to grease an ovenproof dish large enough to take all the cannelloni in one layer. Arrange them in the dish.

Cover with the tomato and mushroom sauce and dot with the remaining butter. Sprinkle with the remaining cheese and bake in the oven for about 15 minutes until bubbling hot. Leave to rest for 5 minutes before serving.

Gnocchi di Patate al Sugo di Pomodoro

Potato Gnocchi with Tomato Sauce

Once again, as with all gnocchi,
if you over-knead this dough you'll end up
with a horribly hard texture.
Be gentle and light of hand and you'll have
lovely soft gnocchi instead of potato bullets!

SERVES 6

1 kg (2 lb) fresh ripe tomatoes
1 onion, peeled and quartered
1 carrot, quartered
1 stick celery with as many leaves as possible
a handful of basil leaves
3–4 sprigs fresh parsley
salt
freshly ground black pepper
1 kg (2 lb) potatoes, peeled and quartered
1 tablespoon unsalted butter
150 g (5 oz) plain white flour, sifted
2 eggs, beaten
100 g (4 oz) Parmesan cheese, freshly grated

Put the tomatoes, onion, carrot, celery, basil and parsley into a saucepan. Cover and place over a low heat. Bring to the boil and simmer for 30 minutes, then remove the lid and simmer for a further 30 minutes. Remove from the heat and push through a food mill or sieve. Season to taste with salt and pepper and set aside. Put the potatoes into a saucepan, cover generously with water and add a pinch of salt. Bring to the boil and cook until the potatoes are completely soft. Drain and mash thoroughly. Return to the saucepan and add the butter. Mix thoroughly over a low heat then remove from the heat and gradually stir in the flour. Add the eggs and stir vigorously. Leave to cool.

Turn the potato mixture on to a work surface and roll it into long sausage shapes. Cut it into 4 cm (1¹/₂ in) sections and roll them against the back of a fork with your thumb to create long indentations on one side. Use a little flour to prevent sticking, if necessary. Be sure you have a light touch to avoid making bullet-hard gnocchi.

Meanwhile, re-heat the tomato sauce and bring a large saucepan of salted water to the boil. Tip the gnocchi into the water and cook for about 3 minutes, just until they float to the surface. Remove them with a slotted spoon and arrange them on a warmed serving dish. Cover with the sauce, sprinkle with Parmesan and serve at once.

Pizza and Polenta

WHAT MAKES a pizza a good pizza? The purists would tell you that you need a proper wood-burning pizza oven for a start, the kind which produces a very high temperature in order to cook the pizza very fast — one minute in some cases! But although some pizza-adoring households in Italy have just such an oven built into their premises, I have never seen one in an ordinary home outside its country of origin. So intense is the feeling in Italy concerning the right oven that there is an inspectorate set up to inspect the premises of restaurants which sell pizza in order to check out the validity of their ovens. In other words, restaurants cannot get away with selling real pizza unless they can cook them in the correct oven. Anything else just isn't pizza. The next point is the thickness of the dough.

Generally speaking, the pizza base is at its most thin and crispy in the south of the country, gradually becoming thicker as you move north. Of course, southern bakers who have moved north and set themselves up in business often take their thin pizzas with them. However, nowhere in Italy will you find the 'deep pan' style of pizza, which is an American invention. To the Italians, the base serves merely as a background for the topping and there isn't even very much of that.

A real Neapolitan pizza is a very thin base coating with just a couple of tablespoons of tomato purée and sprinkled with herbs, salt, freshly ground black pepper and garlic. Even Mozzarella is not included in the original recipe!

In order to recreate the best possible pizza in your own home you should bear in mind that what you are making is something basically very simple. Pizza was invented by a back-street Neapolitan baker as the original fast food. He had the brilliant idea of heating bread and tomato, combined in a sort of sandwich, and selling it directly to passers-by on the street from the wide doorway of his shop. Sadly, nobody can remember the name of the baker, although they can remember the street where the shop used to stand.

Pizza dough is nothing more complicated than ordinary bread dough, enriched with extra olive oil. Like all bread doughs, it needs a lot of kneading and the more effort you put into the kneading, the better the dough will turn out at the end. Hand-made doughs will always differ from one kitchen to another as different bakers have different methods and develop their own style according to their mood. When the dough has risen and been knocked back and kneaded again, it is ready to be flattened out on to an oiled baking tray to cover with a topping. You must never use a rolling pin to flatten it; always use your hands, oiled with a little olive oil, in order to make the dough stretch and flatten out to fill the baking tray properly. The dough will automatically spring back and shrink from the sides, but it is up to you to push and squash it into position.

Having tamed your dough on to the baking tray, it must be rubbed with a little more olive oil. Then comes the topping. Always leave a rim around the edge of the pizza with no topping on it. This is called *la cornice*, the frame, and is a traditional feature of pizza. Cooks make their frames wider or narrower according to personal preference. There are several ideas for toppings in the following chapter, but please don't be afraid to make up your own combinations. A final drizzle of olive oil, a dash of salt and freshly ground black pepper, and the pizza is ready for the oven. Make sure the oven is as hot as possible so that the pizza will cook in the minimum amount of time. Keep an eye on it so that you can turn it around should one side cook faster than the other.

When you take it out of the oven, let it stand for about 30 seconds before you serve it. Ideally each person should have their own whole pizza. Cut it into wedges and then abandon your knife and fork. Once it is all in wedges, pick up a piece with your fingers, either folded in half again or into quarters if you prefer.

I have also included a few recipes for pizzas with the filling inside rather than on top, variations on the stuffed pizza or calzone theme, and a delicious recipe for deep-fried mini pizzas which were always served at parties when I was a little girl.

There is absolutely nothing to substitute for a lovingly made home-baked pizza. However, I have to admit that many supermarket ready-made pizzas have improved enormously since the manufacturers began to understand that the base does not have to have the look and texture of thick blotting paper. The introduction of the 'thin and crispy' to the pizza shelves has made this convenience food a great deal better. I cannot really comment on the standard of those bases which you buy and then cover with your own topping as I have never actually bought one. I would rather not have pizza at all.

The American pizza phenomenon is not to be confused with the original invention on the back-streets of Naples. It obviously came out of the traditions and eating customs which the emigrants took over to the USA with them at the beginning of this century, but it seems to have since developed into something which is almost unrecognisable from the original. I mean, prawns and sweetcorn topping? Surely this is something of a travesty!

If you possibly can, I would recommend that you always make your own pizza from scratch. Apart from anything else, the kneading and working of the dough is very therapeutic!

POLENTA

Classic polenta flour comes in many forms. It can be white or yellow, fine ground or very rough. It is basically dried maize which is ground to a flour. There is no real difference in flavour between the white and the yellow, although in certain parts of Italy they reserve the white variety to serve with fish. Polenta is generally speaking a food which belongs to the north of Italy, although it crops up as far south as Lazio. It is especially popular in the Veneto, Lombardy, Friuli Venezi Giulia and Aosta. As it is the kind of rib-sticking, filling winter food which warms you right through, it is logical that it would appear in areas where the weather is coldest.

Just like bread, potatoes, rice or pasta, polenta functions as a carbo-hydrate base to serve with a protein-rich dish such as meat, fish, vegetable stew or cheese. As a little girl, I also used to eat it with hot milk and a knob of butter. I used to turn it into a real ritual, scooping the polenta and milk around the knob of butter as it melted. The last few bites were the special part, shiny and rich with golden butter.

Old-fashioned polenta flour has to be trickled into boiling salted water and then stirred constantly for 50 minutes until it becomes thick enough to come away from the edges of the pan. It is then turned out on to a flat surface and allowed to set slightly before being cut into thick slabs. The hot polenta is then served alongside a dish of your choice. Polenta on its own is, to say the least, very bland. The quick-cook variety is prepared in exactly the same way but it only takes five minutes. It is nowhere near as good as the old-fashioned version, but it is passable. It reminds me slightly of semolina.

Cooked polenta can also be cut into slices and fried or grilled until hot and crispy. I particularly like hot grilled or fried polenta with a topping of melted cheese, especially something really flavoursome like Gorgonzola. You can also use it in a lasagne-type of dish, cutting it into slices, layering it with cheese and tomato and then baking it. There are also some cake recipes which use polenta flour instead of, or as well as, ordinary flour in order to make a really rich and rather heavy type of cake. In the USA there is something called spoon bread which is very similar to cooked polenta and is served in much the same way.

The general rule for polenta is to remember that it is a bland base and that you should always combine it with ingredients that have a contrastingly strong flavour, such as game, cured meats, stewed salted cod, meat stews with olives and strong herbs and so on. It was never meant to be a sophisticated dish, rather one which was designed to keep out the winter damp and the frosty chills. It is very filling because often there would be nothing else to eat. Like many of the best dishes representative of Italian cuisine, it is born out of peasant poverty and the need to survive.

MAKING BREAD

In order to make Italian bread, you simply have to follow the recipe for Pasta per Pizza (page 141). Just knead the dough into loaves, rolls or plaits and you will get lovely, crunchy, tasty bread. If you like, once you have experimented a bit with this type of dough and seen how easy it is, you can begin to add more things to it. For example, add a handful of coarsely chopped walnuts to make Pane alle Noci, or some stoned chopped olives for Pane alle Olive. You can mix herbs into the dough, or chopped onions, or even a few strips of sun-dried tomatoes. I think that bread-making is something which needs practice, and you need to develop your own knack. I am not a very good baker at all, but I can manage some quite passable rolls with the recipe I have given you for pizza. Sometimes I like to add a bit more oil to get really crispy rolls, at other times I add a bit of milk to make them softer. I hope you do give it a try and start concocting your own ideas from this very simple recipe.

Pasta per Pizza
Basic Pizza
Dough

*It is always best to make pizza with
fresh yeast if at all possible.
However, dried yeast or the new easy-bake type of
yeast can also be used if you cannot get hold of the fresh variety.
You can also use this recipe as a bread dough.*

SERVES 6

15 g (^{1}/$_2$ oz) fresh yeast
250 ml (8 fl oz) warm water
a pinch of sugar
350 g (12 oz) strong plain white flour plus
extra for dusting
1^1/$_2$ tablespoons olive oil
a pinch of salt

Crumble the yeast into a glass and add 6 tablespoons of warm water to dilute it. Stir in the sugar and place the glass in a warm place for about 10 minutes or until the mixture is really frothy. Tip the flour on to the work surface, make a hole in the centre with your fist and pour in the yeast mixture.

Add the oil and salt and knead together very thoroughly and energetically, adding as much of the remaining warm water as is necessary to make a smooth, elastic and non-sticky dough. Punch and knead the dough for as long as possible to incorporate as much air as possible. Dust a bowl lightly with flour, place the ball of dough in the bowl and cover with a lightly floured cloth.

Put in a warm place to rise for 2 to 2^1/$_2$ hours, then knock back and use as required.

Pizza Napoletana
Neapolitan
Pizza

*This is the original and most authentic recipe for pizza,
although to be even more authentic,
it should have crushed dried bay leaves
sprinkled all over it instead of oregano.*

SERVES 6

1 quantity Pasta per Pizza (page 141)
plain white flour for knocking back
1 tablespoon lard (optional)
2 tablespoons olive oil
50 g (2 oz) salted anchovies, boned, rinsed and dried
100 g (4 oz) Mozzarella cheese, cubed
300 g (11 oz) canned tomatoes, drained and chopped
salt
freshly ground black pepper
1 heaped teaspoon dried oregano

Pre-heat the oven to gas mark 9, 240°C (475°F). When the dough is well risen, remove it from the bowl and dust it lightly with flour. Knead it again to knock it back. Using your fingers, flatten out the dough as thinly and as evenly as possible into a 5 mm (1/4 in) thick disc of dough about 30 cm (12 in) across. Lay the dough carefully on an oiled 35 cm (14 in) baking tray. Use your fingertips to tap the dough down energetically. It is traditional to smear the whole of the pizza with lard at this point, but you may prefer to simply use oil. However, if you are using lard, rub the grease all over the surface evenly and then top it with a thin stream of oil. Alternatively, just cover the surface generously with oil. When you top the pizza, remember always to leave a clear space around the edges of the pizza with no topping. Trim the anchovy fillets, cut them into small cubes and scatter them over the pizza. Spread the Mozzarella evenly over the top of the pizza then cover with the tomatoes. Sprinkle generously with salt and pepper then add a generous sprinkling of oregano. Bake in the centre of the oven for 10 to 15 minutes. Serve at once.

Pizza con Funghi e Mozzarella

Pizza with Mushrooms and Mozzarella

A great favourite, you can make this using any kind of mushrooms you like, or a combination of different kinds.

SERVES 6

1 quantity Pasta per Pizza (page 141)
plain white flour for knocking back
2 tablespoons olive oil
100 g (4 oz) dried funghi porcini, soaked in
warm water for 20 minutes
1 tablespoon unsalted butter
300 g (11 oz) canned tomatoes, drained,
de-seeded and chopped
salt
300 g (11 oz) Mozzarella cheese, cubed

Pre-heat the oven to gas mark 9, 240°C (475°F). When the dough is well risen remove it from the bowl and dust it lightly with flour. Knead it again to knock it back. Using your fingers, flatten out the dough into a 1 cm (1/2 in) thick disc of dough about 30 cm (12 in) across. Lay the dough carefully on an oiled 35 cm (14 in) baking tray. Trickle a little more oil all over the pizza and flatten it down securely with your fingertips. Drain the mushrooms and chop them coarsely. Melt the butter in a small saucepan, add the mushrooms and cook them for about 5 minutes, stirring frequently. Stir in the tomatoes, season to taste with salt and heat through for about 5 minutes. Pour the tomato and mushroom mixture over the pizza, leaving a 3 cm (1¹/4 in) border around the edge. Cover with the Mozzarella, drizzle a final coating of oil over the top and place in the oven for about 20 minutes. Serve at once.

Pizza con Ricotta
Pizza
with Ricotta

In this recipe, fresh, creamy, soft Ricotta is
used instead of the more traditional Mozzarella.
For best results, use the best quality ham.

SERVES 6

1 quantity Pasta per Pizza (page 141)
plain white flour for knocking back
2 tablespoons olive oil
500 g (1 lb 2 oz) Ricotta cheese
2 eggs, beaten
25 g (1 oz) Parmesan cheese, freshly grated
salt
freshly ground black pepper
100 g (4 oz) ham, thinly sliced
1 tablespoon milk

Pre-heat the oven to gas mark 6, 200°C (400°F). When the dough is well risen, remove it from the bowl and dust it lightly with flour. Knead it again to knock it back and flatten it thoroughly with your hands. Add another tablespoon of oil to the dough and knead it again. Flatten half the dough into a circle on an oiled 35 cm (14 in) baking tray. Mix the Ricotta thoroughly with the eggs and Parmesan, season to taste with salt and pepper and spread the mixture over the dough leaving a 3 cm (1¹/₂ in) border around the edge. Cover the Ricotta completely with the slices of ham. Flatten the second half of the dough as much as possible with your hands, then lay it on top of the Ricotta. Fold over the edges all the way round very carefully to enclose the filling. Brush with milk and bake in the oven for about 30 minutes until golden brown. Leave to cool for about 5 minutes before serving.

Polenta con Gorgonzola SEE PAGE 152

(Overleaf) Pizza con Salame
SEE PAGE 145

Manzo in Involtini

SEE PAGE 162

Pizza con Salame
Pizza
with Salame

*This pizza has a very strong flavour and
needs a good quality salame,
Milano or Napoletano, for a spicier effect.*

SERVES 6

1 quantity Pasta per Pizza (page 141)
plain white flour for knocking back
90 g (3^1/$_2$ oz) unsalted butter
2 eggs, beaten
a pinch of salt
150 g (5 oz) Mozzarella cheese, sliced
100 g (4 oz) salami, cubed
2 hard-boiled eggs, cubed
1 tablespoon milk

When the dough is well risen, remove it from the bowl and dust it lightly
with flour. Knead it again to knock it back then add 50 g (2 oz) of the
butter, the eggs and salt. Knead this all together very energetically until you
have a very smooth, elastic dough. Butter a 20 cm (8 in) deep baking tin with
the remaining butter. Roll out the dough and carefully line the baking tin with
two-thirds of the dough, reserving the remainder to make a lid. Fill the dough
case with the Mozzarella, salami and eggs. Make a flat lid with the remaining
piece of dough. Cover the filling and bring the edges of both sheets of dough
together to seal the pizza tightly. Put the finished pizza in a warm place to
rise for 2 hours or until it has filled the baking tin completely.

Pre-heat the oven to gas mark 8, 230°C (450°F). Brush the pizza with milk
and bake for about 35 minutes, gradually reducing the temperature every 10
minutes as it bakes. Turn out on to a warmed serving platter and serve at once.

Pizza con Tonno e Pomodoro

Pizza with Tuna and Tomato

A lovely pizza with lots of strong flavours and plenty of texture, this is a perfect recipe for an informal supper with friends.

Serves 6

1 quantity Pasta per Pizza (page 141)
plain white flour for knocking back
100 g (4 oz) lard
800 g (1 lb 12 oz) canned tomatoes, drained,
de-seeded and chopped
4 tablespoons olive oil
salt
freshly ground black pepper
200 g (7 oz) canned tuna in oil, drained and flaked
50 g (2 oz) salted anchovies, boned, rinsed and dried
100 g (4 oz) black olives in oil, stoned and chopped
4 tablespoons salted capers, rinsed, dried and chopped
2 tablespoons milk

Pre-heat the oven to gas mark 6, 200°C (400°F). When the dough is well risen, remove it from the bowl and dust it lightly with flour. Knead it again to knock it back then carefully knead the lard into the dough and work it until it is smooth and elastic. Use two-thirds of the dough to line an oiled 30 cm (12 in) deep cake tin completely. Put the tomatoes into a saucepan with the oil, bring to the boil and simmer for about 10 minutes, stirring frequently. Season to taste with salt and pepper then leave to cool. Mix together the tuna, anchovies, olives and capers then stir the mixture into the tomatoes. Spoon the mixture into the lined cake tin. Use the remaining piece of dough to make a lid and seal the edges carefully. Brush the pizza with milk and bake in the centre of the oven for about 30 minutes until golden brown and crispy. Leave to stand for about 5 minutes before serving.

Pizza di Ventimiglia
Onion and Tomato Pizza

Because this uses no Mozzarella or other cheese,
it is a rather unusual pizza,
relying entirely on the tomatoes and
onions for moisture and flavour.
It is also sometimes called Pizza all'Andrea.

SERVES 6

1 quantity Pasta per Pizza (page 141)
plain white flour for knocking back
4 tablespoons olive oil
2 large onions, peeled and thinly sliced
300 g (11 oz) canned or fresh tomatoes,
skinned, de-seeded and chopped
$1/2$ teaspoon dried oregano
salt and freshly ground black pepper

Pre-heat the oven to gas mark 7, 220°C (425°F). When the dough is well risen, remove it from the bowl and dust it lightly with flour. Knead it again to knock it back then knead in 2 tablespoons of oil and work the dough until it is smooth and elastic and no longer sticky. Using your fingers, flatten out the dough into a disc about 30 cm (12 in) across on to an oiled 35 cm (14 in) baking tray.

Fry the onions and tomatoes together with the remaining oil for about 5 minutes until soft. Spread the warm tomatoes and onions over the dough, leaving a 3 cm ($1^1/4$ in) border around the edge. Sprinkle with the oregano and season generously with salt and pepper. Bake in the oven for 10 to 20 minutes, depending on the thickness of the dough, and serve hot or cold.

La Focaccia
Plain Pizza
with no
Topping

Focaccia can be as thick or as thin as you want it to be.
Usually, thick focaccia is split open and
filled with cooked vegetables or cheese,
ham or salami to make a very tasty sandwich.

SERVES 6

1 quantity Pasta per Pizza (page 141)
plain white flour for knocking back
5 tablespoons olive oil
salt

Pre-heat the oven to gas mark 7, 220°C (425°F). When the dough is well risen, remove it from the bowl and dust it lightly with flour. Knead it again to knock it back then knead in 4 tablespoons of oil. Using your fingers, flatten out the dough on to an oiled 23 cm (9 in) baking tray. Coat with a little more oil and sprinkle generously with salt. Bake in the centre of the oven for about 10 minutes until cooked through and crisp on top without being too brown. Serve hot or cold.

Pizzette
Mini Pizzas

When I was a child, these little pizzas always
used to be served at parties.
They were far more part of the scene than jelly and ice-cream.
Literally hundreds of these tiny pizzas would be
gleefully consumed by noisy kids in the
course of those happy afternoons!

MAKES 18

1 quantity Pasta per Pizza (page 141)
plain white flour for knocking back
4 tablespoons olive oil
2 kg (4 lb 6 oz) fresh ripe tomatoes, skinned,
de-seeded and coarsely chopped
1 teaspoon dried oregano
salt
freshly ground black pepper
olive oil for deep-frying

When the dough is well risen, remove it from the bowl and dust it lightly with flour. Knead it again to knock it back and divide it into 18 small pieces. Flatten each one between your palms to make small pizza shapes. Heat the oil in a saucepan for 5 minutes then add the tomatoes and cook for about 10 minutes, stirring frequently. Add the oregano and season to taste with salt and pepper. Set aside to cool.

Heat the oil until a small cube of bread dropped into it sizzles instantly. Fry the pizzas a few at a time for about 3 minutes. As soon as one side is brown you must turn the pizza over so that the other side cooks. Then scoop them out to drain on kitchen paper. When they are all ready, put a spoonful of tomato sauce on top of each one and serve at once.

Calzone
Stuffed Pizza
Envelope

This is another pizza with the filling inside,
although in this case it is stuffed with
salami and Mozzarella.
As with all the recipes requiring salami,
do make sure you use a good quality Italian salami.

SERVES 6

1 quantity Pasta per Pizza (page 141)
plain white flour for knocking back
4 tablespoons olive oil
200 g (7 oz) Mozzarella cheese, cubed
100 g (4 oz) salami, cut into strips
salt
freshly ground black pepper
1 quantity Basic Tomato Sauce (page 13)

Pre-heat the oven to gas mark 7, 220°C (425°F). When the dough is well risen, remove it from the bowl and dust it lightly with flour. Knead it again to knock it back then knead in 2 tablespoons of oil and flatten out the dough into a disc on an oiled 35 cm (14 in) baking tray. Place the Mozzarella and salami on one half of the dough, season generously with salt and pepper and sprinkle with half the remaining oil. Fold the dough in half and pinch the edges together tightly to seal the filling. Brush with the remaining oil. Bake in the oven for about 20 minutes until cooked through and crisp.

Meanwhile, bring the tomato sauce to the boil. Remove the calzone from the oven and place it on a warmed oval serving platter. Pour a little of the tomato sauce over and around the calzone and serve at once with the rest of the sauce offered separately.

Polenta con Salsicce
Polenta with Sausages

*Best made with traditional polenta flour,
you can use the quick-cook variety for this
dish if you're in a real hurry.
It is one of the most effective winter warmer dishes of them all.*

SERVES 6

3 tablespoons olive oil
2 cloves garlic, peeled
12 Italian sausages
1 onion, peeled and chopped
1 carrot, chopped
1 stick celery, chopped
a handful of fresh parsley, chopped
100 g (4 oz) streaky bacon, chopped
$^1/_2$ tumbler dry white wine
8 tablespoons tomato purée
1.5 litres ($2^1/_2$ pints) water
a pinch of salt
500 g (1 lb 2 oz) polenta
50 g (2 oz) Parmesan cheese, freshly grated

Heat the oil and garlic together over a low heat until the garlic turns dark brown then discard the garlic. Prick the sausages all over with a fork and seal them in the flavoured oil. Remove them from the pan and add the onion, carrot, celery, parsley and bacon and fry for about 5 minutes, stirring occasionally. Return the sausages to the pan, pour over the wine and boil off the alcohol for about 2 minutes. Add the tomato purée and add enough water to make the sauce cover the sausages generously. Bring to the boil, cover and simmer gently for about 30 minutes. Meanwhile, make the polenta. Bring 1.5 litres ($2^1/_2$ pints) of salted water to the boil. Sprinkle in the polenta with one hand so that it falls into the water like fine rain, whisking constantly to prevent lumps. Continue in this way until the mixture begins to thicken then use a wooden spoon to stir constantly for 30 to 50 minutes as the polenta cooks. You will know it is ready when it comes away easily from the sides of the pan. Tip the polenta out on to a board and cover it with a cloth until you are ready to serve. Slice it into generous slices and serve one slice of polenta covered in sauce and 2 sausages for each person. Sprinkle with the Parmesan and serve at once.

Polenta con Gorgonzola
Polenta with Gorgonzola

*This is a very simple but deliciously rich dish,
best made with traditional polenta flour.
You can also make this dish using ripe Fontina cheese.*

SERVES 6

1.5 litres (2¹/₂ pints) water
a pinch of salt
500 g (1 lb 2 oz) polenta flour
100 g (4 oz) unsalted butter
150 g (5 oz) Gorgonzola cheese, thinly sliced

Bring the water to the boil with the salt. Sprinkle in the polenta with one hand so that it falls into the water like fine rain, whisking constantly to prevent lumps. Continue in this way until the mixture begins to thicken then use a wooden spoon to stir constantly for 30 to 50 minutes as the polenta cooks. You will know it is ready when it comes away easily from the sides of the pan. Tip it out on to a board and leave it to cool slightly. Pre-heat the oven to gas mark 6, 200°C (400°F). Cut the polenta into thick slices and make sandwiches with the polenta, butter and Gorgonzola. Place them side by side on a baking sheet and bake for about 8 minutes or until the polenta is heated through and the cheese and butter are melting. Serve at once.

Meat

THE ITALIANS have always respected the nutritive values of meat most highly. I remember very clearly the image of a famous downtown butcher's shop which I would pass twice a day on the school bus. Careering round the cobbled street corner, I would read the big red and white sign outside the doorway which said, *Mangia una bistecca e diventerai un leone!*, 'Eat a steak and you'll become a lion!' At home, whenever we had a nose bleed or a particularly nasty childhood accident which had caused a loss of blood, we would be given steak for dinner almost automatically!

Traditionally, meat has been eaten much more in the north, where it has always been plentiful, than in the south. The arid, drought-ridden south has successfully bred a few pigs, some goats, mules and horses. All these have been eaten in relatively small quantities south of Rome. The household pig has been especially prized thanks to its curing and preserving potential, and preserved meats have kept many hungry families fed through the lean winter months. North of Rome, in Umbria, there is a well-established tradition of skilful breeding and butchering of pigs. Further north again, in Lombardy, the sweet green pasture lands and fertile paddy fields have always yielded fantastic dairy produce, beef and veal. More recently, the ability to afford good meat (roughly translating as beef or veal) has taken on the guise of a major status symbol. It amuses me to see that the rich Milanese industrialists and Piedmontese bankers who can genuinely afford to eat beef twice a day are now so cholesterol-conscious that they are happier as vegetarians!

Whatever one's feelings are about the controversy surrounding the rearing of veal, in no other cuisine anywhere in the world is one meat considered to be of such prime importance. Italians love the fact that it is light and fresh tasting, with all the nourishment and protein value of beef but without the saturated fat content. Also, being a relatively bland flavoured meat, the permutations for its recipes are quite literally endless. Everything from Saltimbocca, meatballs, escalopes, ossobuco, roasts and stews, without even beginning to consider the offal. All this variety makes veal Italy's favourite meat.

When I was a child, pork was never eaten during the summer months *'perché fa venire i vermi'*, 'because it will give you worms'. I have since researched this rather weird idea and have reached the conclusion that it was something to do with hook worm and not being able to keep pork fresh in the summer, therefore it was destined to be used in the winter either cured or fresh or a bit of each. Nowadays, pork is very much more acceptable and is eaten all year round. However, in Italy it is still generally much more prized for its sausages, prosciutto and other cured meats than for fresh meat.

Beef is called *manzo* in Italian, but because of the varying degrees of veal turning to beef, buying a simple steak can present a real problem. The butcher will offer you: *vitella*, female calf; *vitella da latte*, female calf which was still suckling; *vitello*, male calf; *vitello da latte*, male calf which was still suckling; *vitellone*, an older calf; and finally *manzo*. You must not expect Italian beef to be like Scotch beef. For a start they butcher the carcass differently, but the general difference is cultural rather than anything else. If you look at a supermarket joint in Italy called *rosbif*, you can be sure it will not look as you might expect a British roasting joint to appear. But it will taste good!

Lamb is still something of a rarity in Italy except where it has been traditional to eat it because it was one of the few meats available. Especially around Easter, however, lamb does become more readily available. You'll probably be offered *abbacchio* and *agnello*. The former is an older animal up to a year old generally, and the latter is a very young baby lamb. Mutton is considered to be poisonous by certain people and is generally not eaten at all. The main concern about cooking mutton appears to be something to do with the smell it gives off, which needs to be carefully masked with herbs and spices. The smell, more than the far more relevant factors of appearance and flavour, seems to mean that this type of meat is fit only for the very poorest and sorriest of peasant households. Goat meat and horse meat on the other hand have none of these connotations. If anything, they are considered something of a delicacy. The goat has to be extremely young and is called *capretto*. As for horse meat, it is much prized as a iron-rich, sweet-tasting meat which is very good for expectant and nursing mothers, and small children.

BUYING MEAT

As always, with any kind of meat and whatever country you are in, the basic rules of freshness are always the same. The meat should have a pleasant smell; good even colouring; not too much blood (meat which has been insufficiently hung will drizzle blood all over the kitchen); not too much fat; and reasonable tenderness. It is very hard to tell if a piece of meat is going to be tender until it has been cooked, and I must say that Italian meat is generally a lot less tender than I would like it to be. However, you're always safe with veal escalopes and long-cook dishes like casseroles and stews. And there is absolutely nothing to beat a huge Val di Chiana beef T-bone steak cooked on a wood fire!

CUTS OF VEAL AND BEEF

These illustrations should help you when buying meat in Italy or if you want to explain a particular cut to your own butcher. I have found that most butchers will take the trouble to provide you with what you require as long as you give them plenty of notice!

VEAL

1 Small steaks, escalopes, paillards (excellent).

1 (Internal section). Escalopes, paillards, medallions, steaks (superb).

2 Noisettes, loin chops.

3 Saddle of veal, chops.

4 Cheap roasting joint, boiling (good), stewing (good).

5 Boiling (average), stewing (good).

6 Slow roasting joint (passable).

7 Roasting joint (excellent).

8 Escalopes, olives (excellent).

9 Boiling, stewing.

10 Stewing.

11 Stewing.

12 Rolling and stuffing, boiling, stewing (good).

13 Boiling, stuffed 'pocket', rolling and roasting, blanquettes.

13a Cheap roasting joint, boiling, stewing (fair).

14 Ossobuco (excellent!).

15 Cheap roasting joint, stuffed 'pocket' (Cima alla Genovese).

16 Roasting (stuffed only).

17 Roasting (stuffed only).

18 Stewing (good), base for stock.

19 Neck.

20 Head.

BEEF

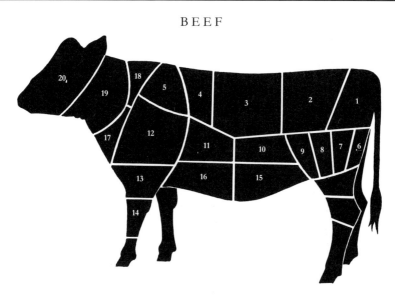

1 Rump steak, braising beef (top quality), paillards.

1 (Internal section). Braising steak (superb), steaks (mediocre).

2 Steaks.

2 (Internal section). Fillets: filets mignon, tournedos, Châteaubriands, steak tartare.

3 Roasting, entrecôtes (excellent).

5 Stock-making, boiling (mediocre).

6 Steaks (mediocre), stewing, braising (excellent).

7 Braising, minute steaks, beef olives, steak.

8 Braising, minute steaks, steaks.

9 Boiling, braising (excellent).

10 Long, slow pot roasting, consommé.

11 Meat sauce for pasta (good), stock or consommé.

12 Boiling, consommé base.

13 Stewing, ragout.

13a Stewing, casseroles.

14 Pot roasting, casseroles, ragout sauces (excellent).

15 Boiling, consommé base.

16 Boiling (excellent).

17 Boiling, bollito (excellent).

18 Stews, casseroles, broths (excellent), stocks (excellent).

19 Neck.

20 Head.

Bistecca alla Cacciatora
Beef Steak
with Marsala and
Caraway Seed Sauce

*An unusual recipe for preparing steaks,
this is very simple and quick to make.
It makes a much more interesting dish than
an ordinary grilled steak.*

SERVES 6

6 x 150 g (5 oz) fillet, sirloin or
rump steaks
2 tablespoons olive oil
salt
freshly ground black pepper
$1/2$ tumbler marsala
$1/2$ tumbler dry red wine
$1/2$ clove garlic, peeled and crushed
a large pinch of caraway seeds
3 tablespoons tomato purée
2 tablespoons chopped fresh parsley

Trim the steaks carefully. Heat the oil in a frying pan large enough to take all 6 steaks, or use 2 or 3 smaller pans. Seal the steaks in the hot oil on both sides for about 4 minutes. Season to taste with salt and pepper. Take them out of the pan and keep them warm between 2 hot plates. Pour the marsala and wine into the pan, stir in the garlic and caraway seeds and boil off the alcohol for about 2 minutes. Stir in the tomato purée.

Arrange the steaks on a warmed serving platter, pour over the sauce and sprinkle with parsley just before serving.

Bistecche di Manzo alla Pizzaiola
Sirloin Steak in a Tomato and Garlic Sauce

A real classic from Naples,
this is very quick and easy to do.
You can use chicken or turkey breasts or
even veal for this recipe if you wish.

SERVES 6

6 x 150 g (5 oz) sirloin steaks
3 tablespoons olive oil
3 cloves garlic, peeled and lightly crushed
1 kg (2 lb) canned tomatoes, drained,
de-seeded and coarsely chopped
salt
freshly ground black pepper
1 teaspoon dried oregano

Trim the steaks and flatten them slightly with a meat mallet. They should be about 1 cm (1/4 in) thick all over. Heat the oil in a wide frying pan and fry the steaks briefly on both sides so that they are browned and sealed. Take them out of the pan and keep them warm between 2 hot plates. Add the garlic to the hot oil and fry until golden. Add the tomatoes and season generously with salt and pepper.

Bring to the boil and let the tomatoes bubble quite fiercely for about 4 minutes. Stir in the oregano and return the steaks to the tomato sauce. Heat through for about 4 minutes then serve at once.

Bollito con Patate
Boiled Beef
with Potatoes

In this dish, the beef is first boiled and then cubed and added to potatoes and other ingredients to make a kind of casserole. It makes a lovely cheap and cheerful family supper dish served with coarse grained mustard.

SERVES 6

1.5 litres (2^1/$_2$ pints) water
salt
750 g (1 lb 10 oz) boiling beef
2 onions, peeled
1 clove
2 large carrots
2 sticks celery
2 small tomatoes
3 tablespoons olive oil
2 heaped tablespoons tomato purée
freshly ground black pepper
1 kg (2 lb) potatoes, peeled and quartered

Bring the water and salt to the boil in a large saucepan. Slide the meat into the water to seal the meat immediately, preventing water from seeping into it while cooking and thus losing flavour. As soon as the water comes back to the boil, lower the heat to a minimum and add 1 onion studded with the clove, 1 carrot, 1 stick of celery and the tomatoes. Cover and simmer for about 1^1/$_2$ hours or until a fork pushed into the meat slides in easily. When the meat is cooked, remove it from the liquid and place it in a bowl. Strain the cooking liquid and discard the vegetables. Just cover the meat with the cooking liquid and leave it to cool.

Cube the meat into walnut-sized chunks and slice the remaining onion, carrot and celery very thinly. Place them in a flameproof casserole with the oil and fry gently for about 5 minutes until soft and golden. Stir in the tomato purée. Re-heat the cooking liquid. Add the potatoes to the other vegetables and add enough of the cooking liquid to cover them generously. Season to taste with salt and pepper, cover and simmer for about 20 minutes until the potatoes are very tender. Stir in the cubed meat and heat through for about 10 minutes. Arrange on a warmed serving platter and serve at once.

Saltimbocca

SEE PAGE 165

Coscetto d'Abbacchio Farcito

SEE PAGE 168

Maiale Uso Caccia

SEE PAGE 172

Pollo alla Salvia

SEE PAGE 177

Braciato alla Lucchese
Braised Beef
with Peas
and Artichokes

A wonderfully tasty braised beef dish
with artichokes and peas,
tradition dictates that this is served with ciabatta bread.

SERVES 6

4 globe artichokes
$^1/_2$ lemon
4 tablespoons olive oil
4 small onions, peeled and finely chopped
$^1/_2$ clove garlic, peeled and finely chopped
6 parsley stalks, finely chopped
300 g (11 oz) lean stewing beef, cubed
300 g (11 oz) shelled fresh peas or frozen petits pois
salt
freshly ground black pepper
$^1/_2$ teaspoon sugar
8 tablespoons beef stock
2 tablespoons butter
6 slices ciabatta bread, cubed

To prepare the artichokes, remove the exterior leaves down to the tender heart and trim the stalk. Prise open the leaves and scoop out the hairy choke with a teaspoon. Cut each artichoke into 8 and put the pieces into a bowl of water into which the lemon has been squeezed and is left floating. Heat the oil and fry the onions, garlic and parsley stalks for about 5 minutes. Add the beef and brown the meat all over. Remove the artichokes from the water and add them to the pan with the peas. Season to taste with salt and pepper, sprinkle with sugar, pour over the stock and stir thoroughly. Bring to the boil, cover and simmer for about $1^1/_2$ hours until the meat is completely tender. Remove the pan from the heat. Melt the butter in a frying pan and fry the cubed bread for a few minutes until crisp. Arrange the beef on a warmed serving platter, scatter the hot fried bread around the edges of the dish and serve at once.

Manzo in Involtini
Stuffed
Beef Olives

*A great classic, this lovely simple dish is full of
flavour and has lots of texture.
The lining of prosciutto crudo inside the beef is
especially important for the flavour of the dish.*

SERVES 6

1 kg (2 lb) minute steak, thinly sliced
100 g (4 oz) prosciutto crudo, thinly sliced
1 large stick celery, sliced into matchsticks
1 onion, peeled and chopped
1 clove garlic, peeled and finely chopped
1 carrot, chopped
2 tablespoons chopped fresh parsley
3 tablespoons olive oil
1 large wine glass dry red or white wine
4 tablespoons tomato purée

Trim and flatten the meat. Cut it into about 12 neat squares and discard the trimmings which can be used for another recipe. Cut the prosciutto to similar-sized squares and lay the prosciutto on the beef. Lay a stick of celery on each square and roll them up. Close them with wooden cocktail sticks. Fry the remaining celery with the onion, garlic, carrot, parsley and oil for about 5 minutes. Add the beef slices and seal them all over. Pour over the wine and boil off the alcohol for about 2 minutes. Add the tomato purée and just enough water to cover the meat completely. Cover tightly and simmer very gently for 2 hours.

Arrange the meat on a warmed serving platter on a bed of mashed potatoes and pour over the juices from the pan. Serve at once.

Arrosto di Vitello
Roast Veal

Although many people prefer not to eat veal for ethical reasons, there is no doubt how delicious and tender a carefully prepared roast joint of veal can be. The vegetables cooked with the meat add flavour and make a delicious gravy to finish off the dish.

SERVES 6

750 g (1 lb 10 oz) joint of veal suitable for roasting
1 large onion, peeled and thickly sliced
1 large carrot, thickly sliced
1 large stick celery, cut into chunks
a handful of fresh parsley, chopped
1 small wine glass olive oil
salt
freshly ground black pepper
50 g (2 oz) unsalted butter
1 large tumbler beef or chicken stock
2 teaspoons cornflour
2 tablespoons marsala

Pre-heat the oven to gas mark 4, 180°C (350°F). Tie the meat securely with cook's string. Place all the vegetables in an oval flameproof dish which fits the meat tightly. Pour the oil over the vegetables and season to taste with salt and pepper. Lay the meat on top. Coat a sheet of baking parchment with the butter and cover the meat loosely with the parchment, leaving a gap at one end. Cover with a lid, leaving an opening on one side. Place the dish over a medium heat until the vegetables begin to sizzle. Transfer the dish to the oven and bake for about 2 hours, turning the meat frequently. Pierce the meat with a long skewer and if you meet no resistance as you push through, you will know it is ready.

Remove the meat from the dish and keep it warm between 2 large hot plates. Skim the fat off the vegetables and cooking juices. Add the stock to the dish and place over a medium heat. Simmer gently, scraping the bottom of the dish as much as possible and stirring together thoroughly for about 2 minutes. Remove from the heat and rub through a sieve into a small saucepan, squeezing hard to extract as much flavour as possible. Mix the cornflour and marsala and stir it into the saucepan. Bring to the boil over a low heat and simmer for a few minutes, stirring constantly, until thick and creamy. Slice the meat thinly and arrange it on a warmed long oval platter. Pour the sauce over the meat and serve at once.

Scaloppine al Marsala
Marsala Escalopes

*A deliciously rich-tasting dish which is actually
simplicity itself to prepare.
You can use sherry or white wine instead of
the marsala to ring the changes every once in a while.
This dish is also very good with thin strips of
pork loin or with turkey escalopes.*

SERVES 6

600 g (1 lb 5 oz) veal or turkey escalopes
salt
freshly ground black pepper
2 tablespoons fine plain white flour
100 g (4 oz) unsalted butter
$^1/_2$ tumbler marsala

Trim and flatten the meat as much as possible without tearing it. Sprinkle it with salt and pepper and dust it very lightly with flour. Do not dust with flour until you are ready to cook the meat as it will become sticky if left to stand for more than about 5 minutes. Melt the butter in a wide frying pan and cook the escalopes for about 2 minutes on each side. Remove them from the pan and keep them warm between 2 hot plates.

Pour the marsala into the pan and simmer for about 2 minutes, stirring and scraping with a spoon to make a smooth sauce. Arrange the meat on a warmed serving platter, pour over the sauce and serve at once.

Saltimbocca
Escalope
with Mozzarella
and Ham

*All my family really love this dish,
whether I make it with veal or chicken.
I have also used flattened strips of
pork loin which taste very good.*

SERVES 6

600 g (1 lb 5 oz) veal or turkey escalopes
a handful of fresh sage leaves
50 g (2 oz) prosciutto crudo, sliced
50 g (2 oz) unsalted butter
salt
freshly ground black pepper
75 g (3 oz) Mozzarella cheese, thinly sliced

Trim and flatten the meat as much as possible without tearing it. Place a sage leaf on top of each escalope. Cut the ham and lay the slices on top of the sage leaves. Use wooden cocktail sticks to keep the sage and ham in place. Melt the butter in a wide frying pan and fry the meat for about 1½ minutes on each side. Season to taste with salt and pepper then cover each escalope with a slice of Mozzarella. Cover the pan and raise the heat to maximum for about 1 minute to allow the Mozzarella to start melting. Arrange on a warmed serving platter and serve at once.

Ossobuco
Ossobuco

Ossobuco consists of sections of beef shin cut into chunks about 6 cm (2¹/₂ in) thick with the central marrow bone circle left in the middle. Ask your butcher to prepare the meat for you and calculate one ossobuco per person.

SERVES 6

150 g (5 oz) unsalted butter
6 ossobuco chunks, total weight about 1 kg (2 lb)
3 tablespoons plain white flour
salt
freshly ground black pepper
1 wine glass dry white wine
2 teaspoons grated lemon rind
2 tablespoons chopped fresh parsley
2 cloves garlic, peeled and finely chopped
1 teaspoon anchovy paste
2 tablespoons tomato purée

Butter a deep frying pan thoroughly with most of the butter. Trim the meat and dust it lightly with flour. Arrange the ossobuco in a single layer in the buttered pan. Place over the heat and brown the meat thoroughly on all sides. Pour over the wine and boil off the alcohol for about 2 minutes. Add just enough water to cover the meat, season to taste with salt and pepper and cover loosely. Simmer gently for about 1 hour.

Remove the meat from the pan and keep it warm between 2 hot plates. Add the lemon rind, parsley, garlic, anchovy paste and tomato purée to the juices in the pan and simmer gently for a few minutes, stirring frequently to make sure the sauce is well amalgamated. Add a little water if it appears to be too thick. Return the meat to the sauce and heat through gently for about 10 minutes. Serve at once.

Abbacchio alla Campagnola
Country-style Roast Lamb

*The strong flavours of anchovies,
garlic and caraway seeds make this a very special
way of roasting lamb – delicious and very rustic.*

SERVES 6

1.25 kg (3 lb) leg of lamb, boned
50 g (2 oz) unsalted butter
2 tablespoons olive oil
3 salted anchovies, boned, rinsed and dried
2 cloves garlic, peeled
1 tablespoon caraway seeds
2–3 tablespoons red wine vinegar
1 tablespoon plain white flour
1–2 ladles of water or meat stock

Cut the lamb into large chunks about the size of a small child's fist. Wash it carefully and pat it dry. Heat the butter and oil in a large saucepan, add the meat and brown it thoroughly all over. Pound the anchovies to a purée with the garlic, caraway seeds and wine vinegar. Drain most of the fat off the browned meat, pour over the anchovy sauce and stir the meat to flavour it thoroughly. Sprinkle with the flour then add 1 ladleful of water or stock. Stir again, cover and simmer gently for about 40 minutes, adding more liquid if necessary. Transfer to a warmed serving platter and serve at once.

Coscetto d'Abbacchio Farcito
Stuffed Leg of Lamb

This recipe makes a really filling and
rich dish for a Sunday roast.
The sausages in the stuffing add a spicy note to the whole dish.

SERVES 6

100 g (4 oz) pearl barley, rinsed
1 tablespoon unsalted butter
6 tablespoons sunflower oil
1 large onion, peeled and thinly sliced
100 g (4 oz) calves' liver, trimmed and cubed
4 Italian sausages, skinned and crumbled
1 x 1 kg (2 lb) leg of lamb, boned
8 tablespoons water
6 fresh sage leaves
salt
freshly ground black pepper

Place the pearl barley in a saucepan with enough water to cover it completely. Bring to the boil and simmer gently for about 1 hour and 10 minutes. Then drain it and stir in the butter. Set it aside. Pre-heat the oven to gas mark 4, 180°C (350°F).

Fry the onion gently in half the oil for about 5 minutes until soft and golden. Drain off as much of the oil as possible into another pan and quickly fry the liver and sausages until sealed. Mix together the pearl barley, onions, sausages and liver and use this mixture to stuff the leg of lamb. Sew up the opening with cook's string. Place the lamb in a roasting tin and pour over the remaining oil. Pour the water around the meat and sprinkle with the sage leaves, salt and pepper. Roast in the oven for about 1¹/₄ hours until cooked through, basting occasionally. Transfer to a warmed serving platter and serve at once.

Costolette d'Agnello alla Bolognese
Lamb Cutlets with Prosciutto and Mozzarella

In this recipe the lamb cutlets are coated in breadcrumbs
and fried until golden and crisp on the outside.
To finish them off they are covered with the ham and
cheese and briefly passed into the oven to melt the cheese.
The result is quite rich and absolutely delicious.

SERVES 6

12 lamb cutlets
3 tablespoons plain white flour
2 eggs, beaten
5 tablespoons dry white breadcrumbs
6 tablespoons olive oil
salt
freshly ground black pepper
100 g (4 oz) prosciutto crudo or
cooked ham, thinly sliced
150 g (5 oz) Mozzarella cheese, cut into 12 slices

Pre-heat the oven to gas mark 7, 220°C (425°F). Trim the cutlets carefully and flatten them as much as possible with a meat mallet. Dip them lightly in the flour, then dip them in egg and finally in the breadcrumbs. Heat the oil until sizzling and fry the lamb cutlets for about 3 minutes on each side until golden brown and crisp. Remove from the pan, drain on kitchen paper and season to taste with salt and pepper. Arrange the cutlets on a baking tray, lay a slice of ham and a slice of Mozzarella on each cutlet and bake in the oven for about 5 minutes or until the cheese begins to melt. Transfer to a warmed serving platter and serve at once.

Costolette d'Agnello Panate
Deep-fried Lamb Cutlets

Because the little lamb cutlets are coated in
breadcrumbs and fried for such a short time,
the inside stays delightfully pink while
the outside goes crisp and brown.
Lovely to eat with your fingers — hot or cold —
the lemon juice cuts through the slight greasiness.

SERVES 6

12 lamb cutlets
2 eggs, beaten
salt
5 tablespoons dried white breadcrumbs
olive oil for deep-frying
2 lemons, cut into wedges

Trim the cutlets carefully and flatten them as much as possible with a meat mallet. Place the eggs in a bowl and submerge the cutlets completely in the eggs. Add a little salt to the breadcrumbs and drain each cutlet a little from the egg before coating in breadcrumbs. Heat enough oil in a large frying pan to cover the cutlets completely.

When the oil is sizzling hot, add the cutlets and fry them carefully on both sides for about 3 minutes until crisp and golden brown. Remove from the pan and drain on kitchen paper. Arrange them on a warmed serving platter and serve garnished with the lemon wedges.

Maiale
Arrosto
Roast Pork

A traditional recipe for preparing a roast joint of pork,
the addition of garlic, rosemary and
pepper gives lots of flavour.
It is important, however, to start off with
a really good, tasty and tender joint of meat.

SERVES 6

1 kg (2 lb) pork loin, boned and rolled
3 cloves garlic, peeled and cut into slivers
5 sprigs fresh rosemary
salt
freshly ground black pepper
2 tablespoons lard
1 wine glass dry white wine

Pre-heat the oven to gas mark 5, 190°C (375°F). Pierce the meat all over with a sharp knife. Insert slivers of garlic and small pieces of rosemary into all the holes. Sprinkle with salt and pepper and spread with the lard. Place the meat in a roasting tin and roast in the oven for about 1¹/4 hours until cooked through, basting with the wine during cooking. Serve either hot or cold.

Maiale Uso Caccia
Pot-roasted Pork

In this recipe, the pork is treated like game and is cooked with various flavourings to make a moist and tasty pot roast.

SERVES 6

750 g (1 lb 10 oz) lean pork loin
75 g (3 oz) prosciutto crudo, thinly sliced
5 fresh sage leaves
1 finger-length strip of lemon rind
$^1/_2$ onion, peeled
3 cloves
6 peppercorns
1 stick celery
$^1/_2$ tumbler water
$^1/_2$ tumbler red wine vinegar
$^1/_2$ tumbler olive oil
salt
1 salted anchovy, boned, rinsed and drained
3 sprigs fresh parsley, chopped

Trim the loin and tie it securely with cook's string. Select a flameproof dish which is large enough to fit the meat tightly. It must be deep and have a tight-fitting lid. Line the dish with prosciutto and sage leaves. Put the lemon rind, onion, cloves, peppercorns and celery into the dish and lay the meat on top. Mix the water, wine vinegar and oil together and pour this over the meat. Cover with foil then with the lid. Place over a low heat and simmer gently for 2 hours without removing the lid.

Remove the meat from the dish and slice it thinly. Strain the contents of the dish and push the mixture through a food mill or sieve. Return it to the dish. Mash the anchovy and add this to the dish with the parsley. Mix it all together thoroughly and dilute with about 6 tablespoons of the cooking stock. Bring to a gentle simmer, return the meat to the dish and heat through for about 15 minutes. Transfer to a warmed serving platter and serve at once.

Poultry and Game

CHICKEN, which used to be regarded as such a rich man's delicacy, has long since become an everyday food for many people. I think this is as true in Italy as it is beyond her boundaries. Yet the humble chicken, with its reputation for eminent stupidity and its role of scapegoat in many different cultures, offers us meat which is low in fat, high in flavour and extremely adaptable and easy to cook in a thousand and one different ways. From the most basic roast chicken, boiled chicken, braised chicken or chicken cacciatora, chicken is at the root of Italian cooking.

There has been much discussion about free-range chickens. To me, as a person who keeps both chickens and guinea fowl, a free-range chicken is a free animal. A chicken likes to scratch around in the ground, peck and cluck and move around at leisure. A chicken doesn't seem to ask for much in life! As a little girl growing up in Tuscany, I remember that both chickens and rabbits were reared for the table. By the time I was seven, I could slaughter and prepare both animals without turning a hair. There is no question in my mind that an animal that is allowed to live freely will result in a meat with far better flavour and texture. Battery chickens cannot possibly be expected to taste the same... after all, you are what you eat, even if you are only a chicken.

But the question of free-range has been incredibly over-complicated. When is a chicken really free-range and when is it not? I don't want to get into the issue in any great depth, but I do know that a happy chicken means a tastier chicken to eat. Frozen supermarket chickens can be used, but only in an emergency as there is little about them worth recommending – although even I have to buy one occasionally!

I think it is worth developing a relationship with a butcher whose poultry you trust as tasting terrific and being good value for money. He may also be able to tell you just how free-range his chickens are!

Chicken, or any other poultry for that matter, used to be served after the antipasto and the pasta course as the main course. Nowadays, with smaller appetites and simply less time to eat such big meals, the main course will often constitute the entire meal. Italians are very keen on boiled chicken, which makes a very low-calorie and healthy meal, and the broth can, of course, be used to make excellent soups or risotto.

It is now possible to enjoy all kinds of very high-quality poultry which can be cooked in lots of interesting ways. In Ancient Rome and right through to the 1500s, stork and peacock would be eaten and enjoyed alongside the more common and usual members of the poultry family. Although these are no longer on our tables, capon, duck, goose and pigeon have retained their position in the huge repertoire of recipes. The introduction of turkey which came to Europe from the New World and found its way on to our tables via the French Jesuit monks, also has an important place in the variety of recipes available.

In this chapter, I have given you just a few of the recipes which cover this huge section of Italian cuisine. They are largely personal favourites, recipes which show off the delicious qualities of poultry to its best advantage. I can only say that to eat a fresh, honestly free-range bird is an experience well worth striving for. I enjoy keeping my chickens enormously. Apart from anything else, they will eat all the cooking scraps and are therefore a marvellously easy way of recycling some of my household waste!

GAME

In Italian, game divides into two very distinct categories: *cacciagione* and *selvaggina*. *Cacciagione* means game with feathers: pheasant, partridge and so on. *Selvaggina* means game which has a furry coat: hare, rabbit, deer and so on.

There was a time in Italian culinary history when the meat of these animals was doubtless considered to be the most valuable and the best to cook. All kinds of amazing recipes have been created through the centuries in order to make the most of these strong, pungent flavours. There is little left of all that now. The open spaces where all game was widely available for hunting are now greatly restricted, nature's seemingly inexhaustible bounty is almost completely diminished and restrictions have been introduced on many different aspects of hunting. Modern tastes, too, lean further towards the easier, blander flavours of veal, chicken or lean pork. Italians are a lot less bloodthirsty than they used to be, and they no longer need to hunt in order to feed their families; they go to the supermarket just like everybody else.

To my mind, in this way one runs the risk of losing a huge range of recipes created out of the game which used to be available. Hunting is now reduced to a seasonal activity and is largely confined to shooting pheasants which have lived out their lives in so-called freedom. Yet hunting used to be a major part of Italian culture and it has left its mark in the hundreds of exciting recipes which still exist but which are very rarely cooked. One could fill an entire book with Italian game recipes, such is the extent of the range. Instead I have chosen to give you a selection of the best, the most exciting and the ones which really deserve not just to be remembered, but to be cooked.

I can remember my mother describing going wild boar hunting with her uncles. Having wounded the animal enough to prevent it from going too far, they would crouch perfectly still in the undergrowth, waiting for the boar to charge. As it broke cover, the final, fatal shot would be quickly fired. And if you have ever eaten wild boar, stewed slowly with fennel seeds, red wine and tomato and served with creamy polenta, you will know why I wish so fervently that game could be more widely appreciated.

Some of the tamer varieties of game such as partridge, quail or pheasant are available at larger supermarkets, otherwise you will have to look for it in specialised butchers where the bounty will be clearly displayed outside the shop. Do bear in mind that game is very seasonal and will only be available during the autumn and early winter months. It is also worth bearing in mind, in these health-conscious times, that venison meat is extremely low in cholesterol with very little fat but packed with flavour.

Pollo
alla Cacciatora
Braised Chicken
with Olives

I love the strong flavours of this dish,
which is really simple to make and tastes excellent with
a fresh green salad and some roast potatoes.

SERVES 6

3 tablespoons olive oil
3 cloves garlic, peeled and lightly crushed
1 kg (2 lb) chicken joints
$1/2$ tumbler dry white wine
2 tablespoons white wine vinegar
20 black olives, stoned
20 black olives, stoned and chopped
1 tablespoon anchovy paste
salt
freshly ground black pepper

Heat the oil and garlic in a shallow saucepan until the garlic is golden brown. Add the chicken joints and brown them all over. Add the wine and wine vinegar and boil off the alcohol for about 2 minutes. Stir in the whole and chopped olives then stir in the anchovy paste and season to taste with salt and pepper. Cover and simmer for about 25 minutes until the chicken is cooked through, stirring and adding a little water from time to time to prevent the chicken from drying out or sticking. Transfer to a warmed serving platter and serve at once.

Oca in Salmi

SEE PAGE 183

(Overleaf) Piccioni di Montecarlo

SEE PAGE 185

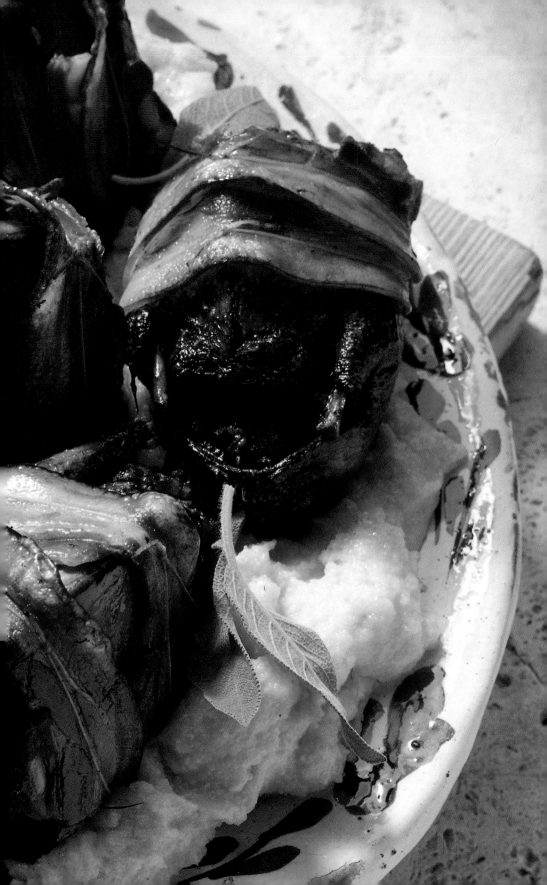

Faraona in Salmi

SEE PAGE 187

Pollo
alla Salvia
Pan-roasted Chicken
with Sage

A marvellously simple chicken dish,
this tastes absolutely wonderful.
It is very good served with carrots and mashed potatoes.

SERVES 6

1 heaped tablespoon unsalted butter
2 tablespoons olive oil
6 large chicken joints, trimmed
1 large wine glass dry white wine
50 g (2 oz) prosciutto crudo, cut into slivers
1 sprig fresh sage, roughly chopped
salt
freshly ground black pepper

Heat the butter and oil in a large frying pan and fry the chicken joints gently until dark golden all over. Drain off as much of the fat as possible, pour over the wine and boil off the alcohol for about 2 minutes. Sprinkle on the prosciutto and sage and season generously with salt and pepper. Mix everything together thoroughly, cover and simmer gently for about 45 minutes, basting occasionally with a little water if the chicken appears to be drying out too much. Serve at once.

Pollo alla Panna
Chicken with Cream

*Another simple and versatile recipe for chicken joints,
this is especially delicious with
glazed baby onions and some steamed spinach.*

SERVES 6

50 g (2 oz) unsalted butter
6 large chicken joints, trimmed
salt
1 large tumbler warm milk
4 tablespoons double cream

Pre-heat the oven to gas mark 4, 180°C (350°F). Melt the butter in a flameproof dish and fry the chicken joints until golden brown all over. Season to taste with salt then pour over the milk. Cover and cook in the oven for about 40 minutes, turning the chicken occasionally. Take the dish out of the oven, transfer the chicken joints to a warmed serving dish and keep them warm. Remove as much fat as possible from the sauce, return to the heat and pour in the cream. Stir over a low heat until just thickened without boiling, pour over the chicken and serve at once.

Filetti di Tacchino ai Funghi
Turkey Fillets with Mushrooms

*This is a slightly more intricate dish to prepare,
so I like to reserve it for occasions that are a
bit more special than just an everyday family supper.
If you want to make it even more special,
use a varied selection of different kinds of mushrooms.*

SERVES 6

6 large turkey fillets, flattened and trimmed
salt
1 egg, beaten
100 g (4 oz) dried breadcrumbs
75 g (3 oz) unsalted butter
1 small tumbler marsala
1 teaspoon cornflour
300 g (11 oz) button mushrooms
2 teaspoons lemon juice

Sprinkle the turkey fillets with salt and lay them in the beaten egg for about 5 minutes, making sure they are well covered. Lift them out of the egg and coat them in breadcrumbs. Melt half the butter in a wide pan, lay in the turkey and fry gently for about 5 minutes on each side. Place the marsala in a small saucepan and stir in the cornflour until smooth. Place over a low heat and continue to stir for a few minutes until you have made a thick smooth sauce. Put the remaining butter in a small saucepan and add the mushrooms. Sprinkle with lemon juice and season to taste with salt. Cook for about 5 minutes until just soft. Arrange the turkey on a warmed serving platter, cover with the marsala sauce and surround with the mushrooms. Serve at once.

Petto di Tacchino alla Napoletana
Turkey Breast with Mozzarella

This is a great favourite with my family.
It is extremely light and easy to
prepare but looks impressive.
As it is also relatively cheap,
it's a good way of feeding larger numbers.

SERVES 6

1 kg (2 lb) rolled turkey breast
1 onion, peeled and quartered
1 carrot
1 stick celery
salt and freshly ground black pepper
200 g (7 oz) Mozzarella cheese, sliced
4 ripe tomatoes, skinned and de-seeded and sliced
50 g (2 oz) unsalted butter
2 tablespoons chopped fresh parsley

Place the turkey breast in a saucepan, cover with water and add the onion, carrot and celery. Season with a little salt and pepper, bring to the boil, cover and simmer gently for about 1 hour until the meat is cooked through. Take the meat out of the saucepan and leave it to cool.

Pre-heat the oven to gas mark 5, 190°C (375°F). Slice the meat and arrange the slices in a flat ovenproof dish. Lay the Mozzarella on top of the meat and lay the tomatoes on top of the cheese. Dot with butter, sprinkle with salt and pepper and bake in the oven for about 20 minutes until the cheese is melting. Serve sprinkled with parsley.

Tacchino Arrosto Ripeno
Stuffed Roast Turkey

*Chestnuts and olives make a wonderful combination in
this stuffing and the unusual flavour works very well
with the delicate flavour of the turkey.
You can use butter instead of the pork fat,
although you will lose some of the intensity of flavour.*

SERVES 6

1 small oven-ready turkey, trimmed
20 chestnuts
20 sweet green olives, stoned
6 Italian sausages, skinned and crumbled
100 g (4 oz) fresh pork fat
salt
freshly ground black pepper

Pre-heat the oven to gas mark 5, 190°C (375°F). Pierce each chestnut with
the point of a sharp knife and lay them on a baking sheet. Bake them in the
oven for about 10 minutes without allowing them to burn. Remove them
from the oven and remove their skins completely. Mix the chestnuts with the
olives and sausage meat. Chop half the pork fat finely and mix this into the
stuffing. Spoon the stuffing into the turkey and sew it closed with cook's
string. Lay a few strips of pork fat on the bottom of a roasting tin and lay
the stuffed bird on top.

  Arrange the rest of the pork fat on top of the turkey. Roast in the oven
for about 25 minutes per 450 g (1 lb) until the turkey is thoroughly cooked,
basting frequently. Transfer to a warmed serving platter and serve at once.

Anatra con Lenticchie
Duck with Lentils

*The combination of game and lentils is a bit unusual, but is one that
works very well. Use the sort of brown continental lentils which do not
need pre-soaking and be sure to skim off the excess fat very thoroughly otherwise
the lentils will become very greasy. Serve the duck with a crisp and
fresh mixed green leafy salad with a lemony dressing.*

SERVES 6

6 duck joints, trimmed
2 bay leaves
2 tablespoons olive oil
50 g (2 oz) ham fat from prosciutto crudo
2 onions, peeled
3 cloves garlic, peeled
2 carrots
2 sticks celery
1/2 wine glass dry red wine
salt
freshly ground black pepper
500 g (1 lb 2 oz) brown lentils
25 g (1 oz) unsalted butter

Place the duck joints in a wide saucepan with the bay leaves, oil and ham fat.
Chop 1 onion, 1 clove of garlic, 1 carrot and 1 stick of celery and add them
to the pan. Fry all this together over a medium heat for about 10 minutes
until the vegetables are soft and the duck is browned all over. Pour over the
wine and season to taste with salt and pepper. Just cover the duck joints with
water, bring to the boil, cover and simmer gently for about 1 hour until the
duck is cooked through, stirring occasionally.

Meanwhile, put the remaining onion, garlic, carrot and celery in a saucepan
with the lentils and just cover with water. Bring to the boil, cover and simmer
gently for about 40 minutes until the lentils are completely soft and they have
absorbed most of the liquid. Remove from the heat, discard the vegetables,
drain off any remaining liquid and stir in the butter. Arrange the lentils on a
warmed serving platter. Place the duck on top of the lentils. Skim off as
much fat as possible from the cooking juices of the duck then spoon a little
over the duck portions and lentils. Serve at once.

Oca in Salmi
Pot-roasted Goose

I really like this recipe because it is completely bone-free when it comes to serving.
I like to serve it with slightly steamed greens or some baby spinach leaves in a salad.

Serves 6

1 oven-ready goose, trimmed
2 tablespoons lard
salt and freshly ground black pepper
4 tablespoons cognac
500 ml (17 fl oz) poultry stock
75 g (3 oz) unsalted butter
1 onion, peeled and finely chopped
1 large carrot, finely chopped
6 parsley stalks, finely chopped
1 bay leaf
a large pinch of peppercorns
1 large wine glass dry white wine
1 tablespoon plain white flour
200 g (7 oz) cooked button mushrooms

Pre-heat the oven to gas mark 5, 190°C (375°F). Rub the goose with the lard and season it generously with salt and pepper. Roast it in the oven for about 30 minutes. Joint the goose carefully and reserve all the extra bones and all the skin. Trim the skinned joints carefully and reserve all the trimmings. Heat the cognac in a flameproof casserole and let it catch light. Flame it briefly for about 1 minute then add a ladleful of stock. Add the goose joints to the casserole, cover with a sheet of buttered baking parchment, cover tightly with a lid and leave to simmer very gently for about 50 minutes.

Meanwhile, melt half the remaining butter and fry the onion, carrot, parsley, bay leaf and peppercorns for about 5 minutes until the vegetables are soft. Pour off the fat, add the wine and boil off the alcohol for 2 minutes. Add the remaining stock, bring to the boil and simmer for about 20 minutes until well reduced. Stir all the reserved bones, skin and trimmings into the pan and heat through. Remove from the heat and sieve carefully, squeezing hard to extract all the flavour. Return the sauce to the pan. Mix half the remain-ing butter with the flour and blend this into the sauce. Remove from the heat and gradually whisk in the remaining butter. Add the mushrooms to the goose, pour over the sauce and heat through without boiling. Transfer to a warmed serving platter and serve at once.

Oca Ripiena
Stuffed Goose

*In the Garfagnana area of Tuscany close to where I grew up,
the goose is always the bird chosen for
celebrations and special occasions.
I must say that is a great deal more flavoursome than some
turkeys which are now available.*

SERVES 6 TO 8

1 x 2 kg (4 lb 6 oz) oven-ready goose
200 g (7 oz) minced pork
200 g (7 oz) minced beef or veal
50 g (2 oz) chicken livers, minced
2 eggs, beaten
salt
freshly ground black pepper
1/2 tumbler good-quality marsala or similar wine
75 g (3 oz) stoned black olives in brine
2–3 tablespoons fresh white breadcrumbs
50 g (2 oz) mushrooms, finely chopped
6 tablespoons vegetable oil
1 wine glass dry red wine

Pre-heat the oven to gas mark 6, 200°C (400°F). Wipe and prepare the goose
for stuffing. Mix together the minced pork, beef or veal, chicken livers and
eggs. Season generously with salt and pepper and stir in the marsala or wine.
Stir in the olives and add enough breadcrumbs to make a solid texture
without allowing the stuffing to become too dry. Mix in the mushrooms then
stuff the goose and sew it closed with cook's string.

Oil the goose all over, place it in an oiled roasting tin and roast in the
oven for about 1¹/₂ hours until cooked through and tender, basting
occasionally with its own fat and with red wine. Serve at once with plenty of
fresh green vegetables and roast potatoes.

Piccioni di Montecarlo
Roasted Pigeons

They say that this recipe dates right back to the eleventh century when the Countess Matilda used to prepare this dish in her house of Vivinaja at Valdinievole.

SERVES 4

4 plump, oven-ready pigeons
4 plump Italian sausages, skinned
8 leaves fresh sage or
1 heaped teaspoon dried sage
salt
freshly ground black pepper
8 rashers streaky bacon or pancetta
6 tablespoons olive oil
1 wine glass dry red wine

Pre-heat the oven to gas mark 5, 190°C (375°F). Wipe the pigeons carefully and remove any odd feather which might still be attached. Insert a sausage and 2 sage leaves inside each bird, season to taste with salt and pepper and wrap them in bacon. Lay them side by side in an oiled ovenproof dish and brush them generously with more oil.

Pour over the wine and roast in the oven for about 1 hour until tender. Serve piping hot with polenta or mashed potatoes.

Quaglie Stufate

Braised Quail

*The simplest possible recipe for quail really shows off
the intensely gamey flavour of these delicious little birds.
I like to serve a selection of steamed or
grilled vegetables with this dish,
which adds both colour and flavour.*

SERVES 6

6 large oven-ready quail
75 g (3 oz) unsalted butter
2 strips belly pork, rinded and cubed
salt
freshly ground black pepper
5 slices ciabatta bread, cubed
1/2 wine glass cognac

Wipe and trim the quail and arrange them in a flameproof casserole with half
the butter and the pork. Season generously with salt and pepper, cover tightly
and place over a medium heat to braise gently for about 25 minutes, turning
the birds over occasionally. Meanwhile, melt the remaining butter and fry the
bread cubes until crisp. Thoroughly warm a second flameproof dish and lay
the fried bread in the bottom. Drain the quail from their fat and lay them on
top of the bread. Skim all the fat from the dish in which the quail were
cooked then pour the cognac into the dish and stir and scrape the dish over
a medium heat for about 4 minutes. Pour this liquid over the quail and
replace the lid. Heat through for a further 10 minutes then serve at once.

Faraona in Salmi
Braised Guinea Fowl

This is the perfect dinner party dish.
If you can't get hold of guinea fowl,
you can use a brace of oven-ready pheasants instead.

SERVES 6

1 large oven-ready guinea fowl, trimmed
1 tablespoon lard
5 tablespoons cooking brandy
500 ml (17 fl oz) strong poultry stock
1/2 onion, peeled and chopped
1 carrot, chopped
1 bay leaf
4–5 parsley stalks
6 peppercorns
100 g (4 oz) unsalted butter
1/2 wine glass dry white wine
1 tablespoon plain white flour

Pre-heat the oven to gas mark 5, 190°C (375°F). Spread the guinea fowl with lard and roast it in the oven for about 20 minutes. Remove it from the oven and leave it to cool completely then cut it into 6 even-sized pieces. Take out the back bones and set them aside with all the skin. Trim and tidy the pieces carefully. Place the brandy in a large, deep flameproof casserole and let it catch light and burn off the alcohol for about 1 minute. Stir in about 2 tablespoons of stock, add the guinea fowl and cover with a sheet of baking parchment. Cover tightly with a lid and simmer over a gentle heat for about 30 minutes until the fowl is cooked. Put the onion, carrot, bay leaf, parsley stalks and peppercorns in a saucepan with 1 tablespoon of butter and fry gently for about 10 minutes until soft and lightly browned. Pour in the wine and boil off the alcohol for about 2 minutes then add the remaining stock. Pound the back bones and skin together in a pestle and mortar then add this to the pan.

Cover and simmer for 10 minutes. Strain the sauce carefully, squeezing hard to extract as much flavour as possible. Mix 2 tablespoons of butter with the flour and whisk this into the sauce over a low heat. Simmer gently for about 10 minutes, skimming and stirring constantly. Remove from the heat and gradually whisk in the remaining butter. Arrange the guinea fowl on a warmed serving platter, pour over the sauce and serve at once.

Coniglio ai Capperi
Marinated Rabbit with Capers

*Lots of really lovely strong flavours combine in this delicious rabbit casserole.
As there are already quite a lot of vegetables in the dish,
you only need a light salad and some boiled potatoes to finish it off.*

SERVES 6

1.5 kg (3 lb 4 oz) rabbit joints
1 wine glass dry red wine
1 wine glass red wine vinegar
2 onions, peeled and thinly sliced
2 carrots, thinly sliced
2 sticks celery, finely chopped
salt
freshly ground black pepper
150 ml (5 fl oz) olive oil
4 salted anchovies, boned, rinsed and dried
50 g (2 oz) salted capers, rinsed and dried
2 tablespoons chopped fresh parsley
1 tablespoon plain white flour
1 tablespoon water

Lay the rabbit joints in a large bowl. Mix together the wine, wine vinegar, 1 onion, 1 carrot and 1 stick of celery and season generously with salt and pepper. Pour this marinade over the rabbit, cover and leave to stand for about 12 hours. Drain the rabbit; strain and reserve the marinade. Pour half the oil into a flameproof casserole and add the remaining onion, carrot and celery. Fry together for about 5 minutes until soft then lay the rabbit in the hot casserole and brown it carefully all over. Pour over half the strained marinade, bring to the boil, cover and simmer gently for about 1 hour until the rabbit is tender.

Meanwhile, make the sauce. Put the remaining oil and the anchovies in a saucepan over a medium heat and mash thoroughly with a fork until you have a smooth brown paste. Add the capers and parsley.

Mix together the flour and water and stir this into the sauce with the remaining marinade. Stir continuously until the sauce thickens then simmer very gently for about 20 minutes. Pour the sauce over the rabbit, mix together and heat through before serving.

Coniglio con le Mele
Rabbit with Apples

This recipe for pot-roasting a whole rabbit
calls for one very important ingredient:
sharp and crisp russet apples.
If you can't get hold of russets,
the only other possibility is to use very small Bramleys.
The recipe also works quite well with chicken.

SERVES 4–6

1 large whole rabbit, skinned and gutted
120 g (4^1/$_2$ oz) unsalted butter
1 kg (2 lb) russet apples
1 large wine glass dry white wine
1 large onion, peeled and finely chopped
salt
freshly ground black pepper

Wipe the rabbit carefully inside and out and rub a thin layer of butter all over it, inside and out. Peel, core and slice about half the apples and put them into a bowl with half the wine. Season to taste with salt and pepper and mix together thoroughly, then fill the inside of the rabbit with sliced apples. Sew the rabbit closed with cook's string. Core and quarter the remaining apples but don't peel them. Season the rabbit thoroughly with salt and pepper. Put the remaining butter into a large deep saucepan with the onion and fry it gently for about 15 minutes. Lay the rabbit on top and seal it thoroughly all over. Arrange the remaining apples around it. Pour over the remaining wine, cover and simmer gently for about 50 minutes.

Lepre alla Sant'Uberto
Hare Casserole with Red Wine

This recipe needs to marinate for 24 hours before cooking.
It is a delicious casserole,
finished off perfectly with the hint of
orange and redcurrant at the very end.
I like to serve it with jacket potatoes and braised leeks.

SERVES 6

1.5 kg (3 lb 4 oz) jointed hare, trimmed
1 large onion, peeled and chopped
1 large carrot, chopped
1 stick celery, chopped
6 tablespoons olive oil
1 clove garlic, peeled and sliced
3 cloves
2 bay leaves
2 sprigs fresh rosemary
1 sprig fresh sage
2 large tumblers dry red wine
1 tablespoon plain white flour
2 teaspoons finely chopped orange rind
2 teaspoons redcurrant jelly
salt
freshly ground black pepper

Lay the hare joints in a bowl and prepare the marinade. Fry the onion, carrot and celery in half the oil for about 5 minutes until the vegetables are soft but not browned. Add the garlic, cloves, bay leaves, rosemary and sage. Add the wine and boil off the alcohol for about 2 minutes. Season to taste with salt and pepper. Strain the marinade carefully, reserving the vegetables and herbs, and leave it to cool completely. Pour the marinade over the hare, cover and leave to marinate in a cool place for 24 hours.

Remove the hare joints from the marinade with a slotted spoon and coat them lightly in flour. Heat the remaining oil in a flameproof casserole and brown the floured hare joints all over. Add the vegetables and herbs from the marinade and continue to cook gently, turning the joints frequently and basting with the marinade. When all the marinade has been added, season to taste with salt and pepper. Cover and simmer for about 1 hour until completely tender. Remove the hare joints with a slotted spoon and arrange them on a warmed serving platter.

Stir the orange rind and redcurrant jelly into the casserole, scraping the bottom of the casserole with the spoon to be certain you have as much flavour as possible in the sauce. Bring to the boil then pour the sauce over the hot hare and serve at once.

Capriolo in Salmi
Venison
Casserole

*Even the toughest piece of stewing venison ends up
tender and intensely flavoured in this recipe.
Serve it with steamed baby potatoes and spinach.*

SERVES 6

1 kg (2 lb) boned venison, cut into chunks
1 large red onion, peeled and thickly sliced
1 large carrot, quartered
2 sticks celery, quartered
a handful of fresh parsley, chopped
1 bay leaf
1 tiny sprig fresh rosemary
1 large leaf fresh sage
freshly ground black pepper
1 large tumbler dry red wine
4 tablespoons olive oil
salt
1 teaspoon plain white flour

Lay the venison chunks in the bottom of a large bowl. Cover with the onion,
carrot and celery. Scatter the herbs on top and season with pepper then pour
over the wine. Cover and leave to marinate for about 2 hours.

Heat the oil in a deep flameproof casserole. Remove the meat from the
marinade with a slotted spoon and seal it all over in the oil, stirring well.
Gradually add all the vegetables from the marinade. Finally add the wine and
season to taste with salt. Bring to the boil and boil off the alcohol for about
2 minutes then add just enough water to cover the meat. Stir well, cover and
simmer gently for about 1¹/₂ hours.

Just before serving, arrange the meat and vegetables on a warmed platter
and keep them warm. If you wish to thicken the sauce, mix the flour with a
little water, stir it into the sauce and simmer for a few minutes. Strain the
sauce carefully, pour it over the meat and serve at once.

Carpa all'Ebraica

SEE PAGE 204

Maccarello in Filetti alla Marinara

SEE PAGE 217

Scampi Arrosto

SEE PAGE 228

Aragosta Arrosto

SEE PAGE 232

Daino
in Salsa di Cigliege
Venison
in Cherry Sauce

*More marinating in this dish – up to three days this time before
you cook the meat! I look upon recipes like this as something of a challenge:
lots of ingredients, quite a bit of work, but my goodness, it certainly is
worth it all in the end! Serve this with steamed crisp green vegetables and
a radicchio and orange salad.*

SERVES 6

1.5 kg (3 lb 4 oz) boned saddle of venison, trimmed
1 large onion, peeled and chopped
1 carrot, chopped
1 stick celery, chopped
a handful of fresh parsley, chopped
$^1/_2$ tumbler olive oil
2 large cloves garlic, peeled and thinly sliced
1 bay leaf
a large pinch of dried mint
a large pinch of dried oregano
a pinch of dried sage
a pinch of dried rosemary
salt
$1^1/_2$ tumblers dry red wine
2 tablespoons red wine vinegar
3 tablespoons unsalted butter
1 tablespoon sunflower oil
1 teaspoon plain white flour
1 orange
$^1/_2$ tumbler marsala
100 g (4 oz) redcurrant jelly
a pinch of ground cinnamon
300 g (11 oz) canned sweet cherries, drained

Slice the meat into thick steaks and beat them lightly with a meat mallet to tenderise them as much as possible. Lay them side by side in a bowl and prepare the marinade. Fry the onion, carrot, celery and parsley in the olive oil over a very low heat for about 30 minutes without letting them brown. Stir in the garlic and all the remaining herbs and season with salt. Fry for a few minutes until the garlic begins to colour. Stir in the wine and wine vinegar, bring to the boil and simmer for a further 5 minutes. Leave to cool completely then pour over the meat. Cover and leave in a cool place, but not the fridge, for up to 3 days, depending on how long the meat has been hanging.

Heat half the butter and the sunflower oil in a large saucepan. Remove the meat from the marinade with a slotted spoon, dry it carefully with kitchen paper and seal each steak in the hot fat. Reserve 1 tumbler of the marinade and gradually add the remainder to the meat, turning the meat and simmering constantly. Cover and simmer for about 45 minutes until the meat is cooked through.

Remove the meat from the pan and put it between 2 hot plates to keep it warm. Skim off the fat in the saucepan and add the reserved marinade, stirring carefully to blend in all the meat juices. Blend the remaining butter with the flour, stir this into the pan and simmer until the sauce has thickened and is smooth and lump-free. Return the meat to the sauce and warm it through without allowing the sauce to boil. Keep the meat hot while you make the cherry sauce.

Pare the rind off the orange carefully without removing any of the pith. Slice the rind very finely into matchstick strips. Squeeze the juice from the orange. Put the orange rind, juice and marsala in a saucepan, bring to the boil and simmer until reduced by half. Stir in the redcurrant jelly, cinnamon and cherries and bring to the boil then transfer to a bowl or large sauce boat and serve with the venison.

Cinghiale in Umido
Stewed Boar

You will need to marinate the boar for 24 hours, and in my experience it really will need it to tenderise the meat unless the boar you are using is commercially reared and very young. I always consider boar to be incredibly tough unless well marinated, although I am assured that some of the farms which breed boar are producing meat which is as tender as the best pork. Even if the meat is already very tender, the marinade will add flavour to the dish.

SERVES 4

1.5 kg (3 lb 4 oz) boned wild boar haunch, skinned
1 large red onion, peeled and chopped
1 large carrot, chopped
1 large stick celery, chopped
a handful of fresh parsley, chopped
2 large tumblers dry red wine
1 bay leaf
a pinch of dried sage leaves
a pinch of dried marjoram
5 tablespoons olive oil
salt
freshly ground black pepper
4 tablespoons tomato purée

Wash and dry the boar carefully and beat it all over with a meat mallet. Do not tie it up. Lay it in a large bowl. Mix together the onion, carrot, celery and parsley and put them into a saucepan with half the wine. Bring to the boil very slowly then add the herbs and simmer for a few minutes. Pour this marinade over the meat, cover with foil and leave in a cool place to marinate for about 24 hours. Remove the haunch from the marinade and tie it securely with cook's string. Strain the marinade and put it to one side. Heat the oil in a saucepan and brown the meat all over. Season to taste with salt and pepper and gradually begin to add the marinade. Mix the tomato purée into the remaining wine and add it to the meat when you have used all the marinade. Cover tightly and simmer very gently, turning and basting the meat occasionally. Cook for about 2¹/₂ hours until the meat is cooked through and tender then remove it from the pan and serve with the cooking juices.

Fish

I T IS QUITE USUAL in Italy for friends or family to get together and
have a huge feast of fish for no other reason than that they feel like it!
Alternatively, fish could be part of the antipasto, it could be in the sauce
which goes with the pasta or in the risotto. Otherwise, it will play the part
of the main course, replacing meat. Sadly, I think that really good, very
fresh fish is so rare to find these days that when one gets the opportunity
to enjoy a feast of fish one should do just that. I am delighted to see that
the marketing of fish has taken such an enthusiastic turn, and I really
hope that more and more people will experiment and discover the
delights of fish in all its guises.

Freshwater fish are found mostly in the northern part of Italy where
drought has never been a problem. The vast Lombard lakes have always
yielded large quantities of fish such as tench, perch, carp and so on. Most
of the recipes I have given you which call for these slightly more unusual
and certainly harder-to-find fish can be cooked with the delicious and
widely available trout. Fresh farmed trout is as popular in Italy as it is elsewhere and because it has a relatively bland flavour, a good firm flesh and
a pleasant appearance, it seems to have become the most adaptable and
flexible of fish – rather like the chicken of the fish world! However, just
because trout is so easy to find and cook that doesn't mean that you should
ignore the more unusual varieties of fish. If you do come across them or
can find them in a local fishmonger's, you should certainly try them.

I can remember when I used to fish from a rowing boat in Ireland
as a little girl, how frustrated I used to get when I caught perch instead of
trout. My parents would help me to throw them back into the lough as

nobody really considered them worth eating, not compared to the bountiful trout anyway, even though the perch seemed to me to be a much more beautiful fish with its brilliant colouring. I wonder if I went back to those fishing pools, would I be able to catch perch now with such nonchalance? Certainly unless you are an angler or are very friendly with one, you are unlikely to get hold of a fresh perch. Carp, on the other hand, is much easier to buy thanks to its popularity in Chinese restaurants.

Pike is another fish which is fairly easy to buy and, of course, you can always catch one yourself! The reservoirs seem to be teeming with these fish and the demand for *quenelles* from smart French restaurants means that it is relatively simple to find. Personally, I feel that the vast quantities of small bones in pike mean that quenelles are the best thing which could happen to it, but I do recall an incident when we sat on a wet and windy bank by an Irish lough, roasting a fresh pike over a wood fire and eating it with our fingers. It is probably fair to say that no fish has ever tasted so good, but I doubt whether that was anything to do with the pike!

Sturgeon lives in the sea and goes up river to spawn. There have been cases of sturgeon being caught in the Seine as far inland as Paris. In the UK, sturgeon is actually the Queen's fish, which means that if you should catch one you need to inform the appropriate authority, such as the Lord Mayor, and go through whatever protocol is involved, as you would do with a swan. In Italy, I have seen them on sale alive at huge wholesale fish markets and have therefore been able to buy and cook this very unusual fish. If you can't find sturgeon, use very firm, thick cod steaks or monkfish tails.

Eel is fairly simple to find, though huss can be used as a substitute should you be unable to buy this much maligned fish. In northern parts of Italy, where rice is grown, eel is extremely popular and widely used. The same damp conditions used to yield delicious freshwater shrimps. They are much less common nowadays; I can only suggest that this might have something to do with modern fertilisers used on the paddy fields.

As far as the saltwater fish are concerned, I don't think any of those mentioned in the following recipes would cause you any problems in terms of finding and buying them, with the notable exception of dentex. It is widely available in Italy, especially in parts of the country where there are rocky coastal areas. I have suggested using cod loin as a substitute, but in fact any delicately flavoured white fish will work for this recipe.

Monkfish is now becoming increasingly popular. It is probably the ugliest fish you can find. In Italian it is called *coda di rospo* because of its monstrous, toad-like appearance, or *pescatrice*, for its practice of hoovering its food up off the ocean floor through its long feelers. The head takes up most of the fish, leaving the deliciously firm-fleshed, bone-free tail, which is often the only part the fishmonger will display. This part of the fish is much sought after and rather expensive, but is stocked by many fishmongers or if not, your fishmonger will be able to get it for you if you give him a couple of days' notice. I have eaten huge, whole monkfish gently poached and with the head being removed before being served warm with a home-made mayonnaise and a fresh green salad. It is a dish fit for kings. Whatever the size of monkfish you buy it is hard to go wrong with it. It is excellent for all kinds of recipes and is very much a favourite in my home.

BUYING FRESH FISH

When you buy fish, whatever type of fish and wherever you are when you buy it, there are a few simple rules which you should follow. Make sure that the fish smells sweet and fresh; look at the eyes and make sure they are bright and sparkling as opposed to dull and darkened; lift the gills and check for a rich pink colouring. Look at the fish as a whole. Is it shiny and are the colours well defined? Does it look fresh and almost alive? If it does, then buy it. Never bother with fish that doesn't look right or smell right.

Finally, my friend Thoby Young has kindly consented to help out should anybody wish to buy and cook a particular fish which they are having trouble finding. The Fresh Food Company is at 100 Bayswater Road, London W2 3HJ. Thoby runs a very good food-finding service by mail order and is dedicated to raising the standard of the enjoyment of food. He will be delighted to help with your enquiries on fish, or indeed any other hard-to-find ingredients for which you may be hunting.

PREPARING ROUND FISH

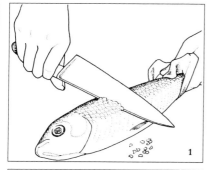

1

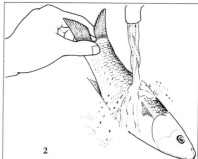

2

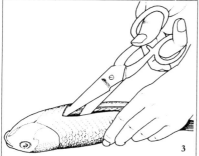

3

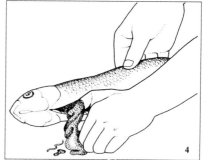

4

You prepare all round fish in the same way. This includes trout, perch, mullet and pike. If the fish is scaly, you'll need to remove the scales before you gut the fish so that you can hang on to it more easily.

Lay the fish on a sheet of newspaper and scrape the scales away with the blunt side of a knife from the tail end towards the head (1). This is a very messy job and if possible should be done outside. When you have scraped off as much as you can, wash the fish thoroughly under running water (2). Then snip off all the fins with a pair of sharp scissors and cut a slit in the white belly of the fish (3). Be careful not to pierce the innards of the fish as if you do, they might taint the flavour of the flesh. Use your fingers or thumb to ease out the innards (4) then quickly wash the fish under running water. You may keep the head of the fish on if you prefer – I think it is best to leave it on – in which case you must make sure that you remove all the innards attached to the head end of the fish. Remove the gills and wash the fish again and then dry it carefully before proceeding.

If you prefer not to open up the fish, you can insert your fingers inside through the gills and pull everything out that way, although this is much more difficult and requires a lot of practice. Once the fish has been prepared, it should be washed and dried carefully.

FILLETING ROUND FISH

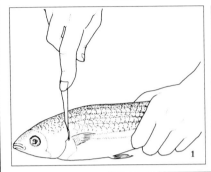

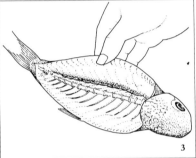

Fishmongers will usually fillet fish, such as mackerel, if you ask them, but if you cannot persuade your fishmonger to fillet the fish for you, you can do it yourself. Gut and wash the fish and pat it dry. Lay it on a work surface with its tail towards you. Hold the fish down firmly with one hand and use a sharp knife to cut round the base of the head in a semi-circular shape (1). Then insert your knife across the backbone and slice down towards the tail, keeping your hand flat on the top of the fish (2). As the knife slices, you should be able to feel the backbone against which it is resting. Now carefully lift the fillet off the fish (3). You will be left with the head, tail and the other half of the fish still attached to the bone. Turn the fish over and repeat the process. You will now have two fillets; the head and bones can be used for stock.

POACHING FISH

Poaching fish is a delicate art. It does not mean boiling the fish. You should gently lower the fish into plain water or court bouillon or a mixture of white wine and water which is cold or just lukewarm. During the cooking time the water must never boil with any vigour, it should be just below boiling point throughout. I like to poach whole fish such as grey mullet in half water and half wine with a thickly sliced lemon, a

PREPARING FLAT FISH

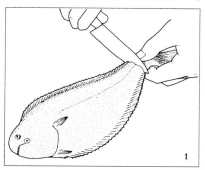

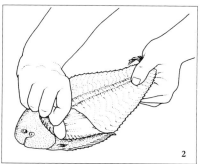

1   2

This includes all flat fish such as brill, plaice, dab and sole. Assuming that the fish has already been gutted, it simply needs to be skinned on either side. If the fishmonger hasn't done this for you, here is how it is done. Lay the fish on a wooden board with the dark-skinned side uppermost and the tail pointing towards you. Cut a nick in the skin near the tail to make a flap which you can hold (1). Take a firm grip on it and pull it away from you firmly in one strong movement (2). When you reach the jaws, turn the fish over and pull the skin up and over the head then continue to pull the skin off towards the tail in one smooth motion. Rinse the fish and pat it dry.

handful of herbs and some peppercorns. Remember to go easy on the salt as most sea fish are naturally salty anyway. If you use fish stock to poach your fish, you will lift even the most ordinary fish into the realms of being a superlative dish.

COOKING SARDINES

I like to coat sardines in beaten egg and breadcrumbs and then fry them in a little oil until crisp and golden. After draining them on kitchen paper, they should be served with lemon wedges to cut through the inevitable oiliness. Because sardines are such an oily fish, they should be cooked with a minimum of oil or fat of any kind. They are ideally suited to grilling because they are protected by their skin which keeps the inside moist and forms a natural crisp crust on the outside. If you cook them under the grill in this way, they will only need to be gutted and washed but not boned. If you grill boned sardines, they taste good coated in fresh breadcrumbs mixed with crushed garlic, grated lemon rind, chopped parsley, salt and freshly ground black pepper. Brush them lightly with oil

PREPARING SARDINES

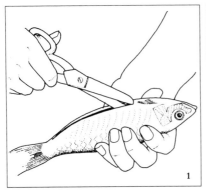 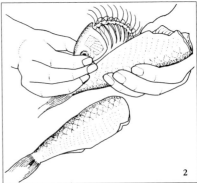

To clean a sardine properly you first need to remove the scales (see Preparing Round Fish, page 199). Remember that the sardine has very tender flesh so it is easy to tear it. Slit the belly open with scissors and ease out the innards (1). Wash and dry the gutted fish and hold it firmly in your hand, belly-side up. With your other hand, grip the head with your thumb and forefinger. Pull the head down through the fish towards you, removing the spine and all the bones, so that you end up with a neat, flat fish (2). Wash and dry the fish very carefully and pat it dry thoroughly. It is now ready to cook. If you are very nimble fingered, it is actually possible to gut the fish through the gills, but this is an expert job and in my opinion should be left to the fishmonger.

before coating them with this mixture so that it will stick to the skins.

The most important thing about sardines is that it is imperative that they should be as fresh as possible. Frozen sardines are now widely available and can be very good, especially if cooked with some kind of a sauce, but every chance should be taken to enjoy sparkling fresh sardines.

GRILLING FISH

Whenever you grill fish, whatever the fish, remember always to pre-heat the grill, oil the rack to prevent sticking, and use tongs or two forks to turn the fish. Also, because fish will not take all that long to cook under a grill, you should have all the sauces, salads and other accompaniments ready so that you can eat the fish very quickly after it has been grilled.

Anguilla Arrosto
Roasted Eel

*Eel is a much maligned fish, probably because it really isn't
a very good-looking animal. But the flavour is quite wonderful so
please give the poor old ugly eel a chance! As children,
we used to fish for them in the deep ditches near our house,
using nothing more than an upturned umbrella and a pair of
very blunt scissors. We then used to cook them as
described below over a precariously balanced grill on an open fire.
As a change, monkfish can also be prepared in this way.*

SERVES 6

18 x 5 cm (2 in) chunks of skinned eel
4 tablespoons olive oil
2 tablespoons white wine or cider vinegar
3 bay leaves
a handful of fresh breadcrumbs
salt
freshly ground black pepper

Arrange the fish in a bowl. Mix together the oil, vinegar, bay leaves,
breadcrumbs, salt and pepper. Pour this mixture over the fish and leave to
stand in a cool place for about 4 hours, turning frequently. Pre-heat the oven
to gas mark 5, 190°C (375°F).

Divide the fish into 6 equal quantities and thread the chunks evenly on to
6 metal skewers. Lay the skewers in a roasting tin and cover generously with
the marinade.

Bake in the oven for about 25 minutes, turning frequently. Serve hot.

Carpa all'Ebraica
Poached Carp
with Almonds
and Sultanas

*Carp decomposes very quickly so ideally it
should still be alive when you buy it.
In any case, be sure that it is as fresh as possible.*

SERVES 6

1.5 kg (3 lb 4 oz) carp, scaled and gutted
salt
400 g (14 oz) onions, peeled and sliced
12 blanched almonds, chopped
50 g (2 oz) sultanas
freshly ground black pepper
2 teaspoons granulated sugar

Rub the fish all over with salt and put it aside to rest for 30 minutes. Wash it thoroughly and cut it into even-sized chunks, including the head and tail. Arrange the onions, almonds and sultanas on the bottom of a fish kettle then place the chunks of fish on top, trying to retain the fish's original shape. Sprinkle with salt, pepper and sugar. Pour over just enough water to cover the fish and put on the lid. Bring to a simmer and simmer very gently for about 30 minutes.

Remove from the heat, take the fish out of the kettle and reconstruct it on an oval platter. Strain and reserve the liquid. Spread the cooked onions over the fish and pour the liquid over and around it. Cool, then chill until the liquid has turned to jelly. Serve cold.

Luccio alla Marinara
Casserole of Pike in Red Wine

Pike can be extremely bland, although this is not the case in this recipe as all the stronly flavoured ingredients certainly overcome that problem. However, there is nothing that can be done about the general boniness of the fish! If you really hate fiddling around with fish bones, choose a different fish altogether.

SERVES 6

1.5 kg (3 lb 4 oz) pike,
cut into walnut-sized chunks
salt
freshly ground black pepper
$1/2$ tumbler olive oil
1 large onion, peeled and sliced
1 clove garlic, peeled and chopped
1 carrot, chopped
a handful of fresh parsley, chopped
1 litre (1 $3/4$ pints) dry red wine
50 g (2 oz) unsalted butter
1 tablespoon plain white flour

Remove as many bones as possible from the fish. Lay it in a saucepan, sprinkle with salt and pepper, pour over the oil and scatter over the onion, garlic, carrot and parsley. Mix everything together very carefully then pour over the wine. Cover and leave to stand for about 3 hours, turning frequently.

Place the saucepan over a medium heat, bring to a simmer and simmer gently for about 20 minutes. Remove the fish, arrange it on a warmed serving platter and keep it warm. Push the remaining contents of the saucepan through a sieve and return to the heat. Simmer until reduced by half. Blend together the butter and flour then mix it into the saucepan. As soon as the sauce is bubbling hot, pour it all over the fish and serve at once.

Pesce Persico alla Massaia
Poached Perch in Cream Sauce

This is a very simple recipe which can be made with any fish you like.
It tastes delicious with carrots and steamed broccoli florets with
a drizzle of olive oil and a squeeze of lemon juice.

SERVES 6

6 x 150 g (5 oz) perch, scaled and gutted
1 tablespoon white wine vinegar
salt
75 g (3 oz) unsalted butter
50 g (2 oz) plain white flour
500 ml (17 fl oz) milk
2 tablespoons double cream
2 hard-boiled eggs, finely chopped
2 tablespoons chopped fresh parsley
freshly ground black pepper

Place the fish in a fish kettle. Pour over just enough water to cover, add the wine vinegar and season to taste with salt. Bring to the boil and simmer for about 20 minutes until the fish is tender and the eyes are white. Remove the fish very carefully from the water and remove the skin gently without tearing it. Return the fish to the hot water and put aside to keep warm.

Meanwhile, melt two-thirds of the butter in a saucepan until foaming then stir in the flour until you have a smooth mixture. Pour in the milk and whisk over a low heat for about 20 minutes, stirring almost constantly, until the sauce is smooth and creamy and no longer tastes of raw flour. Remove from the heat and stir in the remaining butter and the cream. Arrange the fish on a warmed serving platter and pour over the sauce. Sprinkle with hard-boiled eggs, parsley and pepper and serve at once.

Pesce Persico in Filetti al Burro

Fillets of Perch Cooked in Butter

*Although I have suggested that you use
fillets of perch for this recipe,
any fillets will work just as well.
Try fillets of sole for a very delicate flavour,
perhaps serving with wedges of lime instead of lemon.
It is perfect with very thin chips and
Zucchine Fritte Dorate (page 244).*

SERVES 6

3 x 300 g (11 oz) perch, filleted
3 tablespoons plain white flour
2 eggs, beaten
4 tablespoons dried white breadcrumbs
4 tablespoons unsalted butter
2 lemons, cut into wedges

Tidy the fillets as much as possible. Coat them in the flour then in the egg and breadcrumbs. Shake off the excess. Heat the butter until sizzling and fry the fillets for about 3 minutes on each side until crisp and golden brown. Drain on kitchen paper. Arrange on a warmed serving platter, garnish with lemon wedges and serve at once.

Storione con Funghi
Sturgeon with Oyster Mushrooms

Although sturgeon is relatively easy to buy in Italy, it is much more difficult to find in Britain. Good alternatives are cod loin, monkfish tails or very chunky fish steaks.

SERVES 6

6 thick slices sturgeon, skinned
salt
juice of 1 lemon
1 onion, peeled and chopped
3 cloves garlic, peeled and chopped
1 carrot, chopped
2 tablespoons unsalted butter
7 tablespoons olive oil
1 salted anchovy, boned, rinsed, dried and chopped
4 tablespoons chopped fresh parsley
1/2 fresh bay leaf, chopped
1/2 tumbler dry white wine
1/2 tumbler fish stock
1 kg (2 lb) oyster mushrooms, coarsely chopped
2 tablespoons plain white flour
2 eggs, beaten

Sprinkle the fish slices with salt then lay them in a wide dish, pour over the lemon juice and leave to stand for 30 minutes. Fry the onion, 1 clove of garlic and the carrot in half the butter and 1 tablespoon of oil for about 5 minutes until soft but not coloured. Add the anchovy, half the parsley and the bay leaf. Stir in the wine and boil off the alcohol for about 2 minutes. Pour off a little of the fat, add the stock and simmer for about 10 minutes.

Meanwhile, melt the remaining butter with 2 tablespoons of oil, the remaining garlic and parsley. Add the mushrooms, season to taste with salt and fry for about 5 minutes until soft. Transfer the mushrooms to the other saucepan and stir. Drain the fish well then coat in flour then egg. Heat the remaining oil and fry the fish on both sides for about 5 minutes. Drain on kitchen paper then transfer to the saucepan with the mushrooms. Heat through and serve at once.

Trota Cotta al Vapore
Steamed Trout

Trout is a marvellous fish: easy to cook,
easy to eat and delicious!
When you take it to the table,
fillet it carefully to serve.
It is perfect with Porri in Padella (page 248) and
roast potatoes with rosemary.

SERVES 6

1 x 1.25 kg (3 lb) trout, scaled and gutted
salt
freshly ground black pepper
1 onion, peeled and coarsely chopped
1 carrot, coarsely chopped
1 stick celery, coarsely chopped
a handful of parsley stalks, coarsely chopped
1 bay leaf, coarsely chopped
$^1/_2$ tumbler water
100 g (4 oz) unsalted butter
1 wine glass dry white wine or barolo
1 tablespoon plain white flour
5 tablespoons double cream

Pre-heat the oven to gas mark 3, 160°C (325°F). Cut diagonal slits across the fish on both sides and season to taste with salt and pepper. Take the perforated rack out of the fish kettle, arrange the onion, carrot, celery, parsley stalks and bay leaf on the bottom and pour over the water. Replace the rack. Melt about one-third of the butter and brush the rack with some of the butter then brush the fish with butter on both sides. Lay the fish in the fish kettle. Use the remaining melted butter to grease a sheet of baking parchment and lay this over the fish. Cover with a lid and place over a very low heat to cook gently for about 10 minutes then transfer the fish kettle to the oven to bake gently for a further 10 minutes. Turn off the oven.

Return the fish kettle to the top of the stove and remove the lid and the baking parchment. Pour over the wine or barolo and boil off the alcohol for about 2 minutes. Cover and return to the warm oven for about 8 minutes to allow the flavours to develop. Slide the fish carefully on to a warmed serving platter and return it to the oven to keep warm. Push the contents of the fish kettle through a sieve into a small saucepan.

Blend half the remaining butter with the flour and whisk this into the sauce over a low heat. When the sauce is very hot, remove from the heat and gradually whisk in the remaining butter. Re-heat to just below boiling point then remove from the heat and whisk in the cream. Pour the sauce over the fish and serve at once.

Trotelle alla Mugnaia
Pan-fried Trout with Butter and Parsley

*There is nothing quite like the taste of freshly caught trout
and this recipe is very much a no-frills way of cooking the fish to show
off all its flavour and texture without masking them in any way.
Especially if you have caught the trout yourself,
treat yourself to this easy and delicious recipe served with
potatoes and a fresh green salad.*

SERVES 6

6 x 200 g (7 oz) trout, scaled and gutted
salt
freshly ground black pepper
4 tablespoons plain white flour
100 g (4 oz) unsalted butter
3 tablespoons chopped fresh parsley

Season the fish well with salt and pepper. Coat them lightly in flour. Heat three-quarters of the butter until foaming but not brown and lay the fish in the butter. Cook them on both sides for about 15 minutes until golden and crisp. Transfer the fish to a warmed serving platter and sprinkle with parsley. Wipe the pan clean and melt the remaining butter until nut brown. Pour this over the fish and serve at once.

Trota
alla Savoiarda
Pan-fried Trout
with Mushrooms
and Onions

*Although trout farms breed fish which is then
available all year round,
it is not at its best during the months of
November and December.
Avoid buying and cooking fresh trout during these
two months if at all possible,
although you can use frozen trout which has been
caught at another time of year.*

SERVES 6

1 x 1.5 kg (3 lb 4 oz) trout, scaled and gutted
2 tablespoons plain white flour
200 g (7 oz) unsalted butter
3 tablespoons olive oil
500 g (1 lb 2 oz) shiitake or
oyster mushrooms, coarsely chopped
3 tablespoons chopped fresh parsley
salt
freshly ground black pepper
2 tablespoons very fine dried white breadcrumbs
1 small onion, peeled and chopped

Pre-heat the oven to gas mark 6, 200°C (400°F). Coat the fish in flour. Slash
the fish diagonally across the back 4 times on each side. Melt a quarter of the
butter in a wide frying pan until foaming. Lay the fish in the butter and cook
it gently for about 6 minutes on both sides. Turn off the heat, cover the pan

and leave the fish to stand while you prepare the mushrooms. Put 1 tablespoon of butter into a separate pan, add the mushrooms and cook for about 5 minutes until soft. Stir in the parsley and season to taste with salt and pepper. Arrange the mushrooms on the bottom of an oval ovenproof dish large enough to take the fish. Lay the fish on top of the mushrooms and pour over the butter in which the fish was cooked. Season to taste with salt and pepper and sprinkle with breadcrumbs. Bake in the oven for about 7 minutes until the breadcrumbs are golden brown.

Meanwhile, melt the remaining butter in a small pan until golden brown. Stir in the onion, remove from the heat and leave to stand for about 4 minutes. Strain the flavoured butter into a sauce boat and serve with the fish.

Salmone al Pesto
Salmon with Pesto

*As an alternative to cooking salmon in this way,
you could cover the fish in pesto and wrap it in foil.
Place the foil parcels under the grill or in a
hot oven at gas mark 6, 200°C (400°F) and cook them for
about 5 or 6 minutes before serving them for
your guests to unwrap at the table.*

SERVES 6

12 very small salmon tail fillets or
salmon steaks
1 jar very good quality pesto sauce
1 wine glass dry white wine
3 tablespoons olive oil
salt
freshly ground black pepper
4 leaves fresh basil

Arrange the fish in a shallow bowl. Whisk the pesto with the wine and oil until the sauce has emulsified completely. Pour the mixture over the fish and season to taste with salt and pepper. Leave to marinate in a cool place, but not the fridge, for about 5 hours, turning the fish occasionally.

Heat a skillet or heavy non-stick pan rubbed lightly with oil. Cook the fish briefly for about 4 minutes each side, turning frequently. While the fish is cooking, spoon over the pesto sauce so that by the time the fish is cooked, all the sauce is in the pan. Arrange the fish and sauce on a warmed serving platter, and serve garnished with basil leaves.

Cefalo Arrosto al Forno

Roasted Grey Mullet

*Grey mullet can taste a bit muddy which is why
it is important to wash it very carefully.
Make sure you fillet it carefully when you serve it as
a stray fish bone can spoil the enjoyment of fresh fish.*

SERVES 6

2 large lemons, thinly sliced
5 tablespoons olive oil
1 x 1.5 kg (3 lb 4 oz) grey mullet,
scaled and gutted
salt
2 tablespoons chopped fresh parsley

Arrange the lemon slices in overlapping rows all over the bottom of a large oiled ovenproof dish. Brush lightly with a little more oil. Season the fish inside and out with salt and lay it on top of the lemons. Sprinkle inside and out with the parsley, cover loosely with foil and bake in the oven for about 40 minutes until the flesh is tender and the eyes have turned white. Transfer the fish to a warmed serving platter, pour the liquid from the dish over the fish and serve at once.

Dentice all Pizzaiola
Dentex with Tomato Sauce

Delicious with artichokes as an accompanying vegetable, this is a really wonderful way to wake up the flavours of fresh fish using lots of ingredients with good strong tastes.

SERVES 6

6 x 150 g (5 oz) thick slices dentex or cod loin
6 tablespoons olive oil
4 tablespoons chopped fresh parsley
2 bay leaves, cut into strips
1 teaspoon peppercorns
3 tablespoons plain white flour
salt
1 clove garlic, peeled and lightly crushed
500 g (1 lb 2 oz) passata
freshly ground black pepper
4 canned anchovy fillets in oil, drained,
rinsed, dried and chopped
1 teaspoon dried oregano

Lay the fish slices in a wide dish, sprinkle with about half the oil, half the parsley, the bay leaves and peppercorns, cover and leave to marinate for about 2 hours.

Remove the fish from the marinade and shake each slice as dry as possible. Coat the fish slices in flour. Heat the strained oil from the marinade in a wide frying pan and seal the fish on both sides. Sprinkle with salt and cook for about 15 minutes. Remove from the heat and keep warm. In a separate pan, heat the remaining oil with the garlic for a few minutes until the garlic turns brown. Stir in the passata, season to taste with salt and pepper and add the anchovies. Stir all this together, bring to the boil and simmer for about 10 minutes. Arrange the fish on a warmed serving dish, pour over the sauce and sprinkle with the remaining parsley and oregano. Serve at once.

Maccarello in Filetti alla Marinara
Mackerel Fillets with Capers and Olives

I really love the way the capers and anchovies cut through the natural greasiness of the mackerel in this recipe. Definitely one of my favourites!

SERVES 6

150 ml (5 fl oz) olive oil
3 x 300 g (11 oz) mackerel, filleted
6 salted anchovies, boned, rinsed and dried
1 tablespoon salted capers, rinsed and dried
a handful of very fine dried
white breadcrumbs
100 g (4 oz) stoned black olives
3 tablespoons dry white wine
salt
freshly ground black pepper

Pre-heat the oven to gas mark 5, 190°C (375°F). Generously oil an oven-proof dish large enough to take all the fish, and lay the fish in the dish in a single layer. Arrange the anchovy fillets in a lattice pattern over the mackerel, dot with the capers and carefully pour over the wine. Sprinkle with bread-crumbs and surround with black olives. Sprinkle with salt and pepper and bake in the oven for about 20 minutes. Serve at once straight from the dish.

Merluzzo *in Filetti* *al Vino Bianco*
Cod Fillets in White Wine

A really easy way of preparing cod,
the only stipulation with this recipe is that the cod must be as
fresh as possible so that its flavour shines through.

SERVES 6

6 x 150 g (5 oz) cod fillets
100 g (4 oz) unsalted butter
salt
freshly ground black pepper
6 tablespoons dry white wine

Fold the cod fillets in half. Butter a pan thoroughly and lay the fillets in the pan. Heat the pan and cook the fish for about 2 minutes on each side. Season to taste with salt and pepper and pour over the wine. Cover and cook for a further 4 minutes, basting occasionally and turning the fish carefully. Transfer the fish to a warmed serving platter. Boil the liquid in the pan until reduced by half then pour it over the fish and serve at once.

Merluzzo in Filetti al Burro d'Acciuga
Cod Fillets in Anchovy Butter

*If you like the flavour of anchovies,
then this recipe is a good one for you.
There is a marvellous contrast between
the delicate flavour of the cod with the strong,
salty taste of the anchovies.
Serve this dish with boiled potatoes and a green salad.*

SERVES 6

6 x 150 g (5 oz) cod fillets
3 tablespoons plain white flour
2 eggs, beaten
4 tablespoons dried white breadcrumbs
8 tablespoons sunflower oil
6 salted anchovies, boned, rinsed,
dried and chopped
100 g (4 oz) unsalted butter
1 tablespoon white wine vinegar
3 tablespoons chopped fresh parsley

Dip the fish in the flour, then egg, then breadcrumbs. Heat the oil until sizzling hot then fry the fish for about 5 minutes until crisp and golden. Drain on kitchen paper and keep them warm. Put the anchovies, butter and wine vinegar into a small bowl and heat over a pan of boiling water, stirring frequently until you have a smooth brown cream.

Arrange the fish on a warmed serving platter, pour over the anchovy sauce, sprinkle with parsley and serve at once.

Coda di Rospo al Limone
Monkfish in Lemon Sauce

*This is another recipe for which I have to
thank my friend Alvaro Maccione.
He prepares a version in his restaurant La Famiglia,
but this is my own adaptation.*

SERVES 6

2 tablespoons plain white flour
$1/4$ teaspoon salt
1.2 kg (2 lb 12 oz) monkfish tails,
trimmed and cubed
2–4 tablespoons olive oil
juice and grated rind of 1 lemon
1 glass dry white wine
2 tablespoons chopped fresh parsley
freshly ground black pepper

Mix the flour and salt then lightly coat the fish in the mixture. Heat the oil in a wide frying pan and fry the fish until sealed on all sides. Add the lemon juice and rind and the wine and boil off the alcohol for about 2 minutes. Lower the heat and cook for a further 5 minutes, stirring frequently. Sprinkle with parsley and season to taste with pepper. Transfer the fish to a warmed serving platter and keep it warm. Boil the liquid until reduced to about one-third of the original quantity, pour it over the fish and serve at once.

Pesce Spada in Salsa di Pomodoro
Swordfish in Tomato Sauce

Swordfish steaks or shark steaks are so often simply grilled and sprinkled with oil and lemon juice.
This is a slightly more adventurous recipe which is still very easy to make.

SERVES 6

1 kg (2 lb) swordfish steaks
2 tablespoons plain white flour
salt
7 tablespoons olive oil
1 small onion, peeled and finely chopped
1 large clove garlic, peeled and chopped
1 stick celery, finely chopped
2 bay leaves, broken into pieces
2 tablespoons tomato purée
200 ml (7 fl oz) water
$^{1}/_{2}$ wine glass dry white wine
1 tablespoon chopped fresh parsley
1 heaped tablespoon salted capers, rinsed and dried
freshly ground black pepper

Pre-heat the oven to gas mark 7, 220°C (425°F). Coat the fish on both sides in the flour then sprinkle with a little salt. Heat the oil in a flameproof dish and fry the fish for about 3 minutes on each side. Drain the fish on kitchen paper and set aside. Add the onion, garlic, celery and bay leaves to the oil and fry gently for about 6 minutes.

Mix together the tomato purée and water and stir it into the vegetables. Bring to a simmer and simmer gently for about 10 minutes. Lay the fish in the sauce, sprinkle with the wine, parsley and capers and boil off the alcohol for about 2 minutes. Turn over the fish, season to taste with pepper and bake in the oven for about 8 minutes before serving.

Sarde al Finocchio
Baked Sardines with Fennel Seeds

The tastes of fennel and sardine seem almost made for one another;
they really set each other off beautifully.
Although I have specified fresh sardines,
I realise they may be hard to find and you may need to
opt for the frozen variety.

SERVES 6

1 very large onion, peeled and thinly sliced
6 tablespoons olive oil
1 large wine glass dry red wine
500 g (1 lb 2 oz) passata
salt
freshly ground black pepper
150 g (5 oz) dried breadcrumbs
2 heaped tablespoons fennel seeds, crushed
1 kg (2 lb) fresh sardines, scaled, gutted,
boned and headless (see page 202)

Pre-heat the oven to gas mark 4, 180°C (350°F). Blanch the sliced onion in boiling water for 30 seconds then drain and transfer it to cold water. Drain and dry it thoroughly on kitchen paper. Heat half the oil and fry the onion gently for about 6 minutes until golden brown. Add the wine and boil off the alcohol for about 2 minutes. Stir in the passata and season to taste with salt and pepper. Bring to the boil, cover and simmer for about 15 minutes.

Meanwhile, mix together the breadcrumbs and fennel seeds. Spoon half the tomato sauce over the bottom of an ovenproof dish. Top with half the sardines then make a layer of half the fennel and breadcrumbs. Repeat with more sauce, sardines and breadcrumbs. Dribble the remaining oil over the top and bake in the oven for about 30 minutes before serving.

Rombo al Forno
Baked Brill

*I think brill is a delicious fish which
should be used much more frequently.
It is wonderfully white and pure and
is very easy to fillet and serve.
This is an easy way of baking the fish after it
has been marinated in the herbs and oil to
give it moisture and flavour.*

SERVES 6

1.5 kg (3 lb 4 oz) brill, scaled and gutted
4–5 sprigs fresh parsley
2–3 bay leaves
8–9 tablespoons olive oil
salt
freshly ground black pepper
2 tablespoons plain white flour
1 lemon, sliced into thin rounds

Lay the fish in a shallow bowl, cover with the parsley, bay leaves and half the oil and leave to stand in the fridge for about 2 hours. Remove the fish from the oil, sprinkle with salt and pepper and coat with flour. Heat the remaining oil in a flameproof dish until just sizzling then add the fish and seal on both sides. Transfer to the oven and bake for about 30 minutes, basting occasionally. Arrange the fish on a warmed serving platter, garnish with the lemon slices and serve at once.

Seafood

I FRUTTI DI MARE, the fruits of the sea, are very much a part of Italian cuisine. Whether they are eaten on their own, with pasta or in a risotto, they feature strongly as one of Italy's best loved specialities. Although various health problems related to eating seafood have arisen from time to time over the last decade, this has meant that the quality control system and hygiene standards of these goods have now improved enormously.

Mussels are now farmed in specifically designated areas where the quality of the water is regularly tested. The average mussel filters an amazing amount of water in the course of a day, so it is of vital importance that the water should be as edible as the mussel itself! In some areas, the mussels are taken to special tanks for ultraviolet treatment. This sounds dramatic, but is actually very simple. The mussels are tipped into the tanks and left there overnight. Meanwhile, water is pumped into the tanks from a long distance out to sea. The water is subjected to ultraviolet light as it enters the tanks, thus making it completely sterile. The mussels filter the sterile water overnight and are sold the following day. I came across this method in Puglia, where the locals are about as obsessed with the breeding and eating of all manner of shellfish as you can get, most of which they prefer to eat raw with just a squeeze of lemon juice. Personally, I think you need to have the digestive system of a born and bred Barese to be safely able to enjoy a mussel which has been fished out of the harbour at Brindisi, but I know it is considered locally to be a very special delicacy.

Long gone are the days of the delectable *dattero di mare*, the sea date, which looks like a long, thin, brown mussel and tastes so wonderful. When I was a child, we would dive for them off the rocks, dragging stones up to

Cipolline Glassate al Burro

SEE PAGE 255

Spinaci con Groviera e Prosciutto

SEE PAGE 245

the surface and smashing them open on the nearest flat surface. Sea dates burrow into the heart of stones lying on the ocean floor, moving on to bigger stones as they grow larger. They are apparently capable of covering very long distances in this fashion. Nowadays they are a protected species, so you cannot fish for them at all. Perhaps somebody ought to start up a sea date farm alongside a mussel farm!

Oysters are not as common in Italy, although there are some around. The traditional way to eat an oyster is simply to open it up, squeeze a little lemon juice over it, watch it wince, open your mouth and swallow it! I actually prefer to eat them lightly cooked, and I have given you two recipes for cooked oysters in this chapter.

In general terms, it is the smaller varieties of shellfish which tend to be more popular. *Arselle, vongole, vongole di venere*, these are all small shellfish which you are likely to be able to buy in the fish markets of Puglia and Sardinia, along with many others whose names I would not recognise. Puglia and Sardinia are, in my opinion, the two areas of Italy most visibly and obviously dedicated to the enjoyment of seafood. However, there are other parts of the country where they are also very popular. The ubiquitous Spaghetti alle Vongole, for example, is a dish which originated in Naples. This area is also very good for seafood, although localised pollution problems have given rise to concern from time to time.

Crab is extremely popular in northern Italy, particularly in the Veneto and Friuli Venezia Giulia. Further south it is almost unknown, although lobster and crayfish are available, especially in Sardinia.

To my mind, there is absolutely nothing to beat a huge bowl of freshly cooked mussels, flavoured with tomatoes and garlic, tipped out on to a bed of toasted ciabatta bread. My rule for *frutti di mare* is that once you have established (as well as you can) that they are not going to make you ill once they have been cooked with love and care, once you have assembled your friends around the table with you to enjoy them and have chilled the Greco di Tufo to just the right degree of cold... just relax, linger over them, and enjoy!

BUYING FRESH SEAFOOD

Wherever you are buying seafood and whatever type of seafood it may be, the most important aspect of all is that it should be as fresh as possible and that the water from whence it came should be as pollution- and

PREPARING OYSTERS

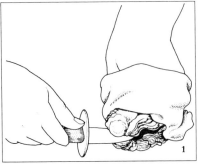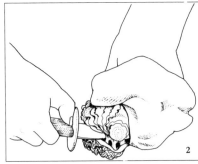

Scrub off and rinse the outside shell of the oysters if necessary. Wear a thick glove or wrap a cloth securely around the hand which will hold the oyster and grasp it firmly, flat side up. Insert a short-bladed knife into the hinge of the shell and wiggle it around gently to open the shell making sure you do not lose any of the liquor (1). When you have the shell open, insert a small sharp knife to prise the flesh of the oyster away from the inside of the shell both top and bottom (2). When this is done, prise off the top shell and discard it. Leave the oyster and the remaining liquor in the bottom shell, but flick off any splinters of shell which may have fallen on to the shellfish. The oyster is then ready to eat as it is, or to be cooked.

disease-free as possible. The shellfish should also be alive when you buy them whenever possible, although this doesn't apply to scallops.

Check with your fishmonger where they are from, as he will be able to tell you if they have been through a purification tank or if the water where they were farmed is clean. Any bivalve, such as an oyster or mussel, should clam up tightly when it is tapped. It should feel heavy and have a pleasant smell.

PREPARING MUSSELS

If you are not sure how to prepare mussels for cooking, refer to page 30.

PREPARING CLAMS

Before you cook with clams, soak them for several hours or overnight in fresh water, changing the water frequently as the clams filter out the mud and clean themselves. Finally, give them a thorough rinse and scrub under cold running water.

PREPARING SQUID

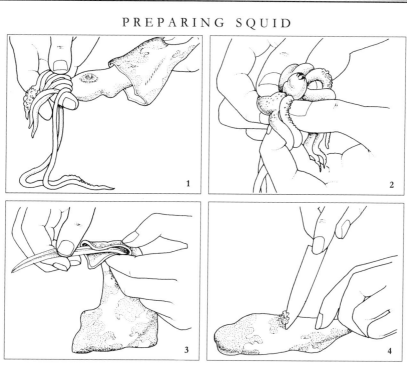

You will often be able to buy squid ready prepared, either fresh or frozen. However, if they aren't, here's how to do it. Pull the head and all the innards out of the body sac (1). Using sharp scissors, cut off the tentacles and take the sharp beak out of the centre of the tentacles (2). Throw away the head and innards. Wash the body sac thoroughly under running water. Pull out and discard the quill (3) and scrape off the membrane which covers the sac (4). Cut off the two side fins. The body sac, the two side fins and the tentacles are all edible. The squid is now ready for use. The sac can be left whole and stuffed, or sliced into rings.

Scampi Arrosto

Roasted King Prawns

*You should make this dish with raw prawns if
you can get hold of them as this is
the only way to get the really sweet flavour of
the fish blending with the savoury ham.*

SERVES 6

1.5 kg (3 lb 4 oz) raw king prawns
4 tablespoons cognac
150 g (5 oz) fatty prosciutto crudo, thinly sliced
a handful of fresh sage leaves
3 tablespoons very fine dried breadcrumbs
salt
freshly ground black pepper
1 lemon, cut into wedges

Remove and discard the heads and shells from the prawns. Put the prawn tails into a bowl and pour over the cognac. Leave to marinate for 1 hour. Wrap each prawn in a small slice of fatty prosciutto. Thread the wrapped prawns on to wooden skewers with a sage leaf between each one. Place them on a grill pan under a medium grill for a few minutes until the fat begins to run on the prosciutto. Sprinkle with breadcrumbs and turn the skewers. Continue to grill until the breadcrumbs are brown and crispy then arrange the skewers on a warmed serving platter, season to taste with salt and pepper and serve garnished with lemon wedges.

Cozze alla Marinara
Mussels with White Wine Sauce

A lovely, rich, creamy dish of mussels!
Make sure you clean them carefully before you begin (see page 30).
Serve them with plenty of crusty bread with which to mop up the sauce.

Serves 6

2 kg (4 lb 6 oz) live mussels, scrubbed and bearded
1 tablespoon olive oil
1 tumbler dry white wine
7 peppercorns
75 g (3 oz) unsalted butter
50 g (2 oz) plain white flour
400 ml (14 fl oz) milk
salt
freshly ground black pepper
3 tablespoons chopped fresh parsley

Place the mussels in a wide shallow pan with the oil, cover and place over a medium heat for about 5 minutes, shaking the pan from time to time to help distribute the heat and open up all the mussels. Remove from the heat and discard any mussels that have not opened. Reserve the cooking liquid. Remove the top shells from the mussels and place the shells containing the mussels on a large warmed serving platter and keep them warm.

Meanwhile, pour the wine into a small saucepan and add the peppercorns. Bring to the boil and leave to simmer over a low heat until it has reduced by half. Remove from the heat and set aside. Melt two-thirds of the butter in a small saucepan until foaming. Tip in the flour and stir together briskly until smooth. Pour in all the milk and whisk vigorously to prevent any lumps. Simmer over a low heat for about 20 minutes, stirring almost constantly, until the sauce no longer tastes of raw flour. Season to taste with salt and pepper. Strain the wine and the mussel cooking liquid into the sauce and blend thoroughly. Remove from the heat and gradually whisk in the remaining butter. Pour the sauce over the mussels and sprinkle with parsley before serving.

Ostriche alla Diavola
Creamy,
Spicy Oysters

If you are like me and prefer your oysters to be cooked rather than raw,
then this is the dish for you. I have described how to open them on page 226.
It is a special occasion dinner-party recipe, using nutmeg and cayenne,
both of which work incredibly well with the fishy flavour of the oysters.

SERVES 6

24 live oysters, scrubbed
25 g (1 oz) plain white flour
25 g (1 oz) unsalted butter
120 ml (4 fl oz) single cream
a pinch of freshly grated nutmeg
a pinch of cayenne pepper
salt
1 tablespoon olive oil
3 tablespoons fresh breadcrumbs

Open all the oysters and reserve the liquid. Remove the oysters from their shells and discard the flat shells. Arrange the concave shells on an ovenproof serving dish. Put the oysters into a small saucepan, pour over their juice and put them over a medium heat until just boiling. Remove from the heat, cover tightly and put aside for 3 minutes then remove them from the saucepan.

Meanwhile, melt the butter until foaming. Tip in the flour and whisk together until smooth then add the cream and 120 ml (4 fl oz) of the oyster liquid. Make up the difference with dry white wine if necessary. Bring to a simmer and simmer for about 20 minutes until the sauce is thick and creamy and no longer tastes of raw flour. Season to taste with nutmeg, cayenne and salt. Pre-heat the oven to gas mark 5, 190°C (375°F).

Heat the oil and fry the breadcrumbs briefly until crisp. Tip the oysters into the sauce then spoon one oyster plus sauce into each concave shell and coat in a thin layer of breadcrumbs. Heat through in the oven for about 6 minutes then serve at once.

Vongole e Piselli in Intingolo
Stewed Clams and Peas

*Be careful when using fresh live clams as they may be rather muddy.
I like to be sure, so I leave them in buckets of water
(preferably clean sea water if I am by the coast)
for several hours or even overnight, changing the water frequently
as the clams squirt out their mud and filter themselves clean.
A good rinsing under running water finishes off the job.*

SERVES 6

1.5 kg (3 lb 4 oz) live clams, soaked and scrubbed
1 large onion, peeled and thinly sliced
3 tablespoons olive oil
1 tablespoon tomato purée
9 tablespoons warm water
1.5 kg (3 lb 4 oz) shelled fresh peas or frozen petits pois
salt
freshly ground black pepper

Keep the clams in cold clean water until required. Fry the onion in the oil for about 6 minutes until soft and golden brown. Stir in the tomato purée and water then add the peas. Bring to the boil, cover and simmer for about 10 minutes until the peas are soft.

Meanwhile, drain and rinse the clams very carefully. Put them in a wide shallow pan, cover and place over a medium heat for about 5 minutes, shaking the pan from time to time to help distribute the heat and open up all the clams. Remove from the heat and discard any clams that have not opened. Remove the clams from their shells and add them to the pea mixture. Strain the remaining liquid through a muslin cloth into the peas. Season to taste with salt and plenty of pepper, heat through for a few minutes and serve.

Aragosta Arrosto
Roast Lobster

Loster is the ultimate treat for me!
This is a recipe which makes the most of
the flavour and texture of this delicious fish.
If you can get hold of those huge American lobster tails,
so much the better.

SERVES 6

1 x 1.5 kg (3 lb 4 oz) lobster
$1/2$ teaspoon English mustard
2 tablespoons chopped fresh parsley
a pinch of dried oregano
salt
freshly ground black pepper
5–6 tablespoons olive oil
1 tablespoon melted unsalted butter
5 tablespoons fresh white breadcrumbs
2 lemons, cut into wedges

Pre-heat the oven to gas mark 7, 220°C (425°F). Cut the lobster in half lengthways and remove all the tail meat in 2 sections. Arrange the tails side by side in a shallow ovenproof dish. Mix together the mustard, parsley and oregano and season to taste with salt and pepper. Add half the oil and the melted butter. Spread this mixture over the top of the lobster tails and cover carefully with the breadcrumbs. Dribble the remaining oil over the top and bake in the oven for about 9 minutes until heated through. Serve at once.

Gamberetti alla Crema
Creamy Prawns

A perfectly simple, delicious way of serving prawns.
As with all prawn dishes,
it tastes so much better if you have started off
with fresh raw prawns.
As an alternative to serving it with plain boiled rice,
you could also serve it on a bed of
tagliatelle dressed with melted butter.

SERVES 6

500 g (1 lb 2 oz) peeled prawns
1 tumbler single cream
100 g (4 oz) unsalted butter
2 tablespoons chopped fresh parsley
salt and white pepper

Put the prawns into a saucepan with the cream and butter. Heat through gently for about 5 minutes, stirring frequently, then add the parsley and season to taste with salt and pepper. Serve at once on a bed of plain boiled rice.

Fritto di Gamberi
e Seppie
Deep-fried Prawns
and Squid

This is a simpler version of the classic Fritto Misto,
which uses all kinds of other fish such as baby sole,
whitebait and baby red mullet.
There is nothing to stop you adding other fish according to
your mood or what is available.
If you buy fresh squid,
refer to page 227 for information on how to prepare it.

SERVES 6

4 tablespoons plain white flour
2 pinches of salt
olive oil for deep-frying
300 g (11 oz) peeled large prawns
300 g (11 oz) unpeeled large prawns
300 g (11 oz) squid rings
1 lemon, cut into wedges

Mix together the flour and salt. Heat the oil in 2 frying pans until a small square of bread dropped into it sizzles instantly. Gently toss the seafood in the seasoned flour and shake off any excess. Tip the prawns into one pan and the squid into the other and fry for about 7 minutes until crisp and golden. Remove from the pans with a slotted spoon and drain on kitchen paper. Arrange on a warmed serving platter, garnish with the lemon wedges and serve at once.

Seppie
alla Napoletana
Stewed Squid
with Garlic
and Tomato

*A real southern dish using all kinds of contrasting flavours
such as sultanas, olives, passata and garlic,
the result is a deliciously gutsy fish casserole with
lots of flavour and texture.
I have described how to prepare squid on page 227.*

SERVES 6

1 kg (2 lb) squid rings
2 cloves garlic, peeled and lightly crushed
4 tablespoons olive oil
500 g (1 lb 2 oz) passata
salt
freshly ground black pepper
a handful of pine kernels
a handful of black olives, stoned
a handful of sultanas
12 small slices ciabatta bread, toasted
2 tablespoons chopped fresh parsley

Dry the squid rings with care. Fry the garlic in the oil for about 4 minutes until golden brown then remove the garlic from the pan, add the passata and season to taste with salt and pepper. Add the pine kernels, olives and sultanas and stir well then add the squid rings. Bring to a simmer, cover and simmer for about 30 minutes until the squid is completely tender. Add a little water if the sauce appears to be drying out.

Arrange the toast on a warmed serving platter and spoon over the cooked squid and sauce. Sprinkle with parsley and serve at once.

Cozze all'Aglio
Mussels
in Garlic

I think the flavour of garlic is perfect with mussels,
so I really enjoy this dish.
You can, of course, cut down the amount of garlic if you prefer.
Make sure you clean the mussels thoroughly before you start (see page 30).
Serve the dish with plenty of crusty bread and chilled white wine.

SERVES 6

2 kg (4 lb 6 oz) live mussels, scrubbed and bearded
4 cloves garlic, peeled and sliced
a handful of fresh parsley, chopped
1 wine glass dry white wine
2 lemons, quartered
salt
freshly ground black pepper

Place the mussels in a wide shallow pan with the garlic, parsley, wine and lemons and season to taste with salt and pepper. Cover and place over a medium heat for about 5 minutes, shaking the pan from time to time to help distribute the heat and open up all the mussels. Remove from the heat and discard any mussels that have not opened. Stir well, then transfer the mussels to a warmed serving bowl and serve at once.

Ostriche, Capesante e Cozze Gratinate

Grilled Oysters, Mussels and Scallops

---

*Any combination of bivalves is suitable for this dish;
you can use razor shells or anything else
you can find and which you enjoy.
Try to stick to the larger shellfish, however,
as the recipe isn't worth the trouble with tiny little
molluscs such as clams.
See pages 30 and 226 for preparation of mussels and oysters.*

SERVES 6

6 live oysters, scrubbed
18 live mussels, scrubbed and bearded
6 live scallops, scrubbed
6 live queen scallops, scrubbed
4 tablespoons fresh white breadcrumbs
2 tablespoons chopped fresh parsley
3 tablespoons olive oil
1 teaspoon grated lemon rind
2 tablespoons dry white wine
salt
freshly ground black pepper

Open the oysters and place the oysters and liquor in a small saucepan. Heat until just boiling then remove from the heat and cover. Place the mussels in a wide shallow pan, cover and place over a medium heat for about 5 minutes, shaking the pan from time to time to help distribute the heat and open up all the mussels. Remove from the heat and discard any mussels that have not opened. Remove the top shells from the mussels and arrange them in their half shell in the grill pan. Return the oysters to their concave shells and place them in the grill pan. Open the scallops and queen scallops and arrange them in the grill pan on their rounded shells.

Mix together the breadcrumbs, parsley, oil, lemon rind, wine, salt and pepper to make a spreadable paste. Smear this over the molluscs and drizzle a little more oil over the top if they appear a bit dry. Flash them all under a very hot grill for about 4 minutes and serve at once.

Vegetables

NOTHING EPITOMISES the diet of Italy quite so well as the marvellously colourful array of vegetable recipes. There are more recipes in which vegetables feature as a central or essential ingredient than any other category. If you wander round a market or go to a real Italian greengrocer, you will be dazzled by the colours and smells of the produce on offer. Tomatoes of every hue of red and in all kinds of shapes and sizes. Massive, fleshy, sweet and juicy peppers and tiny fiery red, flame-like *peperoncinos*. Long and thick braids of onions with red, white or golden skins and lumpy, swelling garlic bulbs of silver and violet. Mounds of green vegetables of every variety, from the huge range of lettuce leaves right through to the long thin strong-smelling black cabbage.

All these marvellous colours, flavours and smells are cooked in a myriad of ways to create dishes which are not only spectacular to look at and taste delicious, but are packed full of vitamins and goodness. When we were children, anybody who looked a bit peaky would immediately be given a diet of boiled spinach, swiss chard or some other sweet green vegetable sprinkled with lemon juice and olive oil.

If you want to create an authentic Italian meal, the vegetables will usually accompany the main course as a side dish. There will normally be only one vegetable and then there will probably be a green or mixed salad as well. But, of course, vegetables might also be part of the antipasto or be an integral part of the pasta sauce. They could be combined with rice and stock to make a risotto. Just because the Italians don't normally serve three or four vegetables with their main course doesn't mean they are not a part of the meal.

Vegetables have a very important role to play in marking the passage of the seasons. Nowadays, supermarkets seem to stock just about everything at any time of the year, and although this does have advantages, I think there are disadvantages as well. Having vegetables which are only available for a brief period whilst they are in season and plentiful means that there is always something to look forward to. For example, if you have eaten frozen peas all winter long, you will appreciate the first of the fresh peas in their pods so much more.

In Italy, seasonal produce tends to be respected a little more than in Britain, although watery greenhouse tomatoes and similar tasteless offerings can be found all year round. I would prefer to use a frozen vegetable out of season and cook it with flair and imagination, rather than to use a financially over-inflated imported vegetable.

There are many vegetables, of course, which seem to have no real season, such as carrots, celery, potatoes and many others. Potatoes, by the way, should be considered a real vegetable, not a staple food. There is an awful lot of life in this humble tuber which goes far beyond the chip, and I would very much like to see more restaurants and home cooks experimenting with the huge variety of potato recipes which are available. I cannot for the life of me understand why the world has gone so chip crazy! *Patate fritte* are delicious, particularly when soaked in several changes of cold water and rubbed dry, then tipped into sizzling hot olive oil flavoured with a branch of rosemary and a couple of whole garlic cloves. But you can have too much of a good thing!

Pulses are also extremely important in Italian cuisine. In fact, the marvellous combination of fresh vegetables with pasta and a single or a combination of pulses is probably the epitome of the most healthy aspect of the Mediterranean diet. Borlotti beans are sold fresh in all Italian markets and greengrocers. Like peas, they simply need shelling and cooking, avoiding the need to pre-soak and pre-boil. All over the country, beans, lentils and chick peas are cooked and eaten in all sorts of imaginative recipes. To me they are much more part of Italian culinary tradition than the expensive and somewhat strange selection of so-called baby vegetables which are now available.

Ceci al Pomodoro SEE PAGE 254

(Overleaf) Insalata del Fattore
SEE PAGE 247

Budino di Pesche

SEE PAGE 269

Peperoni Arrosto
Roasted
Peppers

This is a dish which typifies the strong,
gutsy flavours of the cooking of southern Italy.
Usually part of an antipasto dish,
it should be served with lots of crusty bread to
mop up the juices.

SERVES 6

6 peppers, any colour
salt
6 tablespoons olive oil
3 cloves garlic, peeled and chopped
3 tablespoons chopped fresh parsley
freshly ground black pepper
6 canned anchovy fillets in oil, drained and
sliced in half lengthways (optional)

Bring a large pot of salted water to the boil, toss in the peppers and blanch them for about 30 seconds. Drain the peppers and put them separately into food bags. Close the bags loosely and put them aside for 5 minutes. Take the peppers out of the bags and rub off the outer skin with a cloth. Halve the peppers and remove all the seeds and membranes. Cut them into wide strips and lay them on a grill pan. Brush with oil and sprinkle with garlic, parsley, salt and pepper. Grill on one side for about 5 minutes until slightly blackened and piping hot. Decorate with the anchovy fillets, if liked.

Serve hot or cold with extra oil for those who like it.

Pomodori col Riso
Tomatoes
Stuffed with Rice

*I actually prefer these tomatoes cold and
I like to take them on picnics to eat with salads and bread.
They make a marvellously light, fresh tasting lunch.*

SERVES 6

6 large, ripe marmande or beefsteak tomatoes
150 g (5 oz) cooked long-grain rice
1 tablespoon dried oregano
2 tablespoons pine kernels
1 tender stick celery, finely chopped
9 tablespoons olive oil
2 teaspoons sugar
salt
freshly ground black pepper

Pre-heat the oven to gas mark 3, 170°C (325°F). Slice the tops off the tomatoes and keep them to one side to use as lids. Scoop out and reserve all the insides and turn the tomatoes upside down to drain for about 15 minutes. Then line them up in a lightly oiled ovenproof dish. Divide the rice evenly between the tomatoes, add a little oregano, a few pine kernels and some celery to each one. Drizzle most of the remaining oil into the tomatoes and finish off with a sprinkling of sugar, salt and pepper.

Push the reserved tomato pulp through a food mill or sieve and divide this evenly between the tomatoes. Put on the tomato lids and pour the remaining oil on top of the lids. Sprinkle again with salt, cover loosely with foil and bake in the oven for about 1 hour. Serve hot or cold.

Sedani al Forno
Baked Celery

*This is an ideal dish for a light easy lunch
which doesn't fill you up too much.
Serve it with a green salad and some crusty bread.*

SERVES 6

1 kg (2 lb) celery
salt
75 g (3 oz) unsalted butter
1 large onion, peeled and chopped
1 slice prosciutto crudo,
chopped into julienne strips
$1/2$ teaspoon beef extract
75 g (3 oz) Groviera or
Gruyère cheese, grated

Pre-heat the oven to gas mark 5, 190°C (375°F). Trim the celery very thoroughly and cut all the sticks into 10 cm (4 in) lengths. Wash carefully and strip any strings out of the harder sticks. Bring a large pot of salted water to the boil and boil the celery for about 5 minutes. Drain it thoroughly. Melt half the butter in a large, deep frying pan and fry the onion and prosciutto for about 5 minutes until soft. Stir in the celery and beef extract and fry for 8 minutes. Transfer the mixture to an ovenproof dish and sprinkle with the Groviera or Gruyère. Melt the remaining butter and pour it over the celery. Bake in the oven for about 5 minutes until the cheese has melted.

Zucchine *Fritte Dorate* Golden Fried Courgettes

*A good recipe for showing off the sweet flavour
and firm texture of fresh courgettes,
this is excellent with other deep-fried dishes such as
Fritto di Gamberi e Seppie (page 234).*

SERVES 6

6 courgettes
olive or sunflower oil for deep-frying
2 tablespoons plain white flour
2 eggs, beaten
salt

Cut the courgettes crossways into 13 cm (5 in) pieces then slice them lengthways into thick strips, cutting off a strip of the seeded part. Heat the oil until a square of bread dropped into it sizzles instantly. Toss the courgettes in flour, then in the egg and then fry them in the oil in batches. Fry for a few minutes until golden brown and crispy, then drain on kitchen paper and sprinkle with salt. Serve at once.

Spinaci con Groviera e Prosciutto

Spinach with Groviera Cheese and Ham

*Another deliciously simple dish,
this works well just on its own as a light lunch,
perhaps with some bread and a tomato salad.*

SERVES 6

2 kg (4 lb 6 oz) spinach
100 g (4 oz) unsalted butter
1 small tumbler milk
salt
100 g (4 oz) ham, sliced into strips
100 g (4 oz) Groviera or
Gruyère cheese, grated
50 g (2 oz) Parmesan cheese, freshly grated

Pre-heat the oven to gas mark 4, 180°C (350°F). Steam the spinach for a few minutes until just cooked then drain and squeeze it dry and chop it coarsely. Heat half the butter in a deep frying pan, add the spinach and mix together then add the milk and season to taste with salt. Use the remaining butter to grease an ovenproof dish. Tip the spinach into the dish, sprinkle with the ham and Groviera or Gruyère, then cover with the Parmesan. Bake in the oven for about 8 minutes until the cheese melts. Serve at once.

Insalata
Casalinga
Simple Salad

A lovely fresh salad with plenty of strong flavours,
this makes a very good summer lunch or supper dish,
especially if it is served with
a selection of different cured meats.

SERVES 6

1 medium-sized stale white roll
1 onion, peeled and sliced
1 head cos lettuce, shredded
2 firm, slightly unripe tomatoes, sliced
a handful of black or green olives, stoned
a handful of salted capers, rinsed and dried
6 leaves fresh basil, torn into shreds
4 tablespoons chopped fresh parsley
2 hard-boiled eggs, chopped
4 tablespoons olive oil
1 tablespoon red wine vinegar
salt
freshly ground black pepper

Cover the bread with cold water and leave to soak for about 35 minutes. Drain the bread and squeeze it dry then put it into the bottom of a large salad bowl. Add the onion, lettuce, tomatoes and olives and mix together. Add the capers, basil, parsley and eggs and mix again. Sprinkle with the oil and wine vinegar and season to taste with salt and pepper. Mix it all together once again and serve at once.

Insalata del Fattore
Farmer's Salad

*A salad with a difference! Tuna fish,
green beans and onions make up this
very strongly flavoured salad.
It is best made with fresh green beans
rather than frozen ones.*

SERVES 6

150 ml (5 fl oz) red wine vinegar
a handful of fresh basil leaves,
torn into small pieces
3 tablespoons chopped fresh parsley
1 small onion, peeled and very finely chopped
1 clove garlic, peeled and crushed
100 g (4 oz) canned tuna in oil,
drained and flaked
750 g (1 lb 10 oz) green beans
6 salted anchovies, boned, rinsed,
dried and chopped
5 tablespoons olive oil
freshly ground black pepper

Pour the vinegar into a large salad bowl, mix in the herbs and leave to stand.
Put the onion into a napkin and plunge the napkin into cold water to rinse
the onion. Remove it from the water and squeeze it dry, then mix the onion,
garlic and tuna into the vinegar and herbs. Bring a saucepan of water to the
boil, toss in the beans and boil for about 5 minutes until just tender but still
crisp. Drain them well then add them to the salad bowl. Mix in the
anchovies, cover and leave the salad to cool and allow the flavours to develop
for about 4 or 5 hours, stirring occasionally. Just before serving, add the oil
and season to taste with pepper and mix together once more.

Porri in Padella
Pan-fried Leeks

Leeks need very little doing to them as long as they are fresh and full flavoured to begin with. This is just about the easiest way of preparing them. If you like, add a squeeze of lemon juice and a little grated zest just before serving.

SERVES 6

12 medium-sized leeks
salt
8 tablespoons olive oil

Cut off the green parts of the leeks and reserve them for soup. Bring a saucepan of salted water to the boil and blanch the white parts of the leeks for about 1 minute. Drain and slice the leeks into thin discs. Heat the oil in a wide deep frying pan, add the leeks and sprinkle generously with salt. Sauté the leeks for about 10 minutes until soft and lightly browned. Serve at once.

Rape
allo Zucchero
Pan-fried Turnips
with Sugar

I particularly like turnips cooked like this,
especially when served with pork dishes.
I have also tried cooking parsnips in the same way,
although I leave out the sugar as they are already so sweet.

SERVES 6

50 g (2 oz) unsalted butter
1.5 kg (3 lb 4 oz) turnips,
peeled and thickly sliced
salt
2 tablespoons icing sugar
2 tablespoons plain white flour
300 ml (10 fl oz) chicken or
vegetable stock

Melt the butter in a wide deep frying pan, add the turnips and turn them to coat them thoroughly in butter. Season to taste with salt. Mix together the sugar and flour and sprinkle over the turnips to coat them almost completely. Stir once or twice then pour over the stock, bring to the boil, cover loosely and simmer for about 10 minutes, stirring frequently. The end result should be tenderly soft turnips coated in a smooth, glossy sauce.

Broccoli alla Romana
Pan-tossed Broccoli

If you want to make this dish taste even more fiery,
use chilli oil instead of olive oil, or use a mixture of both.
For a much less spicy dish,
leave the chilli out of the dish altogether.
You can also make the same recipe using cauliflower florets,
but use garlic and lemon juice instead of chilli peppers.

SERVES 6

1.5 kg (3 lb 4 oz) broccoli,
cut into small florets
salt
5 tablespoons olive oil
3 cloves garlic, peeled and crushed
1–2 dried red chilli peppers,
de-seeded and chopped
freshly ground black pepper
1 large wine glass dry white wine

Bring a large pan of salted water to the boil and blanch the broccoli for about 3 minutes, then drain. Heat the oil in a wide deep frying pan with the garlic and chilli for about 4 minutes. Add the broccoli and toss together thoroughly. Season to taste with salt and pepper and add the wine. Cover and simmer for about 8 minutes or until the broccoli is just tender. Mix together thoroughly once more and serve hot or cold.

Carciofi alla Romana
Braised Roman Artichokes

*Artichokes take a little time to prepare and must be
dropped into water and lemon juice as soon as
possible to prevent them from going brown.
They are worth all the trouble, though,
and this is a particularly tasty way of serving them.*

SERVES 6

12 globe artichokes
1 lemon
6 cloves garlic, peeled and thinly sliced
salt
freshly ground black pepper
a small handful of fresh mint leaves, chopped
2 tumblers cold water
$1/2$ tumbler olive oil

Pre-heat the oven to gas mark 5, 190°C (350°F). Remove all the hard exterior leaves from the artichokes and cut off the sharp points of the remaining leaves. Shorten the stalks and peel them until tender. Pull open the inner leaves and scoop out the hairy choke. Pull the artichokes apart so that they appear like an open flower. Rub them all over with half the lemon and drop the prepared vegetables into a bowl of water in which the remaining half a lemon has been squeezed and is left floating. This will prevent the artichokes from turning brown.

When you are ready to cook, pull open the artichoke leaves and insert a few slices of garlic into each one. Sprinkle the insides with salt and pepper and divide the mint leaves evenly between the artichokes. Place them upright in an ovenproof dish, pour the water around and over them and sprinkle with a little more salt. Pour the oil on and around the artichokes, cover and bake in the oven for about 40 minutes, basting frequently. Serve hot or cold.

Carote
Marinate
Marinated
Carrots

*In this recipe, the carrots will need to
bathe in their marinade overnight,
after which they require no cooking at all.
Perfect for taking on picnics,
it is also an excellent dish at a barbecue when you
need a good strongly flavoured salad.*

SERVES 6

1 kg (2 lb) carrots
2 cloves garlic, peeled and chopped
1 teaspoon salt
2 dried red chilli peppers,
de-seeded and chopped
4 tablespoons white wine vinegar
5 tablespoons olive oil
1 tablespoon dried oregano

Scrape the carrots and trim them so they are even-sized. Cover them in cold water and boil them for about 15 minutes until tender but not mushy. Drain them and cut them in half lengthways then cut them into chunks. Mix together the garlic, salt, chilli peppers, vinegar and oil and pour the mixture over the carrots. Sprinkle with oregano.

Cover with foil or cling film and leave to marinate in the refrigerator at least overnight then return to room temperature before serving.

Cavolo
in Salsa d'Acciughe
Cabbage in
Anchovy Sauce

Not the lightest of vegetable dishes,
I would say this is definitely one to reserve for
a meal which is guaranteed to be followed by a long siesta!
Excellent with pork or poultry dishes,
you can serve it with anything that can take on
this very strongly flavoured dish.

SERVES 6

1 kg (2 lb) savoy cabbage, thickly shredded
4 tablespoons red wine vinegar
4 salted anchovies, boned, rinsed,
dried and chopped
1/2 tumbler olive oil
salt
freshly ground black pepper

Steam or boil the cabbage for about 5 minutes until just tender then drain. Put the wine vinegar and anchovies into a large saucepan and mix together over a low heat for about 5 minutes until the anchovies have dissolved into a smooth brown cream. Gradually stir in the oil and season to taste with salt and pepper. Add the cabbage to the anchovy sauce, stir it all together and heat through thoroughly. Serve at once.

Ceci al Pomodoro
Chick Peas with Tomatoes

Adding the bicarbonate of soda will help the chick peas to soften and will make them more digestible. This is a very good one-dish light lunch recipe, delicious with a green salad and some cheese.

SERVES 6

500 g (1 lb 2 oz) dried chick peas,
soaked overnight in cold water
2 litres (3¹/₂ pints) water
¹/₂ teaspoon bicarbonate of soda
1 large onion, peeled and finely chopped
1 clove garlic, peeled and crushed
5 tablespoons olive oil
100 g (4 oz) pancetta or smoked streaky bacon,
coarsely chopped
400 g (14 oz) canned tomatoes,
de-seeded and chopped
salt
freshly ground black pepper

Drain the chick peas then place them in a large saucepan with the water and bicarbonate of soda. Bring to the boil, cover and simmer gently for about 1 hour until tender. Meanwhile, fry the onion and garlic in the oil for about 5 minutes until soft and golden. Then add the pancetta or bacon and fry for a further 10 to 15 minutes.

Stir in the tomatoes and simmer for a further 20 minutes, stirring frequently. Season to taste with salt and pepper. Drain the chick peas and add them to the sauce. Heat through thoroughly, adding extra seasoning if required. Serve piping hot. This recipe is also delicious served cold.

Cipolline Glassate al Burro

Baby Onions Glazed in Butter

This is the ultimate dish to serve alongside
simply grilled calves' liver or
with a dish of pan-fried Italian sausages.

SERVES 6

1 kg (2 lb) small button onions or
pickling onions, peeled
50 g (2 oz) unsalted butter
salt
2 tablespoons sugar
8 tablespoons chicken or
vegetable stock

Soak the onions in cold water for about 1 hour. Drain them carefully. Melt the butter in a large saucepan and tip in the onions, making sure they lie in a single layer. Sprinkle them with salt and sugar. Cover and cook the onions over a low heat for about 30 minutes, turning frequently, until the onions are well browned all over and beginning to soften. Gradually add the stock and continue cooking for a further 10 minutes. Serve piping hot.

Fagioli alla Pancetta

Beans with Pancetta

*A delicious bean casserole with a hint of
vinegar to give the dish an extra tang,
this tastes very good with a lettuce and tomato salad.*

SERVES 6

600 g (1 lb 5 oz) haricot or borlotti beans,
soaked overnight in cold water
4 tablespoons olive oil
100 g (4 oz) pancetta or thick cut bacon, cubed
1 tablespoon red wine vinegar
salt
freshly ground black pepper
2 tablespoons chopped fresh parsley

Drain the beans, return them to a clean saucepan and cover with cold water. Bring to the boil and boil quickly for about 5 minutes. Drain and rinse the beans, cover with clean water and return to the boil. Cover and simmer gently for about 1 hour until completely tender. Do not add salt to the water until the beans are soft as the salt will toughen the skins. Keep the beans in the water until required.

Meanwhile, heat the oil and fry the bacon until crisp and browned. Mix in the wine vinegar and boil off the alcohol for about 1 minute. Remove from the heat and keep warm. Drain the beans and transfer them to a serving bowl. Season with a little salt and plenty of pepper.

Mix together and stir in the parsley. Pour over the fried bacon and all the oil, mix together thoroughly and serve at once.

Tiramisu

SEE PAGE 268

Granita di Caffè

SEE PAGE 273

Finocchi in Sugo di Carne
Fennel in a Meaty Sauce

*Normally, I like to serve fennel with just a
dusting of freshly grated Parmesan and
a little melted butter.
This is a slightly richer recipe which works
well on its own as a light supper dish.*

SERVES 6

8 fennel bulbs
100 g (4 oz) unsalted butter
salt
1 onion, peeled and chopped
2 tablespoons tomato purée
8 tablespoons water
1 teaspoon beef extract
2 tablespoons freshly grated Parmesan cheese

Pre-heat the oven to gas mark 6, 200°C (400°F). Remove any hard exterior leaves from the fennel, wash the bulbs carefully and cut them into quarters. Rinse them again. Put half the butter into a large saucepan and arrange the fennel on top. Sprinkle with salt and cover. Simmer gently for about 15 minutes until tender, adding a little water as required. Do not stir too often.

Meanwhile, melt half the remaining butter and fry the onion for about 8 minutes until golden brown. Stir in the tomato purée, water and beef extract to make a thick sauce. Simmer for about 10 minutes, stirring continuously. Transfer the cooked fennel to an ovenproof dish, pour over the tomato sauce and dot with the remaining butter. Sprinkle with the Parmesan and bake in the oven for about 8 minutes until browned and bubbling.

Melanzane Fritte Filanti
Fried Aubergines with Mozzarella

*A very useful dish for vegetarians,
this is really rather filling so don't serve it
alongside a particularly rich main course.*

SERVES 6

6 medium-sized aubergines, peeled and
cut into 5 mm (¹/₄ in) slices
3 tablespoons plain white flour
8 tablespoons olive oil
2 egg yolks
150 g (5 oz) Mozzarella cheese, diced
4 tablespoons freshly grated Parmesan cheese
salt
2 eggs, beaten
8 tablespoons fine dried breadcrumbs
olive oil for deep-frying

Rinse the aubergines and pat them dry and coat them lightly in flour. Heat the oil until sizzling and fry them briefly until just sealed on both sides. Mix together the egg yolks, Mozzarella and Parmesan and season to taste with salt. Use this mixture to sandwich together slices of aubergine to make several neat sandwiches. Coat these in the egg then in breadcrumbs. Heat the oil until sizzling then deep-fry the sandwiches for about 8 minutes until crisp and golden. Drain on kitchen paper and serve hot.

Patate Arrosto

Roast Potatoes

My favourite way of roasting potatoes,
this leaves them deliciously sweet on the inside
and crisp and salty on the outside.

SERVES 6

18 small red Romana potatoes
a handful of rock salt
6 tablespoons good quality,
strong-tasting olive oil

Pre-heat the oven to gas mark 6, 200°C (400°F). Make sure the potatoes are well washed and free of any eyes and dry them thoroughly. Spread the salt on a work surface and roll the dry potatoes in the salt, pressing slightly to make some of the salt crystals pierce the skins. Put the potatoes in a baking tray with all the remaining salt. Pour over the oil and roll the potatoes around in it to coat them completely. Bake them in the oven for about 50 minutes until tender, shaking the tray occasionally to turn them over.

Piselli alla Sarda
Sardinian Peas

Almost a pea cake,
this is a very good dish on its own for a light meal,
or it can be served with a simple fish dish.

SERVES 6

1.25 kg (3 lb) shelled fresh peas or
frozen petits pois
$^1/_2$ tumbler olive oil
1 large red onion, peeled and thinly sliced
150 ml (5 fl oz) water
salt
1 stale white roll, grated
$1^1/_2$ tumbler milk
6 eggs, thoroughly beaten
40 g ($1^1/_2$ oz) unsalted butter

Put the peas, oil, onion and water in a large saucepan, season to taste with salt and stir well. Bring to the boil, cover and simmer gently for about 30 minutes, stirring frequently and adding a little water now and again if the peas appear to be drying out. Pre-heat the oven to gas mark 5, 190°C (375°F).

Mix the grated bread into the milk then drain the bread and squeeze it dry in your hands. Blend the mixture into the beaten eggs then mix in the cooked peas. Generously butter a 20 cm (8 in) ovenproof dish, pour in the peas and level the top with the back of a spoon. Bake in the oven for about 30 minutes until set. Loosen the edges, turn out on to a warmed serving dish and serve at once.

Desserts, Fruit
and Cakes

JUST LIKE the antipasto course, *il dolce*, the dessert can be made up of ingredients which you can buy ready-made and combined with a dessert wine, which requires no cooking whatsoever. The most typical example of this is the classic Tuscan dish of *Cantuccini*, hard almond biscuits with a glass of Vin Santo, a delicious amber-coloured sweet wine. This is the best kind of dessert, a relaxing, easy-going end to a meal where nothing can go wrong. You simply serve the biscuits and the wine and let everybody dunk the biscuits into the wine as they like. There are other combinations similar to this which also work well. Whatever kind of biscuit or cake you choose, make sure it is fairly dry and crumbly. For example, a crumbly, nutty cake is delicious with chilled Prosecco or with a tiny glass of Nocino liqueur. Another idea worth trying is to serve amaretti biscuits with a coffee-flavoured or almond liqueur, or alternatively to dip them into cups of strong espresso coffee laced with brandy.

Panettone, the classic Italian Christmas cake, also makes a variety of delicious no-cook desserts. Try scooping a hollow out of the middle and filling it with really good quality ice-cream; or fold melted chocolate into whipped cream and then pour it into the hollowed-out panettone. Or you could pour piping hot chocolate sauce over each slice, or fluffy, warm zabaglione.

Gelato, ice-cream, is one of the easiest of all desserts, especially if you have not had to make it yourself! Ice-cream is much more than just a sweet to the Italians, it represents a whole way of life. To amble along the main street of any Italian town at the right time to be seen and to stare at others; to do it while languidly licking an ice-cream cornet is simply part of the scene. Ice-cream therefore becomes much more than just a dessert, it is actually part of the social activity. I think that to serve a variety of different flavoured ice-creams as a dessert to end a classic Italian meal is both authentic and extremely pleasant. The important thing is to use very good quality bought ice-cream or to make your own. Making your own is a much less daunting task since the introduction of all the new easy-to-use ice-cream-makers which are now available.

The important thing to bear in mind is that dessert is not considered such an important and focal part of the meal in Italy. Italians are quite happy to eat something very simple at the end of the meal. Fruit, or perhaps one of the combinations mentioned above, is considered satisfactory. They are often more likely to go and indulge their sweet tooth at a café or *pasticceria* where they can sit around and chat with friends, watching the world go by at the same time. Even at a restaurant, they are unlikely to order a dessert unless the restaurant happens to specialise in making desserts. Unfortunately, many restaurants in Italy now buy in their desserts ready-made, so you end up with very little variety from one establishment to another and a disappointingly uniform flavour. Fortunately, however, the many *pasticcerie*, *gelaterie* and cafés more than make up for this.

At home, a cook will prepare a dessert for her guests is she feels like it, but if she doesn't she can always nip down to her local *pasticceria* and buy something. This is quite standard practice and nobody would hold it against her – the important thing is that it should taste good, whoever made it. Of course, there are many people who love making desserts and there is a huge range of recipes available to them. In this chapter I have included as many of my favourites as possible while trying to give a fair balance between recipes that are very easy to make and those which require more expertise.

I must also mention all the many sweets and cakes which are prepared to celebrate specific occasions. Virtually every saint in Italy has a cake or a biscuit dedicated to their name. To complicate matters, there are different ways to celebrate holy days in different parts of the country! Traditionally, for example, Easter is celebrated by eating La Colomba, a dove-shaped cake sprinkled with sugar crystals which can be bought in all good grocers in a convenient box. At Carnival time, all kinds of light fritters are traditionally enjoyed. The most common are *Frappe* and *Chiacchere*. The reason for all the fried goodies is because in the old days, street sellers used to set up their kiosks in the street and the revellers could enjoy their wares on the way to or from the parties. Carnival used to mean that the cold evening air was perfumed with the scent of frying cakes and icing sugar. The tradition has lingered on in so far as every household will still fry batches of *Frappe* on Shrove Tuesday and all the festivals to celebrate a local patron saint or a village festivity will have their traditionally prepared cakes and goodies to offer to guests and friends.

Finally, I would like to say that my favourite desserts are those which are based around fresh fruit. With such a wide variety of such delicious fruit available in Italy, there is no excuse not to enjoy it. What could be more delicious than a fresh, juicy peach sliced slowly into a glass of red wine to end your meal? Or woodland strawberries dropped into a glass of ice cold Champagne? Or even a variety of fresh fruit sliced into a salad with a scoop of rich ice-cream? Even a really ripe, chilled water melon is very hard to beat. When fruit is in season, it should be enjoyed as much as possible, whether that means using it in a cooked dish or not. I also very much approve of the practice of having a really good *pasticceria* where one can buy a selection of delectable individual pastries to enjoy in the comfort of one's own home. The selection of delicious and cheap fresh fruit and a good cake shop are two things I really miss about Italy.

Sufflé di Albicocche
Apricot Soufflé

A lovely hot and light apricot soufflé with almonds,
I don't usually serve this with cream,
but a scoop of vanilla ice-cream provides an
excellent contrast in texture and flavour.

SERVES 6

350 g (12 oz) apricots
400 g (14 oz) caster sugar
1 teaspoon vanilla essence
8 egg whites, chilled
2 tablespoons unsalted butter
3 tablespoons ground almonds
2 tablespoons icing sugar, sifted

Pre-heat the oven to gas mark 4, 180°C (350°F). Put the apricots and sugar into a saucepan and poach the apricots gently until soft. Remove all the stones and sieve the mixture carefully. Leave it to cool completely. Stir in the vanilla essence. Whisk the egg whites until completely stiff and then fold them lightly but thoroughly into the apricot mixture.

Generously butter the base and sides of a 2 litre (3¹/₂ pint) soufflé dish and coat with the ground almonds. Pour in the apricot mixture and bake in the centre of the oven for about 35 minutes until well risen and fairly firm. Dust with icing sugar and serve at once.

Zabaglione
Zabaglione

Here is the most classic of all the Italian desserts.
It is not as easy to make as it looks and
it will separate very quickly if you haven't cooked it enough.
You can use an electric hand-held whisk to
speed things up a little bit.

SERVES 6

6 egg yolks
4 tablespoons cold water
6 tablespoons marsala
6 tablespoons caster sugar

Put all the ingredients into the top half of a double-boiler and whisk them all together with a balloon whisk off the heat. Fill the bottom of the double-boiler with hot but not boiling water and place the pan over a gentle heat. Whisk constantly at an even rhythm, always beating in the same direction, and keep beating for about 20 minutes until the mixture has become light, foamy and pale yellow. It should be the consistency of semi-melted ice-cream. If you undercook it, the liquid will separate from the egg yolks. If the mixture appears to be scrambling, take it off the heat immediately and beat hard until it is smooth again. Never allow the water in the bottom of the double-boiler to come to the boil. Serve warm or cold in stemmed glasses.

For extra luxury, leave the zabaglione until just cool then fold in 6 tablespoons of whipped cream and chill. It is a good idea to serve some biscuits with this dessert for a contrast in texture.

Crema
Bavarese
Bavarois
Custard

*This is the classic recipe for a marvellously rich and creamy
custard which is used in many Italian desserts,
including the delicious Budino di Frutta which follows.*

MAKES 600 ML (1 PINT)

500 ml (17 fl oz) milk
20 g ($^3/_4$ oz) sheet gelatine
200 g (7 oz) caster sugar
5 egg yolks
1 teaspoon vanilla essence

Place the milk in a saucepan and heat slowly until it reaches boiling point.
Put the gelatine into a cup and cover with cold water. Mix together the sugar,
egg yolks and vanilla essence in a separate saucepan then gradually add the
boiling milk, whisking constantly. Return the custard to a gentle heat and
continue to whisk constantly but do not allow it to come to the boil or the
eggs will scramble. As soon as the custard coats the back of a spoon after
stirring, you can take it off the heat. Take the gelatine out of the water (it
should have soaked for a good 15 minutes). Squeeze it in your hands to
remove as much water as possible. Tip the gelatine into the custard and stir it
thoroughly while it is still hot. Pour the custard into a bowl and allow it to
cool down, stirring it frequently to prevent a skin from forming on the top as
it cools. Use as directed in the recipe.

Budino
di Frutta
Fruit
Pudding

*This is really a sort of fruit trifle finished off
with the delicious creamy Crema Bavarese.
You can make it especially luxurious if you make
it with strawberries soaked in maraschino.*

SERVES 6

500 g (1 lb 2 oz) peeled and chopped fresh fruit
of your choice: pears, bananas, peaches, apricots etc.
5 tablespoons white rum
2 tablespoons granulated sugar
2 teaspoons almond oil
100 g (4 oz) sponge cake, thinly sliced
2 tablespoons strawberry or apricot jam
600 ml (1 pint) Crema Bavarese (page 266)

Put the fruit, rum and sugar in a bowl and stir together. Leave to macerate
for about 30 minutes. Grease a large decorative bowl with the almond oil.
Arrange a very thin layer of the sponge on the bottom of the bowl. Cover it
with a layer of jam, cover the jam with a layer of fruit and then coat with the
crema bavarese. Continue in this way, alternating layers of sponge, jam, fruit,
custard, until you have filled the bowl and used all the ingredients. Finish
with a thick coating of Crema Bavarese.

Tiramisu
Coffee and Chocolate
Mascarpone Dessert

Currently the most fashionable of all the Italian desserts, you can make Tiramisu in individual stemmed glasses if you prefer. It is important to use good quality chocolate and coffee. You can use almost any liqueur for this wonderful dessert. I don't recommend Sambuca, but Amaretto is delicious. It is best if made a day in advance.

SERVES 4

250 g (9 oz) Mascarpone or
very rich cream cheese
4 eggs, separated
4 tablespoons caster sugar
2 teaspoons espresso coffee
100 g (4 oz) bitter cooking chocolate,
broken into small pieces
8 tablespoons weak coffee
6 tablespoons rum, brandy, Tia Maria
or other liqueur
about 20 boudoir biscuits or savoiardi
2 teaspoons cocoa powder
2 teaspoons instant coffee powder

Whisk the cheese until soft and manageable. Beat the egg yolks until pale, then whisk them into the cheese. Very gradually add the sugar to the cheese mixture, stirring and whisking constantly. Pour in the espresso coffee and mix thoroughly. Beat the egg whites until very stiff, then fold them into the egg mixture. Mix the chocolate gently into the mixture. Mix together the weak coffee and the liqueur. Dip half the biscuits in the coffee liqueur mixture one at a time and use them to line the bottom of a bowl. Pour in half the cheese mixture. Dip the remaining biscuits in the liquid and cover the cream layer with soaked biscuits. Pour over the remaining cream. Bang the dish down lightly to settle the layers. Mix the cocoa and coffee powder and sieve over the dessert. Chill for at least 3 hours, preferably overnight.

Budino di Pesche
Peach Pudding

*A pudding which is simplicity itself to make
but tastes perfectly luxurious.
Serve this chilled with sweetened whipped cream.*

SERVES 6

10 ripe peaches
1 large wine glass dry white wine
3 tablespoons granulated sugar
3 egg whites, chilled
1 tablespoon unsalted butter

Put the peaches into a saucepan with the wine and sugar. Poach slowly until
the peaches are soft enough to sieve. Take them off the heat and mix
everything together to break up the peaches then rub it all through a sieve.
Return the sieved peach mixture to the heat and allow it to boil gently to dry
out a little. When it is fairly thick (rather like jam) take it off the heat and let
it cool completely. Whisk the chilled egg whites until completely stiff. Fold
them into the peach mixture. Butter a 1 litre (1³/4 pint) smooth-sided mould
and pour in the mixture. Place the mould over a pan of hot water and cook
for about 45 minutes, never allowing the water to come to the boil. As soon
as the pudding is well set, take it off the heat, leave to cool, then turn it out
on to a dish to serve.

Budino Diplomatico freddo
Diplomats' Dessert

*Another Italian trifle-style dish,
this is very simple to make but with a marvellously
luxurious flavour and a generous hint of
cognac to make it taste very grown up!*

SERVES 6

75 g (3 oz) sultanas
1 small glass cognac
1 tablespoon caster sugar
2 teaspoons almond oil
100 g (4 oz) sponge cake or
boudoir biscuits, finely sliced
75 g (3 oz) mixed candied peel, finely sliced
3 tablespoons apricot jam
600 ml (1 pint) Crema Bavarese (page 266)

Put the sultanas in a bowl with the cognac and sugar. Leave to macerate for about 30 minutes. Oil the bottom of a serving bowl with the almond oil. Arrange a thin layer of sponge on the bottom of the bowl, scatter with a few sultanas, a little candied peel and a few knobs of jam then cover with a layer of crema bavarese. Continue layering the ingredients, ending with a thick layer of Crema Bavarese on top. Chill for 2 to 3 hours before serving.

Gelato di Cioccolato
Chocolate Ice-Cream

*There is something very satisfying about
preparing your own ice-cream,
even though there are so many good quality brands
available at the supermarket these days.
If you don't have an ice-cream machine,
I think it is well worth the investment.
Home-made ice-cream has never been easier to make.*

SERVES 6

50 g (2 oz) potato flour
400 ml (14 fl oz) milk
50 g (2 oz) butter, softened
50 g (2 oz) caster sugar
50 g (2 oz) bitter cooking chocolate
100 ml (3^1/$_2$ fl oz) double cream

Blend the potato flour and milk together in the top of a double-boiler until completely smooth. Place the boiler over hot water and stir in the butter, sugar and chocolate over a gentle heat until completely blended and smooth. Remove from the heat and blend in the cream. Leave to cool completely then pour into a freezer mould and freeze for 2 hours, mixing it thoroughly with a spatula about every 30 minutes to prevent ice crystals forming.

Alternatively you can pour the cooled mixture into an ice-cream machine and proceed as directed in the instructions.

Crema al Mascarpone Chilled Mascarpone Cream

*Mascarpone cheese is the richest,
creamiest dairy product there is!
In this dessert it is used to blend with egg yolks and
a generous dash of rum or maraschino to
make a very luxurious pudding.
You will only need to serve very small
quantities as it is very rich.*

SERVES 6

4 egg yolks
100 g (4 oz) caster sugar
4–5 tablespoons rum or maraschino
150 g (5 oz) Mascarpone cheese
12 light biscuits such as
langues de chat

Beat the egg yolks until pale yellow then gradually add the sugar. Blend in the rum or maraschino. Beat the Mascarpone until light and creamy then very lightly and carefully blend it into the egg mixture. Pour into 6 individual stemmed glasses and chill for about 2 hours before serving with light biscuits.

Granita
di Caffè
Coffee
Granita

Most cafés in Italy make delicious coffee granita
which you can languidly eat as you sit and
dream at a pavement table...
I won't promise that this one will taste quite the same,
but it is a wonderful dessert.

SERVES 6

500 ml (17 fl oz) cold water
150 g (5 oz) caster sugar
300 ml (10 fl oz) very strong black coffee
200 ml (7 fl oz) whipping cream
2 tablespoons icing sugar

Heat the water and sugar together for about 15 minutes, stirring occasionally, until it forms a smooth syrup. Stir in the coffee. Pour the mixture into a bowl or metal mould, allow to cool and freeze for at least 2 hours, stirring every 30 minutes to prevent ice crystals forming. Whip the cream, blend in the icing sugar and chill. Divide the granita into 6 stemmed glasses and cover each one with whipped cream. Serve immediately.

Torta Margherita Teatime Cake

The most basic and classic of simple tea time cakes, this is the Italian version of a plain sponge cake.

SERVES 6

3 eggs
6 egg yolks
100 g (4 oz) caster sugar
1 teaspoon vanilla essence
100 g (4 oz) plain white flour plus
extra for dusting
100 g (4 oz) potato flour
75 g (3 oz) unsalted butter, melted,
plus extra for greasing

Pre-heat the oven to gas mark 8, 230°C (450°F). Break the eggs into the top half of a double-boiler over hot water. Add the egg yolks, sugar and vanilla essence. Beat these ingredients together with a balloon whisk until the mixture is well blended and has reached blood temperature. Remove from the heat and continue to whisk constantly, lifting the whisk up high to incorporate lots of air in order to make the mixture as light and airy as possible. You must keep whisking until the mixture forms a smooth ribbon when you lift up the whisk. At this point substitute a wooden spoon for the whisk. Sift together the flour and potato flour and gradually add it to the egg mixture, stirring constantly with the wooden spoon. When all the flour has been blended in, slowly pour in the butter and mix it in gently. Butter and flour a 2 litre (3½ pint) round or rectangular cake tin. Pour in the cake mixture and bake in the centre of the oven for 5 minutes.

Open the oven door and cut a cross right across the top of the cake from side to side. Lower the temperature to gas mark 5, 190°C (375°F) and continue to bake for about 1 hour, gradually lowering the heat every 10 minutes. The cake is ready when a wooden skewer inserted into the centre comes out completely clean. Leave to cool on a wire rack before serving.

Pane Dolce alle Noci
Sweet Walnut Bread

*For a real contrast in flavours,
serve this sweet bread with some ripe Gorgonzola or
with slivers of fresh Parmesan.*

SERVES 6

500 g (1 lb 2 oz) plain white flour
2 teaspoons baking powder
100 g (4 oz) caster sugar
2 eggs
350 ml (12 fl oz) milk
a pinch of salt
150 g (5 oz) chopped walnuts
1 tablespoon unsalted butter

Pre-heat the oven to gas mark 4, 180°C (350°F). Sift the flour and baking powder together and mix in the sugar. Gradually beat in the eggs and enough milk to make a smooth texture rather like a thick batter. Add the salt and mix in the walnuts. Butter a 28 cm (11 in) loaf tin thoroughly. Pour in the cake mixture and bake in the oven for about 1 hour 20 minutes.

The cake is ready when a wooden skewer inserted into the centre comes out clean. Take it out of the oven and leave to cool before serving thinly sliced and spread with unsalted butter.

Pizza
Pasquale
Simple
Easter Cake

*This savoury cake is traditionally served with a selection of
Salame and hard-boiled eggs to celebrate Easter.
You can also add sugar and halve the amount of
flour to make a sweet version.
I have given large quantities here so that you can
feed all your Easter guests.*

SERVES 12

1 kg (2 lb) plain white flour
8 eggs
a large pinch of ground cinnamon
300 g (11 oz) Ricotta cheese
a pinch of salt
grated rind of 2 lemons
800 g (1 lb 12 oz) bread dough, risen and knocked back
2 tablespoons lard

Pile the flour on to the work surface and plunge your fist into the centre. Break the eggs into the hole and add the cinnamon, Ricotta, salt, lemon rind and bread dough. Knead all this together very thoroughly with both hands, beating the dough as you do so. When you have a single, very elastic, smooth dough which comes off the work surface in a single ball, it can be considered ready. Grease 1 or more loaf or cake tins with the lard. However many you use, please remember that the mixture must only fill the tins to just under the half-way mark. Cover loosely and place the dough in a warm place to rise for about 2 hours until it has doubled in size.

Pre-heat the oven to gas mark 4, 180°C (350°F). Bake the loaves in the oven for about 50 minutes, depending on the size of the loaves. They are ready when a wooden skewer inserted into the centre comes out clean. Serve cold or warm with sliced Salame and plenty of red wine.

Rocciata d'Assisi
Assisi Pastry

This is a deliciously fruity cake,
with marsala to lend it a very special flavour.
Serve it in thin slivers with some chilled dessert wine.

SERVES 6

250 g (9 oz) plain white flour plus extra for dusting
275 g (10 oz) caster sugar
6 tablespoons sunflower oil
a pinch of salt
175 ml (6 fl oz) water
50 g (2 oz) currants
75 g (3 oz) sultanas
100 g (4 oz) walnuts, chopped
100 g (4 oz) prunes, stoned and chopped
100 g (4 oz) dried figs, chopped
100 g (4 oz) hazelnuts, chopped
2 apples, peeled, cored and sliced
6 tablespoons marsala
100 g (4 oz) blanched almonds, cut into slivers
4 tablespoons icing sugar

Pre-heat the oven to gas mark 4, 180°C (350°F). Blend the flour with 1 table-spoon of sugar, $1^1/2$ tablespoons of oil and the salt. Add enough water to make a smooth pliable dough. Roll it out on a floured work surface until it is as thin as possible without tearing. Mix all the fruit and nuts together with the remaining sugar and blend in the marsala. Use this mixture to fill the centre of the pastry sheet. Roll the pastry up on itself to encase the fruit and nut mixture. Carefully seal the edges all round then bend the filled pastry to make a horseshoe shape. Use half the remaining oil to grease a baking sheet. Lay the pastry on top and rub the remaining oil over the surface. Bake in the centre of the oven for about 40 minutes until crisp and golden brown. Leave to cool on a wire rack then dust with icing sugar just before serving.

Torta Meringata
Meringue
Cake

*The lovely jam and meringue topping on
the light sponge make this a very unusual cake.*

SERVES 6

100 g (4 oz) unsalted butter, softened,
plus 1 tablespoon for greasing
120 g (4¹/₂ oz) caster sugar
2 eggs, separated
100 g (4 oz) plain white flour plus
1 tablespoon for dusting
1 teaspoon baking powder
3 tablespoons milk
2 egg whites, chilled
50 g (2 oz) blanched almonds, finely chopped
4 tablespoons apricot jam
4 tablespoons icing sugar

Pre-heat the oven to gas mark 4, 180°C (350°F). Cream the butter thoroughly
then blend in 100 g (4 oz) of sugar until the mixture is pale and fluffy. Blend
in the egg yolks one at a time. Mix together the flour and baking powder and
gradually sift them into the cake mixture. Add the milk to soften the mixture.
Whisk the egg whites until stiff and carefully fold them into the cake mixture.
Line, butter and flour a 20 cm (8 in) spring-loaded cake tin. Pour in the
mixture and bake in the centre of the oven for about 40 minutes. Meanwhile,
whisk the remaining egg whites until stiff and blend in the remaining sugar
and the almonds. Take the semi-cooked cake out of the oven and spread the
jam over the surface. Top with the meringue mixture and even it up with a
spatula. Lower the temperature to gas mark 3, 170°C (300°F) and return the
cake to the oven for a further 20 minutes until the meringue is crisp. Take
the cake out of the cake tin and leave on a wire rack to cool completely
before serving dusted with icing sugar.

Coffee, Aperitifs and After-Dinner Tipples

C APPUCCINO is enjoying tremendous popularity at the moment. You can even (although I can't imagine why you would want to) buy instant Cappuccino... just add hot water? Real Cappuccino, made in a bar, consists of a good, strong espresso coffee to which frothy milk is added. The ground chocolate on the top is simply an added extra.

You can also have a *Cappuccino con Panna*, which is an ordinary Cappuccino to which a mound of softly whipped, sweetened cream has been added. Some powdered chocolate can be sprinkled on top of the cream in this instance, but what you ought to know is that no self-respecting Italian would dream of drinking Cappuccino after 11.00 a.m. Cappuccino is strictly a breakfast time drink. One simply does *not* drink Cappuccino after a meal.

Caffé Espresso

Espresso coffee forms the basis for all Italian coffee. In its own right, it consists of a very small, strong and dark cup of coffee. If you like, you can have a decaffeinated version of the same thing. Italian coffee is always very highly roasted, which means that it has an extremely intensive flavour and can sometimes be bitter. Italians tend to have a little cup of espresso almost 'on the run', standing up at the bar and knocking it back when they need a quick refreshment to keep them going through the day. Often it is drunk with a cold water chaser, or even with a shot of something stronger. It is also drunk at the end of a meal, in which case sometimes cold milk can be added to it in order to smooth and soften the flavour and the effect.

CAFFÈ LUNGO

This is an espresso coffee to which more water is added to make the drink longer and slightly weaker. If the water added is cold, then it becomes a *caffè lungo tiepido.* You can also have a decaffeinated version of a *caffè lungo* and it is drunk in the same cases as espresso.

CAFFÈ DOPPIO

Not for the faint-hearted, this is a double espresso and tends to be very strong. I have found it very good for keeping me awake through long hours, but of course you can always have a decaffeinated version. This is a drink most usually ordered at the bar during the course of the day, so you would probably drink it either mid-morning or mid-afternoon.

CAFFÈ RISTRETTO

This is an espresso coffee made with less water, which makes it even darker, stronger and more concentrated. This is a drink for real coffee fanatics and needs to be made on an espresso machine by somebody who really knows what they are doing. Usually drunk either mid-morning or mid-afternoon, it can be made with decaffeinated coffee so you can order a *caffè ristretto decaffeinato, per piacere.*

CAFFÈ CORRETTO

Caffe corretto is a cup of espresso coffee (which can be *ristretto, lungo* or *doppio* as long as it's black) to which a shot of spirits has been added to make it alcoholic. Brandy, Fernet Branca, Sambuca, Amaretto, Whisky and Grappa are all drinks which are sometimes added to an espresso to make it *corretto.*

CAFFÈ FREDDO

This is an iced coffee served in a glass and consists of strong espresso coffee diluted with iced water and ice cubes or crushed ice. It is almost always made with sugar syrup added to the coffee so it tends to be quite sweet. In Italy, one would drink this in the course of the day, either mid-morning or mid-afternoon or after a meal as a cooling pick-me-up. It really serves as a summer alternative to ordinary espresso.

CAFFÉ MACCHIATO

This is a cup of espresso (either *ristretto*, *doppio* or *lungo* if you prefer it that way) to which a small drop of frothy milk has been added. The frothy milk just floats on the surface of the coffee, making a stain; hence the name, which means stained coffee. If you add cold milk it is called *caffè macchiato al latte freddo*. The distinction is necessary because ordinary cold milk will not float on the surface like the hot milk which has been frothed up.

LATTE MACCHIATO

This is the reverse of a *caffè macchiato*. It is a glass of warm or cold milk served in a tall glass with a drop of hot espresso coffee dropped on to the top to make a stain; hence the name, stained milk. If the milk is hot, it will be called *caffè caldo macchiato*. Cold milk prepared in this way is called *caffè macchiato freddo*. This is really a sort of alternative to Cappuccino, a breakfast or elevenses drink, or perhaps a bedtime toddy. It is often prepared for children to give them the flavour of coffee and make them feel more grown up.

CAFFÉLATTE

Also traditionally prepared in a tall glass, this is a combination of espresso coffee and hot milk but without the froth of the Cappuccino. Normally this is a breakfast drink with none of the fancy pretension of Cappuccino, but very weak *caffélatte* can be drunk as a bedtime toddy. When you make breakfast at home, adding home-made coffee to hot milk makes *caffélatte* but you need to go out to the bar for Cappuccino.

APERITIFS

There are lots of different types of Italian pre-dinner drinks designed to get the gastric juices flowing and set the scene for the meal to follow. Vermouth is a combination of wine and herbs and it is one of the most popular types of pre-dinner drink. The specific recipe is to this day a complete secret, but there is a school of thought which says that it is based on a recipe from Ancient Rome for a pre-dinner drink. It was called Absintium Romanum and was created by Apicius. In the old days, most of the wine produced in Italy's deep south would be shipped up to Piemonte where companies such as Martini Rossi and Cinzano would use it to make vermouth. Here are a few of my favourite aperitifs:

MARTINI ROSSO

I love this poured over ice with a slice of lemon... perfect.

MARTINI SECCO

Pour this over crushed ice with a slice of lime, or add just a dash of soda for a longer drink.

PUNT E MES

This tastes quite medicinal until you get used to it. It is delicious with ice and a slice of orange. Or you can try Fiammetta's Mess: 2 parts Punt e Mes, 1 part Martini Secco, 1 part gin, 1 part freshly squeezed lemon juice, ice – stirred not shaken.

CYNAR

Cynar is a very strange drink made with artichokes. I quite like it, but it has to be diluted with soda for my taste.

CAMPARI

Campari is a very old favourite. I love it mixed 2 parts Campari with 3 parts fresh grapefruit or orange juice, or with soda. I don't think it is very nice neat and I detest it with lemonade.

WINES

Prosecco makes a very light and pleasant pre-dinner drink, especially when the weather is hot. Non-sparkling white wine can also be served chilled before a meal, as can a very light red wine or, of course, a rosé. Some of the new types of marsala wine coming in from Italy have shaken off their sticky, dessert wine image and are emerging as tantalisingly dry and fragrant sherry-type wines to rival anything from Jerez. Vernaccia is a wine which is very similar to sherry. It comes from Sardinia and is very dry and delicious.

NIBBLES WITH APERITIFS

I think it is always nice to serve little nibbles with your aperitifs, and that doesn't have to mean a handful of peanuts or some crisps. Crostini are very good to serve as a little teasing taster, and if you must have olives then serve a variety of different ones to add interest. I think sun-dried tomatoes are nice to chew on while you wait for your food, although they can be a bit oily if you are using the type you buy in jars. If you place some sun-dried tomato paste and/or olive pâté in little bowls and serve some *grissini*, breadsticks, I think it will be easier for everybody to eat them.

AFTER-DINNER DRINKS

DIGESTIVI AMARO

A rather medicinal-tasting drink made with various herbs, amaro is reputedly very good for the digestion. It is made in various parts of Italy. In my opinion, the best brand is Averna. Fernet Branca falls into this category, as does the unbelievably fiery Unicum.

BRANDY

Italy is not a brandy-making nation so their brandy is passable without being outstanding. Vecchia Romagna and Stock are the best brands and both are quite good when added to espresso coffee.

GRAPPA

From the coarse, harsh drink of our forefathers, Grappa has evolved into a very sophisticated up-market drink which comes in a variety of flavours and in beautifully designed bottles. Basically, it is a distillation of the skins, seeds and pulp left over after the wine has been made. I think it is still largely an acquired taste, although the varieties made from sweet dessert wine grapes are easier on the palate.

SAMBUCA

As a tourist attraction, this syrupy aniseed-flavoured drink is often set alight and served flaming, with a few coffee beans as a decoration. This is completely unnecessary and does nothing to enhance the flavour of the drink. It should either be drunk straight or poured over ice. In the latter case, the drink goes cloudy.

STREGA

Named after the witches who, according to legend, used to inhabit the city of Benevento, this tastes to me rather as I would expect a witches' brew to taste! I think there are better drinks available.

Innovations

IN THIS CHAPTER, I have basically let my imagination take flight and have departed from the classics of Italian cuisine. The rest of the book contains recipes which are very much classics and most often appear in their original guises in many an Italian cookery book. The following recipes are different because they combine ingredients which are slightly more unusual, to create a new set of flavours, colours and appearance.

Generally speaking, modern eating habits call for dishes which are considerably lighter and smaller than old-fashioned large helpings. Therefore most of these dishes are extremely light and presented in relatively smaller proportions than some of the classics.

I begin with five antipasti, all of which can be served together for a complete meal or separately to begin the meal. These are followed by four pasta recipes and one risotto. It is very easy to be wild and imaginative with pasta as it is doubtless the most versatile of foods. There is then one recipe for duck breasts which is as simple as can be. This main course recipe can be combined with Insalata di Spinaci (page 287) in the antipasto category to create a healthy and wonderfully tasty combination of flavours and textures. Two very pretty and fruit-based desserts complete this short section which I hope gives you an idea as to just how excitingly different and imaginative Italian cuisine can be.

There are many young chefs all over Italy who are cooking dishes just like these. Although the concept of nouvelle cuisine never really took off in Italy, there has certainly been a desire to lighten much of the style of cooking and to give it a more up-to-date image. That is not to say that the old classics should be abandoned, far from it. Those dishes have a very definite place in Italian, and hopefully worldwide, cuisine which cannot be ignored and which has lasted the test of many decades, even centuries in some cases. But there is room for a lighter and more colourful style of Italian cooking and the recipes which follow are merely a few examples of my idea of *la cucina moderna.*

Insalata di Spinaci
Fresh Spinach Salad

*An intensely flavoured salad which is perfect for
an antipasto or as a light meal in itself.*

SERVES 4

300 g (11 oz) fresh spinach leaves
120 g (4^1/$_2$ oz) pancetta, cubed
7–8 tablespoons olive oil
200 g (7 oz) rye bread, cubed
3 teaspoons balsamic vinegar
100 g (4 oz) Parmesan cheese, freshly grated
salt
freshly ground black pepper

Arrange the washed and dried spinach leaves in a salad bowl. Fry the
pancetta for about 8 minutes until the fat runs and the pancetta is crispy.
Heat about 3 tablespoons of oil and fry the bread until crispy. Mix together
the remaining oil, balsamic vinegar and Parmesan and season to taste with
salt and pepper to make a dressing. Pour the pancetta and bread over the
spinach, pour over the dressing and serve at once.

Salvia Fritta

Deep-fried Sage Leaves

Here is the perfect recipe if you need
a surprisingly unusual and very tasty little snack to
serve with a glass of sparkling Prosecco or
other wine before a meal.

SERVES 4

32 fresh sage leaves
2 tablespoons anchovy paste
40 g (1¹/₂ oz) plain white flour
5–6 tablespoons water
salt
1 egg white, chilled
150 ml (5 fl oz) olive oil

Sandwich together pairs of sage leaves with a little anchovy paste. Beat the flour with enough water to make a batter the consistency of double cream. Season to taste with salt. Beat the egg white until stiff then fold it into the batter. Dip the leaf sandwiches into the batter to coat them. Heat the oil until sizzling and fry the sage leaf sandwiches for a few minutes until golden and crispy. Drain on kitchen paper and serve hot.

Rocciata d'Assisi

SEE PAGE 277

Torta Meringata

SEE PAGE 278

Fiori di Zucchine Ripieni
Stuffed Courgette Flowers

*Rather a fiddly antipasto, this is none the less very impressive.
As an alternative, you could omit the shallots and use
a few anchovy fillets instead of mushrooms.*

SERVES 4

20 fresh courgette flowers,
washed and dried carefully
50 g (2 oz) unsalted butter
200 g (7 oz) mushrooms, chopped
2 shallots, peeled and chopped
salt
freshly ground black pepper
175 g (6 oz) Mozzarella cheese, finely cubed
3 tablespoons freshly grated Parmesan cheese
2 eggs
2 tablespoons plain white flour
450 ml (15 fl oz) milk
olive oil for deep-frying

Open out the flowers very gently and remove the pistils inside if they are particularly large. Melt the butter and fry the mushrooms and shallots gently for about 5 minutes until soft. Season with salt and pepper. Mix together the mushrooms, Mozzarella and Parmesan. Use this mixture to fill the flowers but do not overfill them. Whisk together the eggs, flour and milk to make a smooth batter and season with a little salt. Immerse the flowers in the batter. Heat the oil until a small cube of bread dropped into the oil sizzles instantly. Take the flowers out of the batter and shake off any excess.

Drop them a few at a time into the oil and fry them for a few minutes until crisp. Drain on kitchen paper and serve hot.

Fagottini di Melanzane
Aubergine Parcels

*The wonderful minced lamb stuffing in the aubergines makes this a
rich and filling dish. Serve it as a main course with a salad or
on its own as an alternative to the pasta course.*

SERVES 4

2 aubergines, sliced lengthways into finger-thick slices
salt
1 onion, peeled and chopped
2 salted anchovy fillets, boned, rinsed, dried and chopped
4 tablespoons olive oil
2 canned tomatoes, de-seeded and chopped
12 green olives, stoned and chopped
200 g (7 oz) minced lamb
1 small wine glass dry white wine
1 clove garlic, peeled and chopped
1 dried red chilli pepper, finely chopped
freshly ground black pepper
a handful of crust-free white bread
1 tumbler milk
olive oil for brushing

Lay the aubergines in a colander and sprinkle with salt. Cover with a plate
and lay a weight on the top. Leave them to drain for about 30 minutes then
rinse and dry them. Meanwhile, fry the onion and anchovies in the oil for
about 5 minutes until soft. Stir in the tomatoes, olives, lamb and wine and
boil off the alcohol for about 2 minutes. Add the garlic and chilli peppers,
season to taste with salt and pepper, cover and simmer for about 30 minutes.
Soak the bread in the milk then squeeze it dry and mix it into the other
ingredients. Pre-heat the oven to gas mark 4, 180°C (350°F).

Arrange pairs of aubergine slices in cross shapes on a greased baking tray
and place a little of the meaty filling in the centre of each cross. Fold the 4
ends of each cross together and hold the parcels closed with cocktail sticks.
Bake in the oven for about 20 minutes until the aubergines are soft and
pulpy, brushing occasionally with oil as they cook. Serve piping hot.

Orecchiette al Mascarpone e Pomodori Secchi
Orecchiette with Mascarpone and Sun-dried Tomatoes

You can use any type of pasta you like for this dish,
but orecchiette really does do it justice.
If you can't get hold of Mascarpone, use any rich cream cheese.

SERVES 4

1 small onion, peeled and finely chopped
$^1/_2$ clove garlic, peeled and chopped
3 tablespoons olive oil
150 g (5 oz) canned tomatoes, drained,
de-seeded and chopped
salt
freshly ground black pepper
400 g (14 oz) orecchiette
100 g (4 oz) Mascarpone cheese, cubed
12 sun-dried tomatoes, chopped
4–5 leaves fresh basil

Fry the onion and garlic in the oil for about 5 minutes until soft. Stir in the tomatoes and season to taste with salt and pepper.

Meanwhile, bring a large saucepan of salted water to a rolling boil, toss in the orecchiette and give it one good stir. Cover the pan and bring the water back to the boil. Remove the lid and cook until *al dente*; brands vary but 5 minutes should be about right. Drain the orecchiette thoroughly and return it to the warm empty saucepan. Pour over the tomato sauce and toss together thoroughly. Add the Mascarpone and toss again then add the sun-dried tomatoes and toss again. Transfer to a warmed serving bowl, tear the basil leaves into pieces, scatter them on top and serve at once.

Risotto
al Melone
Melon Risotto

The flavour of this risotto is extremely unusual,
but I think it is delicious!
In Italy, risotto is often made with all kinds of fruit
such as strawberries, raspberries or cherries.

SERVES 4

1 medium-sized Charentais melon,
peeled and cubed
1 wine glass port
90 g (3¹/₂ oz) unsalted butter
1 small onion, peeled and finely chopped
300 g (11 oz) risotto rice
1 litre (1³/₄ pints) chicken stock
100 g (4 oz) prosciutto crudo, finely chopped
25 g (1 oz) Parmesan cheese, freshly grated
freshly ground black pepper

Place the melon in a bowl, pour over the port and put aside to macerate. Melt half the butter and fry the onion for about 5 minutes until soft but not browned. Add the rice and stir it around until it is heated through and shining. Then add the first ladleful of stock. Stir until the stock has been absorbed, then add some more. Always add small amounts and always wait for the rice to absorb the stock before you add any more. After 10 minutes, drain and reserve the melon and stir the port into the rice. After a further 10 minutes, add the melon and prosciutto to the rice, stir and remove from the heat. Add the remaining butter and the Parmesan and season to taste with freshly ground black pepper. Cover and leave to rest for 5 minutes before transferring to a warmed serving platter.

Conchigle Fuxia
Fuchsia
Pasta Shells

A very easy pasta dish, this has a fabulous colour and great flavour.
You can use any shape of pasta you like,
although I would recommend you stick to something short
and stubby rather than a long shape such as spaghetti.

SERVES 4

1 onion, peeled and finely chopped
4 tablespoons sunflower oil
40 g (1^1/$_2$ oz) unsalted butter
2 medium-sized boiled beetroot,
finely cubed, juice reserved
1 wine glass dry white wine
200 ml (7 fl oz) single cream
salt
3 teaspoons lemon juice
400 g (14 oz) pasta shells
25 g (1 oz) Parmesan cheese, freshly grated
3 tablespoons chopped mixed fresh basil,
parsley, chervil and chives

Fry the onion gently in the oil and butter for about 5 minutes until soft. Add the beetroot and all the juice. Add the wine and boil off the alcohol for about 2 minutes. Purée the beetroot mixture, gradually adding the cream. Season with a little salt. Return the sauce to the heat and heat through for a few seconds, stirring in the lemon juice.

Meanwhile, bring a large saucepan of salted water to a rolling boil, toss in the pasta shells and give them one good stir. Cover the pan and bring the water back to the boil. Remove the lid and cook until *al dente*; brands vary but 10 minutes should be about right. Drain the pasta carefully and return it to the warm empty saucepan. Pour over the sauce and mix together thoroughly. Add the Parmesan and mix again. Transfer to a warmed serving bowl, sprinkle with the herbs and serve at once.

Fazzoletti al Basilico

Basil Pasta Squares

*Although this is a bit fiddly to prepare,
it looks very impressive and tastes fantastic;
a very unusual but truly wonderful pasta dish.*

SERVES 4

2 tablespoons chopped fresh parsley
a handful of fresh basil
3 large leaves fresh spinach, shredded
25 g (1 oz) Parmesan cheese, freshly grated
3 tablespoons sunflower oil
250 ml (8 fl oz) double cream
50 g (2 oz) pine kernels
salt
freshly ground black pepper
500 g (1 lb 2 oz) plain white flour
5 eggs
25 g (1 oz) unsalted butter

Put the parsley, half the basil, the spinach, Parmesan, oil, cream and half the pine kernels in a food processor and process for about 40 seconds until smooth and greenly creamy. Season to taste with salt and pepper and set aside until required. Chop the remaining basil. Pile the flour on to a work surface and plunge your fist into the centre to make a hole. Break the eggs into the hole. Using your fingers, beat the eggs roughly into the flour then use your hands to knead everything together thoroughly until you have a smooth pliable ball of dough. Transfer to a clean food processor and knead for a couple of minutes with the remaining basil which will fleck the dough with green speckles. Roll out the dough as thinly as possible then fold it in half and roll it out again. Continue to do this until the dough is elastic, smooth and shiny and the rolling pin snaps as it rolls over the fold. Roll it out again and cut it into 10 cm (4 in) squares. Bring a very large saucepan of salted water to a rolling boil, toss in the pasta squares a few at a time and boil for 3 minutes. Remove from the pan and drain thoroughly.

Use the butter to grease a warmed serving dish and stand it over a pan of hot water in order to keep everything as hot as possible while you create the dish. Arrange a layer of warm pasta squares in a slightly overlapping sheet in the base of the dish. Pour a little green sauce over the pasta and scatter a few of the remaining pine kernels on top. Repeat with another sheet of pasta squares, more green sauce and a few more pine kernels. Continue until all the ingredients have been used up then serve at once.

Petti d'Anatra alla Mostarda
Duck Breasts with Mustard

*I think duck breasts are a very simple solution for
cooking dishes that are impressive without
being in any way complicated to prepare.
This is a deliciously easy recipe which results in
a lovely dish with good strong flavours.*

SERVES 4

4 duck breasts with skin
2 large cloves garlic, peeled and thinly sliced
salt
freshly ground black pepper
2 teaspoons French mustard
1 egg, beaten
5 tablespoons fine white dried breadcrumbs

Cut slashes through the skin on the duck breasts and insert slivers of garlic.
Season them all over with salt and pepper. Fry them briefly on both sides in
a non-stick pan, putting them skin side down first, until browned and sealed.
Remove from the pan and brush generously on both sides with mustard. Dip
them in beaten egg then cover in breadcrumbs on both sides. Place them
under a medium grill for about 20 minutes until cooked through and golden,
basting occasionally with their own fat.

Fichi al Forno
Baked Figs

*This combination of fresh figs and zabaglione
makes a very impressive dessert.
You could also use a bed of
fresh raspberries covered with zabaglione.*

SERVES 6

12 large ripe black figs
1 teaspoon almond oil
4 egg yolks
4 tablespoons marsala or
medium sherry
4 tablespoons caster sugar

Wipe the figs clean and cut them into quarters. Loosen the flesh from the skin to the halfway point and then open the figs out like stars. Brush a flat ovenproof dish very lightly with almond oil and lay the figs in the dish. Beat the egg yolks, marsala or sherry and caster sugar together with a balloon whisk in the top of a double-boiler over hot but not boiling water for about 20 minutes until light and foamy. Spoon the zabaglione all over the figs and place under a hot grill for about 2 minutes to heat through. Serve at once.

Gelatina
nel Mandarino
Mandarin
Jelly

*A delicately flavoured and very refreshing dessert.
I like to make the same jelly in halved lemons and
blood oranges to create a good contrast of
flavours and colours.*

SERVES 6

6 large juicy clementines,
satsumas or mandarins, halved
3 sheets gelatine
10 leaves fresh mint
4 tablespoons water
75 g (3 oz) caster sugar

Squeeze the juice from the fruit, keeping the skins as intact as possible. Scoop out all the white pith and membranes as carefully as possible. Soak the gelatine in cold water for about 15 minutes. Put the juice, water and sugar into a saucepan and heat gently for about 5 minutes until syrupy, stirring constantly. Take the gelatine out of the water, squeeze it dry in your hands and stir it into the liquid until completely dissolved.

Divide this between the halved fruits, cool then chill until set.

Italian Cheeses

THERE IS A LOT MORE to Italian cheese than the plastic tub of pre-grated 'Parmesan cheese' on offer in so many shops and super-markets. Thank goodness, most of the larger stores now stock proper lumps of Parmigiano or Grana cheese which one can grate oneself!

One of my favourite meals consists of some kind of thick soup like Pasta e Fagioli or Minestrone, followed by a selection of cheeses with a great big green salad, lots of crusty bread and a big bowl of fruit. For me, this is by far the best way to enjoy cheese, and many households in Italy serve cheese like this in place of the main course.

There are certain types of cheese which seem to have more obvious companions. For example, Mascarpone and ripe pears are fantastic; Italian grapes at the beginning of their season taste incredible with fresh Parmigiano; and fresh Ricotta tastes delicious with avocadoes or apricots. I also love to eat cheese with fresh walnuts or hazelnuts.

Italian cookery uses a lot of cheese; too much if you believe what Elizabeth David says in her *Italian Food*. You only have to think of all the pasta recipes which call for cheese, the way cheese is added to risottos and the way some meat and poultry dishes have cheese melted over them or combined into stuffings for them. This is without considering the way both Ricotta and Mascarpone are used in desserts.

The famous and fabulous Tiramisú, for example, currently everyone's favourite Italian dessert, uses Mascarpone, and those marvellously rich and creamy Cannoli pastries from Sicily are filled with Ricotta mixed with sugar and candied fruit.

If you are choosing cheese in a delicatessen, special store or off a market stall, the likelihood is that you'll be allowed to taste a tiny wedge before buying a large amount. This is by far the best way to do it, especially if the person you are buying from is enthusiastic enough to help you try out the cheeses which may be unfamiliar.

I think buying cheese should be an enjoyable occasion, one which means taking your time. I buy my cheeses from a shop in Bury St Edmunds where each cheese is patiently sliced, tasted, weighed and individually wrapped. I have spent up to two hours in there – and what fun it was!

If you have to buy your cheese vacuum-packed, then do make sure you unwrap it quite a long time before you want to eat it so that the flavours can develop. I would recommend that you buy a large vacuum-packed piece of Grana Padano or Parmigiano when you are next in Italy as it will travel better that way.

As far as storage is concerned, wrap the cheeses in foil and keep them in a cool place but preferably not in the fridge unless the weather is really hot.

Finally, a word about imitations. I have already told you about the dreadful stuff in plastic tubs which masquerades under the name Parmesan cheese (except when it has those two magical words, freshly grated) which is to be avoided. The other notable imitation is those horrible, rubbery, flavourless, ivory-colour slabs called Mozzarella or Pan Carré Mozzarella (which is square). Whatever you choose, make sure it is Italian and that it is moist and wet and pure white.

ASIAGO

A semi-hard cheese with irregular smallish holes and a sweet, milky flavour, this is a very popular table cheese which is not used a great deal in cookery. It is produced in northern Italy. A similar cheese exists called Vezzena, which can be aged for up to two years and then grated like Grana.

BAGOSS

A semi-hard cheese from Lombardy, Bagoss is pale primrose yellow with a dark ochre rind with the name of the cheese printed on it in white lettering. It has a strong, pungent flavour. It is usually served in thin wedges rather like Grana and can be grated like Grana when aged.

BEL PAESE

This is a very mild, widely produced cheese which can work as an alternative to Mozzarella in cookery. Pale yellow, with a silver paper cover round the rind and a greenish paper map on the top, it is widely available.

BITTO

A buttery, slightly soft cheese from Valtellina with a greyish rind, this is made with a combination of cows' and goats' milk.

CACIOTTA

This is a collective term for various types of country-style cheeses. It basically refers to all kinds of unsophisticated semi-hard cheeses regardless of the area from which they come.

CAPRINI

This is a deliciously soft and creamy cheese made with a mixture of cows' and goats' milk. It must be eaten fresh within three days, or it can be matured for two to four weeks. The fresh cheese is white and spreadable. As it matures it makes an orangey crust and the flavour becomes a great deal more piquant. The cheeses are sometimes sold in jars, covered in oil, with bay leaves and peppercorns to flavour them.

CRESCENZA

A soft white cheese made entirely from cows' milk, this is made under warm conditions so that it ferments and swells. It is white and rindless with a gentle, milky flavour. It belongs to the Stracchino family.

FONTINA

A cheese produced exclusively in the Valle d'Aosta, this is a sweet and pungent cheese with a soft, silky texture. It is matured in caves deep inside the mountain sides and is used in the local speciality of Fonduta, a variety of cheese fondue, and many other recipes throughout the country.

GORGONZOLA

A creamy, strongly flavoured cows' milk blue cheese, Gorgonzola exists in two versions. The 'sweet' variety is matured for sixty days, whilst the more 'natural' version is matured for up to one hundred days. Delicious melted with milk and butter and used as a sauce on pasta, it also makes a wonderful risotto with the addition of some red wine.

GRANA LODIGIANO

Grana is the collective name for all the gritty, hard, grating cheeses known collectively around the rest of the world as Parmesan. Grana Lodigiano is a very rare version of this hard cheese which comes from the Lodi area of Lombardy and is matured for two to three years. There is another type which is much smaller and is only matured for three to four months. This Grana is then shaved into translucent ribbons and is eaten as a particular local speciality.

GRANA PADANO

This is probably the most famous of all the Lombard cheeses. It is a hard, grainy, grating cheese which is matured for one to two years. Used extensively in cooking, this is the first cheese to be awarded the DOC label (*Denominazione di Origine Controllata*) and as such is protected by a consortium dedicated to the upkeep of its quality. Another version of this cheese is called Grana Trentino and comes from the region of the same name.

GROVIERA

This is the Italian version of Gruyère and is practically identical.

MASCARPONE

A very creamy, white cheese made from soured cows' milk, Mascarpone must be eaten within two days of purchase as it tends to deteriorate quite quickly. It is used extensively in all forms of cookery, including desserts, and is widely available.

MOZZARELLA

A white, doughy kind of cheese, Mozzarella is sold floating in whey in order to keep it fresh. It has a delightful elastic texture which goes very stringy when it melts in cooking. It must always be eaten as fresh as possible. Mozzarella di Bufala is the more expensive and, sadly, increasingly rare version of this cheese, and as the name suggests it is made with buffalo milk. The more common and very widely available variety is made with cows' milk and the name of the cheese varies only according to its shape. A *treccia* is a Mozzarella which has been braided, *cigliegine* are tiny, cherry-sized cheeses, *ovoline* are small, egg-shaped cheeses and so on.

PANNERONE

A rather rare cylindrical, semi-hard cheese peppered with lots of holes, Pannerone has a sweet flavour with a faint hint of bitterness. It is pale yellow with an orangey rind.

PARMIGIANO REGGIANO

This cheese is produced in a wide area in the vicinity of Parma, which includes parts of Emilia and Lombardy. The main difference in terms of production when you compare it with Grana Padano is that Parmigiano is made from hillside-grazed cattle, and this alters the flavour of the cheese if not the appearance and texture. This is a completely natural product which is used a great deal in cooking and is also served in small wedges with fruit, nuts or wine.

PECORINO

This is reputed to be the oldest of all the Italian cheeses. It is a hard, grating ewes' milk cheese. The original version, known as Pecorino Romano, has a black rind. It is used a lot in pasta dishes, grated over the finished dish, but is also delicious with bread, fruit and wine or cured meats. It has a very strong, piquant flavour and a characteristically pungent smell. Another very well known variety of this cheese comes from Sardinia and is called Pecorino Sardo.

PROVOLONE

A long, sausage-shaped cheese which comes in two versions either sweet, *dolce*, or spicy, *piccante*. The cheeses come in varying sizes, weighing from just a few hundred grammes right through to 100 kilos. The sweet version is a golden yellow colour; the spicy cheese is almost white and has a harder texture. It is good for use in cooking as it melts rather like Mozzarella. It has a consortium to protect its authenticity and the mark of the consortium appears on every cheese.

RICOTTA

A white, slightly crumbly cheese with a wet texture typical of fresh cheeses, Ricotta is very useful in cooking, including desserts and cakes. It is best eaten as fresh as possible and is widely available.

ROBIOLA

Robiola is a creamy, soft, white cheese packed individually in small irregularly rounded shapes. There is also a version made with smoked salmon incorporated into the cheese.

SCAMORZA

These are Mozzarellas which have been allowed to dry out and become hard and slightly leathery. A very mild cheese, especially popular in the south, it is delicious when grilled until just melted and soft. Scamorza affumicata is the smoked version of the same cheese. A larger version of a very similar type of cheese is called Caciocavallo.

TALEGGIO

A unique, square-shaped cheese with a soft, creamy, golden texture and colour, Taleggio has a soft, slightly darker skin and is a full fat table cheese. This is another cheese protected by its own consortium.

Salvia Fritta

SEE PAGE 288

(Overleaf) Conchigle Fuxia

SEE PAGE 293

Fichi al Forno

SEE PAGE 297

*V*ino

I WRITE THIS CHAPTER very much as a wine lover and drinker rather than as a wine expert. All I have done is to experiment with dishes I particularly enjoy and wines that I love and I have come up with combinations which I feel work rather well. It therefore follows that all the wines mentioned here will be personal favourites. I am very keen that Italian wines should gain the position of respect and honour which they deserve, and therefore I am always keen to introduce as many people as possible to the huge range of really top grade wines which the country now produces and exports. I welcome this opportunity to write about the wines of Italy in a format where they work alongside some of the dishes in the recipe sections as good companions for the flavours and textures of the food.

However, I must stress that this is not a wine book and I am not a wine expert. If you need to find out more about the wines I have mentioned alongside the dishes, you will have to look them up elsewhere, for I do not have the space here to go into each and every wine in detail. I have tried to give you a mixture of very well known wines and others which are less famous. I know that some might be hard to get hold of if you are not in Italy, but I have still included them so that you might seek them out whilst you are in Italy and give them a try.

ANTIPASTI

Salame	Young Chianti
	Frecciarossa Rosato
La Caprese	Ischia Bianco
	Greco di Tufo
Insalata di Fagioli e Tonno	Chiaretto del Garda
Cozze alla Maionese	Cinqueterre Bianco
Crostini all'Aringa	Greco di Tufo
Stuzzicarelli	Valpolicella
Bresaola all'Olio	Sassella
Insalata di Mare	Torbato
La Bagna Cauda	Young Barolo
	(as dictated by Piedmontese tradition)
Crostini di Polenta con Gorgonzola	Frecciarossa Rosso

SOUPS

La Stracciatella	Soave
Minestrone	Young Chianti
Zuppa de Cipolle e Vino	Rosatello Ruffino
Pappa al Pomodoro	Capri Bianco
Minestra di Fagioli con Riso e Verdura	Calmasino
	Rosatello Ruffino
Minestra di Zucchine	Teroldego Rotaliano
	Rosato
Minestra di Fagioli e Fontina	Cortese Bianco
Zuppa de Ceci	Pomino Bianco
Zuppa di Sedani	Gambellara
Zuppa di Lenticchie	Rosato del Salento
Zuppa Pavese	Bardolino
Pasta Reale	Bardolino
Zuppa di Fave	Cecubo

RISOTTO

Risotto alla Milanese	Riesling dell'Oltrepo
Risotto alle Erbe	Soave
Risotto con i Fegatini	Valpolicella
Risotto alle Verdure Miste	Bardolino
Risotto al Pollo e Pisellini	Bardolino
Risotto con le Cozze	Müller-Thurgau
Risotto con i Gamberetti	Riesling
Risotto con le Seppie	Riesling
Risotto d'Asparagi	Arbia
	Nipozzano

PASTA

Spaghettini al Burro e Limone	Colli Albano Bianco
Spaghettini con Pomodore e Mozzarella	Capri Bianco
Spaghetti alla Carbonara	Cerasuolo
Spaghetti Aglio e Olio	Frascati
Spaghetti al Pomodoro	Capri Bianco
Spaghetti al Tonno	Vernaccia
Spaghetti allo Scoglio	Torbato Secco
Spaghetti alle Vongole	Ischia Bianco
Spaghetti con Funghi e Piselli	Chiaretto del Garda
	Maccarese Bianco
	Marino Secco
Spaghetti alla Menta con il Maiale	Merlot Trentino
Bucatini all'Amatriciana	Rosato del Salento
Bucatini alla Puttanesca	Rosata del Salento
Penne all'Arrabbiata	Est! Est! Est!
Penne al Salame	Frecciarossa Rosato
	Bonarda
Maccheroni al Sugo Napoletano	Capri Bianco
Maccheroni al Quatre Formaggi	Chianti Classico
Chiocciole con Noci e Mascarpone	Chianti Classico
Vermicelli con Peperoni e Melanzane	Martinafranca Rosso

Tagliatelle al Ragú Bolognese	Sangiovese Rosso
Tagliatelle al Prosciutto	Fiorano Bianco
Pappardelle alla Lepre	Gutturnio
Maltagliati all'Anatra	Barbera di Romagna
Trenette al Pesto	Coronata
	Campochiesa
	Rossese Rosato
Lasagne al Forno	Valpolicella
Tortellini alla Bolognese	Sangiovese Rosso
Ravioli alla Genovese	Chianti Colli Senesi
Cannelloni Ripieni de Carne	Rosatello Ruffino
	Pusterla Rosato
Cannelloni con Ricotta e Spinaci	Greco di Tufo
	Ciro Bianco
Gnocchi di Spinaci	Calmasino
Gnocchi di Semolino	Frascati
Gnocchi di Patate al Sugo de Pomodoro	Bardolino
	Irpinia Rosato

PIZZA AND POLENTA

Pizza Napoletana	Greco di Tufo
	Locorontondo Red
Pizza con Funghi e Mozzarella	Pinot Oltrepo Pavese
	Soave
Pizza con Ricotta	Traminer Collio
Pizza con Salame	Lambrusco di Sorbara
	Peroni (Italian lager)
Pizza con Vongole	Greco di Tufo
	Locorontondo Bianco
Pizza di Ventimiglia	Riesling Renano Alto
	Adige
La Focaccia	Soave
	Frascati
	Orvieto
Polenta con Salsicce	Recioto Amarone della Valpolicella

Polenta con Gorgonzola	Taurasi
	Grignolino
	Cannonau Rosato

MEAT

Bistecca alla Cacciatora	Chianti Classico
Bistecche di Manzo alle Pizzaiola	Valpolicella
Bollito con Patate	Barbera del Monferrato
	Oltrepo Pavese
	Sassella
Stufato al Vino Rosso	Barolo
	Inferno
	Oltrepo Pavese
Manzo in Involtini	Chianti dei Colli Aretini
Arrosto di Vitello	Franciacorta Rosso
	Bardolino
	Parrina Rosso
Fettine all'Uccelletto	Grignolino
	Matino Rosato
Scaloppine al Marsala	Grignolino
	Gavi
Ossobuco	Cellatica
	Valpolicella
Abbacchio alla Campagnola	Pinot Nero Collio
	Merlot de Aprilia
Coscetto di Abbacchio Farcito	Marzemino
	Cabernet di Breganze
Costolette d'Abbacchio Piccanti	Cabernet di Pramaggiore
	Valpolicella
Costolette d'Agnello Panate	Franciacorta Rosso
	Santa Maddalena
Lombatine di Maiale al Pomodoro	Chiaretto del Garda
	Grignolino

POULTRY AND GAME	
Pollo alla Cacciatora	Cabernet di Pramaggiore
	Marzemino
	Merlot
Filetti di Tacchino ai Funghi	Lagrein Rosato
	Grignolino Tacchino
Arrosto Ripeno	Nebbiolo d'Alba
Chianti Classico	
Anatra con Lenticchie	Cabernet Colli Berici
	Valcaloppio Rosso
Oca in Salmi	Gutturnio
	Donnaz
Oca Ripiena	Carmignano
	Barbaresco
Piccioni con Piselli	Torgiano Rosso
	Teroldego
	Brunello di Montalcino
Quaglie Stufate	Carema
	Vino Nobile Montepulciano
Faraona in Salmi	Nebbiolo d'Alba
	Carmignano
Coniglio ai Capperi	Bardolino
Coniglio con le Mele	Valpolicella
Lepre alla Sant'Uberto	Inferno Valtellina
Lepre alla Marengo	Superiore
	Donnaz
	Teroldego Rotaliano
Capriolo in Salmi	Refosco Colli Orientali
	Sassella
Daino in Salsa di Cigliege	Vino Novile Montepulciano
Cinghaiale in Umido	Vino Novile Montepulciano

FISH

Anguila Arrosta	Bardolino
	Sangiovese di Romagna
Carpa all'Ebraica	Riesling Oltrepo Pavese
	Pinot di Franciacorta
	Bianca di Custoza
Luccio alla Marinara	Sangiovese di Romagna
	Riviera del Garda Rosso
Pesce Persico alla Massaia	Riesling Oltrepo Pavese
Pesce Persico in Filetti al Burro	Tocai Collio
	Pinot di Franciacorta
Storione con Funghi	Pinot Grigio
Trota Cotta al Vapore	Lugana
Trotelle alla Mugnaia	Gavi
Trota alla Savoiarda	
Salmone al Pesto	Montecarlo Bianco
	Pinot Bianco Breganze
	Cinqueterre
Cefalo Arrosto nel Forno	Bianchello del Mataura
Dentice alla Pizzaiola	Sauvignon Collio
Merluzzo in Filetti al Vino Bianco	Verdicchio
	Castelli di Jesi
	Bianchello del Metauro
Merluzzo in Filetti al Burro d'Acciuga	Verdicchio
	Castelli di Jesi
	Bianchello del Metauro
Coda di Rospo al Limone	Pomino
Sarde al Finocchio	Trebbiano di Romagna
	Gambellara Bianco

SEAFOOD

Scampi Arrosto	Torgiano Bianco
	Verdicchio di Matelica
Cozze alla Marinara	Cortese di Gavi
Ostriche alla Diavola	Ischia Bianco Superiore
Vongole e Piselli in Intigolo	Ischia Bianco Superiore
	Frascati
Aragosta Arrosto	Prosecco di Conegliano
	Torbato
Gamberetti alla Crema	Bianchello del Matauro
	Erbaluce di Caluso
Seppie alla Romana	Bianco di Pitigliano
	Verdiccho Castelli di Iesi
Fritto di Gamberi e Seppie	Vermentino
	Malvasia di Casorso d'Asti

VEGETABLES

It is very hard to choose wines to go with vegetables, as usually the vegetables are accompanying the main dish – whatever that might be. However, many people, and not just the ever-growing number of vegetarians, enjoy eating vegetables without meat, poultry, game or fish, so I cannot just ignore the combination of vegetables and wine. Here are just a few general suggestions for wines to drink with vegetables.

Asparagus	Cambellara
	ParrinaBianco
Aubergines	Nuragus di Cagliari
	Ciro Bianco
	Sauvignon Alto Adige
Courgettes	Müller-Thurgau Valle Isarco
	Montecarlo Bianco
	Etna Bianco
Courgette Flowers	Traminer Aromatico
	Orvieto Abboccato
Funghi Porcini	Riesling Trentino
	Dolcetto d'Alba

Lettuce	Marino
	Valdadige Bianco
Onions	Albana di Romagna
	Valdadige Bianco
	Parrina Bianco
Peppers	Rossese di Dolceacqua
	Merlot Colli Berici
Pulses	Lago di Caldero
	Chiaretto del Garda
Spinach	Malvasia Collio
	Riesling Renano Alto Adige
Tomatoes	Trebbiano d'Abruzzo
	Martina Franca
	Alcamo Bianco

DESSERTS

Most desserts can be enjoyed with a small glass of a dessert wine such as Moscato or Malvasia. Alternatively, you can drink something with bubbles such as a Castello Gancia or an Asti Gancia. Here are a few of my favourite combinations. Just a few words of warning about desserts which contain chocolate: they will simply not go with wine, whatever the wine. Chocolate and wine means either spoiling the dessert or wasting the wine, so don't bother.

Dry cakes	Moscato di Siracusa
Almond cakes	Moscato di Cagliari
Creamy cakes and pastries	Moscato Rosa Alto Adige
Pudding-type desserts	Moscato d'Asti
	Moscato Trentino
Other great favourites	Mammertino
	Malvasia delle Lipari
	Ambrato di Comiso
	Moscato di Sorso Sennori
	Vernaccia di Serrapetrona

CHEESE

These are just some generalised ideas as it is very hard to choose wines to suit each individual cheese.

Fresh soft cheeses	Lugana
	Soave
	Trentino Reisling
	Bianco del Pitigliano
	Orvieto
	Vermentino
	Colli Euganei Bianco
Medium mature cheeses	Cannonnau Rosato
	Grignolino
	Casteller
	Castello di Diano d'Alba
Very mature cheeses	Chianti Classico
	Torgiano Rosso
	Valtellina Superiore
	Inferno
	Teroldego Rotaliano
	Grave del Friuli Merlot
Extremely mature cheeses	Falerno
	Cannonnau
	Marsala Vergine
	Vin Santo Toscano

Index